July 27 —

LEO

Temple

9/880

Dry

OH

D. H. Lawrence at Work
The Emergence of
the *Prussian Officer* Stories

At last, after heaving at himself several times, for he seemed to be a mass of inertia, he got up. But he had to force every one of his movements from behind, with his will. He felt cold, and dazed, and helpless, ~~but not beaten~~. Then he clutched hold of the bed, the pain was so keen. And looking at his thighs, he saw the darker bruises on his swarthy flesh and he knew that, if he pressed one of his fingers on one of the bruises, he should faint. But he did not ~~mean~~ want to faint – he did not ~~mean~~ want anybody to know. No one should ever know. It was between him and the Captain. There were only the two people in the world now – he had lost the old world, with comrades.

Slowly, economically, he got dressed and forced himself to walk. Everything was obscure, except ~~just what he had his hands~~ *the fiery pain revived his dulled senses* on. But he managed to get through his work. The worst remained yet. He took the tray and went up to the Captain's room. The officer, pale and heavy, sat at the table. ~~So~~ The orderly *as he* saluted, ~~he~~ felt ~~himself go out of existence~~ ~~himself annihilated, annihilated~~. He stood still for a moment ~~submitting to his own annihilation – then he gathered himself, on the rebound gather himself together~~; and then the Captain seemed to grow vague, unreal, and the young soldier's heart beat up with pride. He clung to this sensation – that the Captain did not exist, so that he himself might ~~live~~ ~~live~~. ~~But~~ When he saw his officer's hand tremble as he took the coffee, he felt everything falling, shattered. And he went away, feeling as if he himself were coming to pieces, disintegrated. And when the Captain was there on horseback, giving orders, while he himself stood, with rifle and knapsack, sick with pain, he felt as if he must shut his eyes and ~~not be there~~ *gone* – as if he must shut his eyes on ~~existence~~ *them, existence*. It was only the long agony of marching with a parched throat that filled him with one single, sleep-heavy intention: ~~to free himself of the Captain, to save~~ *to get~~know~~ the Captain, to save* himself ~~from~~ the Captain.

2.

He was getting used even to his parched throat. That the snowy peaks ~~were radiant among~~ ~~gleamed out of~~ the sky, that the whitey-green glacier river twisted through its pale shoals, in the ~~wide~~ *valley* below, seemed ~~not even to exist~~ ~~but~~ quite natural, ~~but~~ he was going mad with fever and thirst. He plodded on, ~~to~~ uncomplaining. ~~He would~~ *He did not want to complain, not to* ~~to that~~. There were two gulls, like flakes of water & snow, over the river. The scent of green rye soaked in sunshine ~~came into~~ *came like a dizziness* ~~was real felt sick~~. And the march continued, monotonously, almost like a sleep.

D. H. Lawrence at Work

The Emergence of
the *Prussian Officer* Stories

Keith Cushman

The Harvester Press

Hassocks

The Harvester Press Limited
2 Stanford Terrace, Hassocks
Nr. Brighton, Sussex
Copyright © 1978 by the Rector and Visitors
of the University of Virginia

First published 1978

Frontispiece: A page from the holograph manuscript
of "Honour and Arms," the original version of
"The Prussian Officer." (Courtesy of the Humanities
Research Center, The University of Texas at
Austin, and of Laurence Pollinger Ltd. and the
Estate of the late Mrs. Frieda Lawrence.)

British Library Cataloguing in Publication Data

Cushman, Keith
    D. H. Lawrence at work.
    1. Lawrence, David Herbert. Prussian officer,
    and other tales.
    I. Title
    823'.9'12   PR6023.A9P/
      ISBN 0-85527-614-2

Printed in the United States of America

To my father,
and to the memory of my mother

Contents

Preface

The stories collected in *The Prussian Officer and Other Stories,* published in 1914, include the best short fiction from Lawrence's early career. Though most of the stories date from his first years as a writer, they achieved their final form only after a lengthy and complicated process of revision. These revisions—and what they demonstrate about Lawrence's developing art—are my subject.

E. M. Forster once wrote a charming review of *Authors at Work,* a volume richly illustrated with photographs of manuscripts of major writers. His conclusions about the value of studying such manuscripts have bearing on Lawrence's 1914 revisions of the *Prussian Officer* tales:

> Thanks to these wobblings of authors can we not learn something about them which they did not wish us to know?
>
> I do not think we can, for the reason that creative writers do not wobble centrally. Their variants are on the margin, in the region where they are trying to present their ideas or dreams to the reader, not in the deeper region where ideas and dreams have birth. But this is an arguable point.[1]

Lawrence's late revisions of *The Prussian Officer* prove that Forster's point is indeed arguable. The revisions of the lesser stories in the collection tend to bear him out: most of the revisions of these tales are marginal retouchings. However, there is nothing at all wobbly about the revisions of the important stories, which do emanate from "the deeper region where ideas and dreams have birth." Lawrence recast these stories so extensively precisely because his fundamental conception of their

---

1. E. M. Forster, review of *Authors at Work: An Address Delivered by Robert H. Taylor at the Opening of an Exhibition of Literary Manuscripts at the Grolier Club* (New York, 1957), in *The Library: Transactions of the Bibliographical Society,* 5th ser., 13 (1958), 142.

materials had changed so radically. It is unlikely that everyone will agree with Edmund Malone's vehement assertion that "the minute changes made in their compositions by eminent writers are always a matter of both curiosity & instruction to literary men, however trifling and unimportant they may appear to blockheads."[2] But the *Prussian Officer* revisions allow us to examine in detail the crucial turning point in the work of a major twentieth-century writer.

The years of the making of the *Prussian Officer* stories are also the years of Lawrence's literary apprenticeship and of the great artistic advance he made as he grappled with and completed *The Rainbow*. The final revisions of the *Prussian Officer* stories play an important role in this great artistic transition. My study of the revisions of these stories aims to illuminate the process by which Lawrence left his apprenticeship behind and came into his own as a writer of fiction.

Parts of my argument presuppose a general familiarity with Lawrence's life, especially his early years. No detailed knowledge is necessary, but the reader who can differentiate Jessie Chambers, Louie Burrows, and Frieda von Richthofen will have an advantage. In Appendix C, I have provided a calendar for the *Prussian Officer* volume, chronicling the evolution of all twelve of the stories as well as important dates in Lawrence's personal and artistic life. I would recommend Harry T. Moore's authoritative *The Priest of Love* (New York, 1974) to readers who desire a full biographical account. Mark Schorer's "Life of D. H. Lawrence," included in his *D. H. Lawrence* (New York, 1969), is an excellent brief introduction to Lawrence's life.

2. Quoted in James M. Osborne, *John Dryden: Some Biographical Facts and Problems* (New York, 1940), p. 131.

Acknowledgments

The array of gratitude at the beginning of scholarly books always seemed like an empty convention to me until I tried to write a scholarly book myself. It has been a pleasure to learn how wrong I was.

My largest debt is to Charles Ross, whose suggestions were so acute that sometimes as he reads these pages he is apt to feel like a collaborator. A. Walton Litz helped shape the earliest form of this book, and he has been a sustaining presence and good friend ever since. The book has also profited from readings, at various stages, by Merlin Bowen, Allen Fitchen, David Gordon, Stephen Miko, James E. Miller, Jr., Janel Mueller, Sheldon Sacks, and Robert Streeter.

I would like to acknowledge the long-standing support and encouragement of James C. Cowan, David Farmer, and Harry T. Moore. I deeply regret that John Baker did not live to see this book. My wife Judith has been cheerfully tolerant while D. H. Lawrence has occupied so much space in my life for such a long time. My daughters Phoebe and Brett have gladly made room as well.

I am grateful to the National Endowment for the Humanities for a Younger Humanist Summer Grant that allowed me to return to England to examine some manuscripts. I am also grateful to the University of North Carolina at Greensboro for two grants that helped me complete this project. One of these grants was from the Research Council.

Portions of this book first appeared in articles published in *The D. H. Lawrence Review, Journal of Modern Literature, Modern Philology* (© 1972 by The University of Chicago), and *Studies in Short Fiction.* In each case the material has been significantly altered. My thanks to these periodicals for permission to use this material.

I am indebted to the following institutions for permission to quote from unpublished materials in their collections: The Bancroft Library of the University of California, Berkeley; the Henry W. and Albert A. Berg Collection of the New York Public Library and the Astor, Lenox and Tilden Foundations; the Humanities Research Center, The University of Texas at Austin; the Local Studies Library of the Nottinghamshire County Library; and the University of Nottingham Library. My special thanks to George Lazarus for permission to study and quote from his "Daughters of the Vicar" materials, for his gracious hospitality, and for sharing his considerable expertise.

I wish to thank Laurence Pollinger Ltd. and the Estate of the late Mrs. Frieda Lawrence for permission to quote from the published and unpublished works of D. H. Lawrence. I am also indebted to The Viking Press, Inc., and Messrs. William Heinemann Ltd. for permission to quote from Lawrence's writings. Finally, my thanks to the Macmillan Publishing Co., Inc., of New York, publishers of *The Variorum Edition of W. B. Yeats,* edited by Peter Allt and Russell K. Alspach (copyright 1903, 1906, 1907, 1912, 1916, 1918, 1924, 1928, 1931, 1933, 1934, 1935, 1940, 1944, 1945, 1946, 1950, 1956, 1957), for permission to quote the Yeats poem that serves as one of my epigraphs. I am also indebted to M. B. Yeats, Miss Ann Yeats, and the Macmillan Co. of London and Basingstoke for permission to use the same poem.

Editions Used

Generally I have used the most easily accessible editions of Lawrence's works. The first edition of *The Prussian Officer* is the main exception to this rule, and I have also used the first editions of *The Trespasser* and *The Widowing of Mrs. Holroyd*. References to works for which an abbreviation appears below in the left-hand column will be incorporated into my text.

CL *The Collected Letters of D. H. Lawrence.* Harry T. Moore, ed. 2 vols. Viking, 1962.

CP *The Complete Poems of D. H. Lawrence.* Vivian de Sola Pinto and F. Warren Roberts, eds. Viking Compass paperback, 1971.

CSS *The Complete Short Stories.* 3 vols. Viking Compass paperback, 1961.

 Fantasia of the Unconscious in *Psychoanalysis and the Unconscious* and *Fantasia of the Unconscious.* Viking Compass paperback, 1960.

 Kangaroo. Viking Compass paperback, 1960.

LL *Lawrence in Love: Letters from D. H. Lawrence to Louie Burrows.* James T. Boulton, ed. Nottingham, 1968.

AH *The Letters of D. H. Lawrence.* Aldous Huxley, ed. Heinemann, 1932.

 The Lost Girl. Viking Compass paperback, 1968.

 Phoenix: The Posthumous Papers of D. H. Lawrence. Edward D. McDonald, ed. Viking Compass paperback, 1972.

 Phoenix II: Uncollected, Unpublished, and Other Prose Works. Warren Roberts and Harry T. Moore, eds. Viking Compass paperback, 1970.

PO *The Prussian Officer and Other Stories.* Duckworth, 1914.

H *The Prussian Officer and Other Stories:* proof set. Lawrence sent these proofs, which contain some holograph revision, to W. E. Hopkin in January 1915. Now in the collection of the Nottinghamshire County Library.

R   *The Rainbow.* Viking Compass paperback, 1961.

SL   *Sons and Lovers.* Viking Compass paperback, 1958.

T   *The Trespasser.* Duckworth, 1912.

         Twilight in Italy in *D. H. Lawrence and Italy: Twilight in Italy, Sea and Sardinia, Etruscan Places.* Viking Compass paperback, 1972.

WP   *The White Peacock.* Southern Illinois University, 1966.

WMH   *The Widowing of Mrs. Holroyd.* Mitchell Kennerley, 1914.

D. H. Lawrence at Work
The Emergence of
the *Prussian Officer* Stories

. . . It is pleasant to see great works in their
seminal state, pregnant with latent possibilities
of excellence; nor could there be any more delightful entertainment than to trace their gradual growth and expansion, and to observe how they
are sometimes suddenly advanced by accidental
hints, and sometimes slowly improved by steady
meditation.

Samuel Johnson, "The Life of Milton"

The friends that have it I do wrong
When ever I remake a song,
Should know what issue is at stake:
It is myself that I remake.

W. B. Yeats

The copy of *Sons and Lovers* has just come—I am
fearfully proud of it. . . . I shall not write quite
in that style any more. It's the end of my youthful period.

D. H. Lawrence to Edward Garnett, 19 May 1913

Chapter I

Introduction
The Growth of an Artist

"I am going through a transition stage myself"

It is impossible to think of D. H. Lawrence without thinking of the way he looked: the red beard of course, the deep-blue, penetrating eyes, and the "Bohemian" clothes—an odd mixture of casualness and formality—loosely draped over the lanky, tubercular frame. This appearance was a form of self-advertisement and self-expression, a way of asserting his identity and of distinguishing himself from the mob. When one memoirist found him looking uncharacteristically "the well-dressed and smart man-about-town," she wondered why he did not dress stylishly more often: "His lean figure lent itself to well-cut clothes, but I remember him saying that he hated orthodox clothes and dressed in the blue coat and odd things because he liked to create attention. 'I like people to look at me,' he said once."[1] Although this physical presence remains an unmistakable component of today's Lawrence mystique, there is another Lawrence who is still relatively unknown, a young man and writer who antedates the popular image of the writer. The question of how the young provincial became the bearded visionary has rarely been given serious and sustained consideration.

The young man in question is the collier's son who first bettered himself by reading for his teacher's certificate at Nottingham University and then went to the London suburbs to teach elementary school. This young schoolteacher, ambitious to make his mark on English literary life, was the author of two novels, *The White Peacock* and *The Trespasser,* as well as of numerous short stories and poems. The young man can be seen in a photograph taken on his twenty-first birthday in 1906, several months after beginning his first novel. He is clean-

1. Cecily Lambert Minchin in *D. H. Lawrence: A Composite Biography,* ed. Edward Nehls, I (Madison, Wis., 1957), 505.

shaven and looks earnest and rather uncomfortable in the
stiff white collar: in Lawrence's own words, this is a photograph of a "bright young prig in a high collar like a curate."[2]
In another photograph, taken six years later, the young man,
now twenty-six and sporting a moustache, looks handsome
and confident in his elegant three-piece suit. It is this Lawrence
who transformed the draft of a novel called *Paul Morel* into
Sons and Lovers and eloped to the continent with Frieda Weekley
in the spring of 1912, determined to make his living by writing
and by nothing else.

Lawrence first grew a beard, mostly out of convenience,
when he was in bed with pneumonia in 1912. On December 11
of that year he wrote Louie Burrows that he had "shaved off
[his] red beard" (LL 153).[3] When she complained, Lawrence
replied in no uncertain terms: "Why do you regret my red
beard? I hate it. Oh, no more of it for me. I shaved again today"
(LL 154). Lawrence's decision to again grow a beard in the
autumn of 1914 was an important symbolic action intended to
signify personal change and development.[4] He described his new
beard to his friend Catherine Carswell in October of that year:

2. Stephen Potter, *D. H. Lawrence, a First Study* (London, 1930), p. 7. The
same photograph appears in "A Modern Lover," where it "had been
called the portrait of an intellectual prig" (CSS 8).

The Complete Short Stories of D. H. Lawrence. Copyright 1922 by Thomas
Seltzer, Inc., renewed 1950 by Frieda Lawrence. Copyright 1928 by Alfred A.
Knopf, Inc., © 1955 by Frieda Lawrence Ravagli. Copyright 1933 by the
Estate of D. H. Lawrence, © 1961 by Angelo Ravagli and C. Montague
Weekley, Executors of the Estate of Frieda Lawrence Ravagli. Copyright
1934 by Frieda Lawrence, © 1962 by Angelo Ravagli and C. Montague
Weekley, Executors of the Estate of Frieda Lawrence Ravagli. Reprinted by
permission of Laurence Pollinger Ltd., the Estate of the late Mrs. Frieda
Lawrence, and The Viking Press, Inc.

3. *Lawrence in Love: Letters from D. H. Lawrence to Louie Burrows,* edited by
James T. Boulton (Nottingham, Eng.: University of Nottingham Press,
1968). Copyright 1968 by Angelo Ravagli and C. M. Weekley, Executors
of the Estate of Frieda Lawrence Ravagli. Reprinted by permission of
Laurence Pollinger Ltd. and the Estate of the late Mrs. Frieda Lawrence.

4. In much the same way, Henry James had signaled that he was a new
man who would be writing about a new century when he shaved his
beard in May 1900, just at the time he was beginning *The Ambassadors.* See

"Oh, by the way—I was seedy and have grown a beard. I think I look hideous, but it is so warm and complete, and such a clothing to one's nakedness, that I like it and shall keep it" (CL 293).[5] Lawrence kept the beard to clothe his nakedness the rest of his life, and there is no mistaking how he felt about it. Richard Lovat Somers, the authorial self-projection in *Kangaroo*, has the same attitude toward his own beard: "He said in his heart, the day his beard was shaven he was beaten, lost. He identified it with his isolate manhood."[6] Surely the growing of the beard was also a symbolic act of allegiance to his bearded father, a way of demonstrating for all the world to see that he was no longer his mother's son.

I do not mean to be facetious in beginning this study with a discussion of Lawrence's facial hair. My analysis of the evolution and development of the best of the stories collected in the *Prussian Officer* volume is designed to show Lawrence's own development during these years. The gradual transformation of Lawrence's appearance mirrors the great personal and artistic transformation that was taking place at the same time. This transformation is but a visible—and to a large degree conscious —manifestation of an inner development. The *Prussian Officer* collection has never received adequate critical attention, even though it contains some of Lawrence's finest stories and estab-

---

Leon Edel, *Henry James: The Treacherous Years, 1895–1901* (Philadelphia, 1969), pp. 355–56.

5. *The Collected Letters of D. H. Lawrence,* edited by Harry T. Moore. Copyright 1932 by the Estate of D. H. Lawrence and by Frieda Lawrence. Copyright 1933, 1948, 1953, 1954, and each year 1956–1962 by Angelo Ravagli and C. M. Weekley, Executors of the Estate of Frieda Lawrence Ravagli. Reprinted by permission of Laurence Pollinger Ltd., the Estate of the late Mrs. Frieda Lawrence, and The Viking Press, Inc.

Few beards are so well documented. John Middleton Murry remembers that he "inherited" Lawrence's "excellent razor and strop" at this time. See Nehls, I, 255.

6. From *Kangaroo,* p. 227. (Copyright 1923 by Thomas Seltzer, Inc., renewed 1951 by Frieda Lawrence. Reprinted by permission of Laurence Pollinger Ltd., the Estate of the late Mrs. Frieda Lawrence, and The Viking Press, Inc.) This passage is found in the "Nightmare" chapter; Somers is afraid the authorities will cut off his beard.

lished him "in the front rank of contemporary English short-story writers."[7] More important to my study, however, is the unique perspective on Lawrence's early years and his growth to artistic maturity offered by the best of the stories.

The Prussian Officer and Other Stories was published by Duckworth in December 1914. In their earliest versions, the first of the twelve stories to be written date back to 1907. Eleven of the twelve appeared in magazines before they were collected in 1914, and an early version of the twelfth was published in 1934. All of these magazine texts are different—often strikingly different—from the versions published in *The Prussian Officer*. Considerable manuscript materials are extant for the stories, as well as a set of unpublished proofs dating from July 1914. In addition, prototypes for three of the stories are found in *The White Peacock*. All these texts (plus a few others) add up to an especially rich lode of materials for investigating Lawrence's artistic growth. The study of the various versions of the best of the twelve tales is a study in miniature of Lawrence's apprenticeship and of his development to artistic maturity.

Even at this late date, it is not general knowledge that Lawrence revised his writings. Innumerable memoirists have commented on the ease and spontaneity with which he wrote, and his enormous output in a relatively short career also testifies to his literary facility. The image of the bearded novelist sitting beneath a tree in Tuscany, pouring words into the copybook on his knee, is romantic-sounding but nevertheless accurate. Aldous Huxley is merely typical when he deduces that Lawrence was unable to revise because he was "determined that all he produced should spring direct from the mysterious, irrational source of power within him" (AH xvii). It is well to begin by laying this myth to rest.

Huxley was right about spontaneity, but not about revision itself. Not only did Lawrence revise, but revision was essential to his creative method. To Lawrence, writing was both process

7. Emile Delavenay, *D. H. Lawrence, the Man and His Work: The Formative Years, 1885-1919,* tr. Katharine M. Delavenay (Carbondale, Ill., 1972), p. 205.

and act of discovery. Genuine art could not be achieved with scissors and paste: his revisions do not consist of mechanical repairs and patchwork. The flow of true art could be produced only by a total immersion of self in the experience of composition. However, Lawrence's habit of composition made it unlikely that he would get a piece of fiction right on the first attempt. We should believe him when he complains in the midst of that early draft of *The Rainbow* that he is "doing a novel which I have never grasped. Damn its eyes, there I am at page 145, and I've no notion what it's about" (CL 203).

After his first draft, he would engage himself anew with the words he had written, improving them and refining the insights he had gained from the initial encounter. The revision might be a totally fresh start, or it might be a quick run-through for the purpose of minor verbal alterations. However, even when he was beginning all over again, as in the well-known case of the three versions of *Lady Chatterley*, he always built on the foundation of the earlier draft. The final product became a sort of palimpsest as each successive layer of composition modified the layers that had come before.

Frank Kermode has commented on Lawrence's "habitual method" of confronting "the text again and again": "He worked under pressure, producing many drafts, all widely different. . . . Each rewriting involved another struggle with the text: deletions, additions, remodelings, further qualifications of doctrine. There is a kind of creative opportunism in this, a desire to catch the momentary flux of life rather than comply with the dictates of 'form.' "[8] The process of revision was as fresh and spontaneous for Lawrence as the original composition. His holographs—with their nervous alterations and emendations, their added paragraphs written in a tiny but always legible hand, squeezed into whatever available margin—are further testimony to the speed and spontaneity with which he wrote and revised.

The revisions of the *Prussian Officer* stories are especially revealing. They span the years of Lawrence's early manhood

8. Frank Kermode, *D. H. Lawrence* (New York, 1973), p. 29.

and literary apprenticeship, the years of this greatest personal and artistic development. These were the years when he was actively engaged in the search for his own literary voice. These were also the years in which he worked to heal the wounds left by the struggle between his collier father and his more genteel mother.

Accidents of publishing history account for most of the revisions of the stories. At this point in his career it was his habit to revise an unsold story before trying again to place it—a kind of artistic updating. He also revised all the magazine versions of the stories in the early summer of 1914, after the contract for the *Prussian Officer* volume was signed. These revisions were the most important of all. Instead of merely gathering up the magazine texts and getting on with his other work, he revised all the stories and recast the finest so thoroughly that they became strikingly different works of art. He refused to release his first collection of short fiction to the world without having it accord as fully as possible with the new artistic vision that was taking shape in the process of creating *The Rainbow*.

Another important aspect of the best of the *Prussian Officer* stories is their close relation to the experience of Lawrence's childhood and early manhood. My analyses are based in part on Leon Edel's belief that "a writer of novels and tales . . . in the act of creating universal works is at the same time telling us parables about himself."[9] Lawrence has an emotional stake in the material. As he "grew up" and changed, the stories, especially the best of them, changed along with him.

The young man who submitted his first stories to a newspaper contest in 1907 will seem somewhat unfamiliar to many readers. At the time he was still in the midst of the long, frustrating relationship with Jessie Chambers, the original of Miriam in *Sons and Lovers*, and was very much under the dominion of his mother. By 1914, the key date in the history of the *Prussian Officer* stories, he had come into his own. His mother had been dead over three years; he had been with Frieda for two. He had completed three versions of *The Rainbow*. Insights

9. Edel, *Henry James: The Treacherous Years*, p. 17.

that went into the composition of the novel, insights garnered from the experience with Frieda, insights expressed in an important letter about character he wrote to Edward Garnett—all these played a part in the sweeping transformation of the major stories in the collection in the early summer of 1914. These late revisions directly reflect the emergence of the vision and of the particular novelistic talents that produced *The Rainbow* and *Women in Love*. Lawrence meant what he said when he wrote his literary mentor Edward Garnett in the spring of 1914 that there was "something deep evolving itself out in me" (CL 273).

My starting point is a remark made by R. E. Pritchard about the *Prussian Officer* stories: "In these stories which, in their revised form, mark the beginning of the 'true,' unmuffled Lawrence, conventional understanding of morality, personality and even life are transcended in search of the dark reality buried in the body, where consciousness, individuality and sexuality are absorbed in the nonhuman source of life."[10] My purpose is to illustrate and define the developmental process by which he reached that "beginning." I will be charting the progress of the six best stories in the collection: "Odour of Chrysanthemums," "Daughters of the Vicar," "The Shades of Spring," "The White Stocking," "The Thorn in the Flesh," and, to a lesser extent, "The Prussian Officer" itself. ("The Prussian Officer" is a special case; for reasons that will be apparent, most of my discussion of the text of this story can be found in Appendix A.) These are the stories Lawrence was imaginatively most deeply engaged with, and these are the stories that display the most revealing pattern of revision. I have omitted discussion of the more negligible stories in the volume: "Goose Fair," "Second Best," and "A Sick Collier." "The Shadow in the Rose Garden" and "A Fragment of Stained Glass," interesting second-line stories, are excluded in the interest of avoiding excessive detail and repetition.[11] The

10. R. E. Pritchard, *D. H. Lawrence: Body of Darkness* (London, 1971), p. 66.
11. I discuss "The Shadow in the Rose Garden" in "D. H. Lawrence at Work: 'The Shadow in the Rose Garden,'" *D. H. Lawrence Review*, 8 (1975), 31–46.

twelfth story is "The Christening," a satiric *jeu d'esprit*. It does not merit full-scale treatment, but its amusing biographical sources are explored in Appendix B.

My method is essentially comparative. For each of the stories considered in detail, I will be comparing the various extant texts—manuscript, magazine, proof, and *Prussian Officer*—focusing primarily on thematic development. The study of the successive versions of these stories reveals a Lawrence growing in emotional maturity at the same time he was learning how to dramatize his particular beliefs with greater precision, clarity, and craftsmanship. The technical advances—stronger narrative coherence, more natural dialogue, more complex characterization—and the major changes in Lawrence's attitudes are ultimately two sides of the same coin. I will be focusing on the transformation of these attitudes and on the continuous process of artistic refinement rather than attempting to run down and account for every inconsequential verbal alteration. My overriding theme is the final emergence of the stories—and of their author as well.

The remainder of this introductory chapter attempts to set the scene. I will speak briefly about Lawrence's early novels to help provide a context for the consideration of the short stories that follows. My findings would be of limited value unless they led to a richer understanding of Lawrence's distinctive achievement as a novelist. This chapter then concludes with a comparison between two related scenes in *The White Peacock* and *The Rainbow*, by way of providing a sort of map of the progress Lawrence made during these years.

Chapter II offers a working history of the *Prussian Officer* volume and deals in detail with the question of its relation to *The Rainbow*. The five chapters that follow are substantive analyses of the six major stories I am treating. These chapters are ordered in a way that parallels the personal and biographical development I am tracing. I have chosen this arrangement because I believe my "biography" of Lawrence's art is perhaps the most important news I have to offer. I begin with "Odour of Chrysanthemums," a story that directly engages the writer's feelings about his parents. "Daughters of the Vicar" also examines his family background and colliery origins. The chapter on "The Shades of Spring" presents the history of Lawrence's reappraisal of his first love; that story is very much a postscript to *Sons and Lovers*. "The White Stocking" offers a vision of mature, married love, and so in its way does "The Thorn in the Flesh," a story set in Germany and composed after the elopement with Frieda. "The Prussian Officer" itself also reflects Lawrence's German experience and contains a major early formulation of ideas basic to the structure and meaning of *The Rainbow*. The final chapter attempts to "place" the *Prussian Officer* volume in Lawrence's career and to consider some of its overall artistic implications.

The key turning-point in Lawrence's lifetime of development came between 1912 and 1915—that is, from the completion of *Sons and Lovers* to the publication of *The Rainbow*. Although my analysis of the six individual *Prussian Officer* stories will follow their progress from inception to final text, my primary emphasis will be on the sweeping revisions of 1914. If *Sons and Lovers* were the last of Lawrence's novels we possessed, he would be remembered as a remarkable footnote to early modern literature, a regional writer who wrote a vivid autobiographical novel in the tradition of the Victorian *Bildungsroman*. The year 1914, Lawrence's *annus mirabilis*, marked his great launching out. He discovered and formulated what he was trying to achieve in *The Rainbow* as he worked toward the completion of that novel. He drafted the *Study of Thomas Hardy*, his first real attempt to define his "doctrine." The final revision of the *Prussian Officer* stories was an important component of Lawrence's artistic development during this transitional year, and in the process some enduring works of short fiction finally came into being.

The White Peacock was begun in 1906 and completed in 1910. *The Trespasser* was written in 1910 and rewritten two years later. These novels are contemporary with the early versions of the *Prussian Officer* stories, and a brief consideration of some of their limitations can help provide a sense of what the Lawrence of 1914 had learned as an artist and an observer of human experience. The sensibility on display in the two books would come as a great surprise to most readers of Lawrence. As Julian Moynahan has put it, there is something almost scandalous about the rapid development of "a hapless provincial from a colliery village" into an "artistic genius."[12]

Although both novels show promise, the overall impression is of a young novelist writing over his head and not managing to control his materials. Lawrence doesn't seem to trust his own voice. Both novels—the earlier with its secondhand Nietzsche and Schopenhauer, the later with its self-conscious pastiche out of Wagnerian opera—strain awkwardly for profundity. Consider the brooding *Weltschmerz* of Cyril, the narrator of *The White Peacock:* "I sat by my window and watched the low clouds reel and stagger past. It seemed as if everything were being swept along—I myself seemed to have lost my substance, to have become detached from concrete things and the firm trodden pavement of everyday life. Onward, always onward, not knowing where, nor why, the wind, the clouds, the rain and the birds and the leaves, everything whirling along—why?" (WP 93).[13] The accidental pun contained in "concrete things and the firm trodden pavement" is only the most striking evidence of artistic immaturity. Even more amazing is Siegmund's soliloquy in *The Trespasser* when he cuts his thigh while swimming—which lurches into unintentional comedy: "That is I, that creeping red, and this whiteness I pride myself on is I, and my black hair, and my blue eyes are I. It is a weird thing to be a person" (T 49).[14]

12. Julian Moynahan, *The Deed of Life: The Novels and Tales of D. H. Lawrence* (Princeton, N.J., 1963), p. 1.

13. *The White Peacock* (Carbondale, Ill.: Southern Illinois University Press, 1966). Copyright 1911, 1921 by D. H. Lawrence and copyright 1930 by Frieda Lawrence. Copyright 1966 by Angelo Ravagli and C. Montague Weekley, Executors of the Estate of Frieda Lawrence Ravagli. Reprinted by permission of Laurence Pollinger Ltd. and the Estate of the late Frieda Lawrence.

14. *The Trespasser* (Mitchell Kennerley, 1912). Reprinted by permission

In these passages and many more like them in the two novels, Lawrence's speculations about the riddle of life are self-conscious and embarrassing. One of the important forward steps in *Sons and Lovers* was the discovery that he could give larger resonance to a novel by discarding such borrowed scaffolding and by confronting his own experience more directly. [15]

Frank Kermode has spoken of the "flourishing regional culture" in the Midlands "founded on the chapel, the free library, and a flow of visits from great speakers." [16] This is true, but if we can judge from the early lectures, "Art and the Individual" and "Rachel Annand Taylor," and from *The White Peacock*, the hallmark of this culture (as understood by the young Lawrence and his friends) was self-conscious conversation packed with allusions to all the latest in painting, poetry, music, and literature. The following passage in which Lettie and Leslie plan marriage is typical: "I'm not one of your souly sort. I can't stand Pre-Raphaelites. You—You're not a Burne-Jonesess—you're an Albert Moore. I think there's more in the warm touch of a soft body than in a prayer. I'll pray with kisses" (WP 95). A passage like this underscores the youth and isolation of Lawrence and the young Midlands intellectuals. The same holds true of the Wagnerian allusions systematically introduced into *The Trespasser*. Again the impression is of earnest self-consciousness—and of a young writer floundering about in search of his voice. The always purple prose achieves nearly sublime heights of Wagnerian ludicrousness in the passage in which Helena picks up a light bulb that floats in to shore:

As he watched her lifting her fingers from off the glass, then gently stroking it, his blood ran hot. He watched her, waited upon her words and movements attentively.

of Laurence Pollinger Ltd. and the Estate of the late Mrs. Frieda Lawrence.

15. The avoidance of his own experience in *The White Peacock* is notorious: he elevates his family to the middle class and kills off his father in the fourth chapter.

16. Kermode, *D. H. Lawrence*, p. 5.

"It is a graceful act on the sea's part," she said. "Wotan is so clumsy—he knocks over the bowl, and flap-flap-flap go the gasping fishes, *pizzicato!*—but the sea——"

Helena's speech was often difficult to render into plain terms. She was not lucid. (T 64)

Lawrence realized quite early that his first two books were false starts. In the autumn of 1910 Lawrence described *The White Peacock* as a "florid prose poem" and *The Trespasser* as "a decorated idyll running to seed in realism" (CL 66–67).

When Lawrence injected Burne-Jones and Wagner—and Rossetti and Maeterlinck and Beardsley and Tchaikovsky—into his earliest novels, he was demonstrating that he belonged to the cultivated world of literature and had risen above the spiritual and intellectual deprivation of his working-class origins. "Culture" is a calling card by which he seeks entrée into official literary society. This is the idea of culture that Lawrence himself would come to condemn in later works, embodying it in such characters as Bertie, the Scotch barrister and reviewer in "The Blind Man," the collecting couple in "Things," and Clifford Chatterley and his crowd at Wragby Hall. The conflict between nature and this shallow notion of culture is a major source of irresolution in the two early novels. The subsequent redefinition of culture and resolution of the conflict were essential to Lawrence's developing artistry.

Sons and Lovers was obviously a major advance. Lawrence's professed purpose in writing the book was therapeutic, and indeed at one level the novel can be seen as his attempt to exorcise his household demons. *Sons and Lovers* plays an important role in Lawrence's developing personal mythology. He wrote the novel with the belief that "one sheds one's sicknesses in books—repeats and presents again one's emotions, to be master of them" (CL 234). When the book was completed, he felt that the sicknesses had, in fact, been shed. The act of working through his problems in fictional form convinced him, at least at the time, that he had successfully resolved the problems. Furthermore, Frieda was at his side when he made the final revisions in Italy. After the difficult and frustrating experiences with Jessie Chambers and Louie Burrows, he had at last found his woman. As a writer and as a man, he felt for the first time that his feet were solidly on the ground.

The artistic gain Lawrence achieved with *Sons and Lovers* was something he could not have predicted. He had discovered that the kind of fiction he had to write must begin as a search for self. From the beginning he had been drawn to using the novel as a medium for exploring the largest questions of man and his relation to the created universe. Now he was armed with the knowledge that any such exploration must begin with a voyage inward.

Though *Sons and Lovers* contains passages of visionary brilliance and though the perspective is sometimes cosmic, there is as yet no systematic basis to the vision. Surely some of the novel's most vivid scenes dramatize man in his relation to the powerful, supercharged energies of the universe: Mrs. Morel in the garden, locked out by her husband; Paul in the cherry tree; Paul's experience with the flowers before breaking off with Miriam; Paul and Clara making love in the field as the peewit calls and the stars wheel. Nevertheless, Lawrence has not yet entered into the artistic world of *The Rainbow*. Part of the problem comes down to his muddle concerning his parents, for he had not mastered his feelings in *Sons and Lovers* as well as he imagined. Indeed it is a critical commonplace that no coherent attitude toward Mr. and Mrs. Morel can be found in the novel.

As Mark Schorer puts it, "Lawrence . . . loves his mother, but he also hates her for compelling his love; and he hates his father with the true Freudian jealousy, but he also loves him for what he is in himself. . . ."[17] Lawrence cannot decide whether Paul is saved by his ability to commune with the otherness of the natural world, a trait learned instinctively from his father, or by the Puritan grit, inherited from his mother, that sends him toward the lighted city. (The famous "drift towards death" letter [CL 160–61], written to Garnett

17. Mark Schorer, "Technique as Discovery," in *The World We Imagine: Selected Essays* (New York, 1968), p. 13.

in November 1912, indicates that Lawrence wasn't even convinced that Paul has managed to survive at all.) The scenes of intense response to nature, impressive as they are, finally do not offer a coherent path through the novel. In *Sons and Lovers* Lawrence for the first time creates the full-fledged Lawrentian universe, but he does not yet seem to fully comprehend it. He is moving toward the ideas he would use and develop in the fiction and expository prose of the succeeding years. But in *Sons and Lovers* the ideas have not been worked out, and the novel suffers.

The nature-culture conflict is part of the confusion. At the time of *Sons and Lovers*, Lawrence's father represented a natural grace and vitality to him, but he also stood for the crude provinciality that the young writer was trying to escape. The mother's willfulness and rigidity stood directly in opposition to her husband's life-giving qualities, but she was also Lawrence's representative of culture and gentility, the values he aspired to through his pursuit of a literary career. The conflict is found in the novel right through the final paragraph. If there is reason for Paul's survival, it is that he is enough his father's son to prevail over his mother's attempts to devour him. Yet on the last page, his "salvation" is signaled by a walk toward the light of the city—motion away from the dark countryside of the father toward the genteel, rational world of the mother. No subsequent Lawrentian protagonist finds strength in walking toward a city.

In Lawrence's later fiction, one of his major character types is the willful woman, resistant to the flow of life and to the fulfillment of the passional self: he was no longer his mother's son. Characters like John Thomas Raynor in "Tickets, Please," Henry Grenfel in "The Fox," Joe Boswell the gypsy, and Oliver Mellors the gamekeeper are related to Lawrence's new perception of—and identification with—the father figure. A fundamental change of attitude was involved. The new ideal was polarity, but more often than not after *The Rainbow* and *Women in Love* it is the male figure who is the bringer of life to the unawakened female. The balance Lawrence achieved at the time of his two greatest novels was not one he could maintain for long.

The great watershed in Lawrence's career falls between *Sons and Lovers* and *The Rainbow*. It is in *The Rainbow* that he leaves behind traditional notions of form and conventional representations of scene, character, and story. We know from Lawrence's strenuous quarrel with Edward Garnett while writing *The Rainbow* that he himself felt that he was making a sharp break with his literary past. He had considered *Sons and Lovers* a great achievement, but he quickly changed his tune. Just before launching into the final revision of the novel in the summer of 1912, three months after the elopement with Frieda, he wrote Garnett a letter about fighting "tooth and claw to keep" his "mate" (CL 135) and closed by saying that he loathed the novel he hadn't even quite completed. In March 1913, before *Sons and Lovers* had been published, he wrote that his new novel was a great advance, "a stratum deeper than I think anybody has ever gone, in a novel" and "quite unlike *Sons and Lovers*" (CL 193). By January of the next year he was surer about what he was attempting in his new novel, and he was also surer about the break between his work in progress and the novel that preceded it: "I have no longer the joy in creating vivid scenes, that I had in *Sons and Lovers*. I don't care much more about accumulating objects in the powerful light of emotion, and making a scene of them. I have to write differently" (CL 263). Garnett had been given carte blanche to make the final revision of *Sons and Lovers*, and in fact he reduced the novel by approximately 10 percent. But Lawrence broke with his mentor over *The Rainbow*, feeling that Garnett was unable to follow him into the new fictional territory he was staking out.

Lawrence found his way for the first time in *Sons and Lovers*, but the true turning point came afterwards. The crucial transition in his art can be located by studying the making of *The Rainbow* and *The Prussian Officer and Other Stories*. Before proceeding to the short story collection, however, I need to clarify what I mean by Lawrence's "maturity." I will do so by contrasting two related scenes—one from *The White Peacock*, the other from *The Rainbow*—to illustrate the great progress during these years.

Like all prolific novelists, Lawrence often reworked scenes he had previously made use of. The tableau of the miner washing his back before the fireplace is almost archetypal in his fiction, and so is the culminating action of flight into destruction. The murder in "The Prussian Officer" and the fight between Paul and Baxter Dawes in *Sons and Lovers* both seem rewritings of the staircase battle between Edward Severn and Joe Thomas in "The Old Adam." As we shall see in Chapter III, variations on the corpse-washing scene that concludes "Odour of Chrysanthemums" can be found in Lawrence's writings from an early poem through *Lady Chatterley's Lover*. When two such reworkings are closely enough related, a comparison can measure Lawrence's artistic development. That is what I propose to do here, using scenes from *The White Peacock* and *The Rainbow*. Once again my purpose will be to demonstrate how much Lawrence had learned about his art during the years that span the making of the *Prussian Officer* stories.

The scenes both take place in a barn, and both involve a male character deeply rooted in agricultural life: George Saxton in *The White Peacock*, Tom Brangwen in *The Rainbow*. Both scenes strive to establish the barn as a vividly experienced alternative to the world of middle-class society. In the earlier novel Cyril gives George the bad news that Lettie and Leslie are "practically engaged" (WP 99) while George is in the barn milking. In *The Rainbow* Tom carries the young Anna out to the barn with him. He feeds the cattle and tries to quiet her while her mother is in labor. In *The White Peacock* "the cattle stirred in their stalls; the chains rattled round the posts . . ." (WP 98). In *The Rainbow* "there was a noise of chains running, as the cows lifted or dipped their heads sharply . . ." (R 74). [18]

The later scene clearly contains a memory of the earlier. [19]

The setting of the scene in *The White Peacock* is its most impressive feature:

> The lamp hung against the barn-wall, softly illuminating the lower part of the building, where bits of hay and white dust lay in the hollows between the bricks, where the curled chips of turnip scattered orange gleams over the earthen floor; the lofty roof, with its swallows' nest under the tiles, was deep in shadow, and the corners were full of darkness, hiding, half hiding, the hay, the chopper, the bins. The light shone along the passages between the stalls, glistening on the moist noses of the cattle, and on the whitewash of the walls. (WP 99)

The scene is brilliantly particularized, and much about it—the "quickness" of the sentence rhythms, the interplay of light and dark, the use of color, the luminous, "visionary" gleam of the total effect—suggests the later Lawrence. Yet the rest of the scene fails to pick up on the implications of the setting. The meaning of the scene is essentially social: Lettie's engagement to Leslie cuts off George's avenue of escape to gentility and seals his fate. Lawrence actually interrupts his barn scene to bring George and Cyril in for tea to emphasize this meaning. In the parallel scene in *The Rainbow*, the merely social meaning is quickly left behind. In *The Rainbow* the visionary intensity of the scene in the barn connects with the grandest metaphysical reverberations contained in the novel. This larger meaning seems almost to be there *in potentia* in *The White Peacock*, but in 1910 Lawrence seems unable to recognize it. [20] George Saxton yearns to escape his agricultural

19. In turn the scene in *The Rainbow* is a trial run for the great barn scenes in "The Blind Man."

20. In this context consider Annable, the brutal gamekeeper with his philosophy of the untrammeled natural life. Cyril is very uneasy with Annable, and Lawrence seems unhappy too: he unexpectedly kills off the character midway through the novel. But the Annable type will reappear in subsequent fiction once Lawrence's attitudes about nature and society have become clearer. Annable is an awkward intrusion in the first novel, but he points forward remarkably to the fiction from *The Rainbow* onward.

lot, but he truly belongs in the barn: this is his defeat. Communion with the elemental forces alive there cannot lead him to self-fulfillment. In contrast the ritual scene of feeding in *The Rainbow* provides Tom Brangwen and his stepdaughter with renewed strength as they come into contact with the mysterious source of life itself. In *The White Peacock* the barn is only a prison, and the rattling chains enslave George as much as they do the cattle.

Most of the rest of the scene in *The White Peacock* consists of awkward dialogue between George and Cyril. The cattle seem to be present in order to crudely symbolize the women George has such difficulties with: " 'Stand still!' he shouted, striking her on the haunch. She seemed to cower like a beaten woman. He swore at her, and continued to milk. She did not yield much that night; she was very restive; he took the stool from beneath him and gave her a good blow; I heard the stool knock on her prominent hip bone" (WP 99–100). One of the cattle knocks George on the cheek with her nose, and he bemoans the fact that he can understand neither cattle nor women. This sort of symbolism is obviously the work of a beginner.

For the most part the language of the scene is rather flat. The charged language of the parallel in *The Rainbow* expresses a full-scale vision of man's place in the cosmos, but the scene in *The White Peacock* possesses no such vision, and the language rarely transcends the commonplace. Lawrence's feelings about his characters are decidedly mixed. George is a man caught in between, and imaginatively that is where Lawrence seems to find himself. *The White Peacock* was written at a time when he was making his own break with his own past of colliery and countryside, and George's inability to make his escape and to realize his potentiality is the center of the tragedy of Nethermere. At the same time the autobiographical Cyril—detached, effete, and deracinated—is evidence enough that Lawrence also had misgivings about the urban literary life that was his goal. He endorses neither the natural nor the cultural, for each alternative has serious drawbacks. The language in the barn scene in *The White Peacock*, indeed of much of the novel, seems somewhat tentative partly because Lawrence is never quite sure of the meaning of the book he is writing. He labored on the novel from 1906 through 1910, yet he was never able to wrestle it into coherence. One aspect of the difficulty was Lawrence's own confused identity at this point in his life.

The cattle-feeding scene in *The Rainbow* is one of the most moving in all of Lawrence. One winter night Lydia Brangwen goes into labor, and Anna, her young daughter, is terrified. Tom decides to take the child out to "supper-up the beast" (R 73) in order to put her terror at rest. I must quote the first part of the scene at some length, for, like all the great scenes in *The Rainbow*, it defies abridgment:

He opened the doors, upper and lower, and they entered into the high, dry barn, that smelled warm even if it were not warm. He hung the lantern on the nail and shut the door. They were in another world now. The light shed softly on the timbered barn, on the whitewashed walls, and the great heap of hay; instruments cast their shadows largely, a ladder rose to the dark arch of a loft. Outside there was the driving rain, inside the softly-illuminated stillness and calmness of the barn.

Holding the child on one arm, he set about preparing the food for the cows, filling a pan with chopped hay and brewer's grains and a little meal. The child, all wonder, watched what he did. A new being was created in her for the new conditions. Sometimes, a little spasm, eddying from the bygone storm of sobbing, shook her small body. Her eyes were wide and wondering, pathetic. She was silent, quite still.

In a sort of dream, his heart sunk to the bottom, leaving the surface of him still, quite still, he rose with the panful of food, carefully balancing the child on one arm, the pan in the other hand. The silky fringe of the shawl swayed softly, grains and hay trickled to the floor; he went along a dimly-lit passage behind the manger, where the horns of the cows pricked out of the obscurity. The child shrank, he balanced stiffly, rested the pan on the manger wall, and tipped out the food, half to this cow, half to the next. There was a noise of chains running, as the cows lifted or dropped their heads sharply; then a contented, soothing sound, a long snuffing as the beasts ate in silence.

The journey had to be performed several times. There was the rhythmic sound of the shovel in the barn, then the man returned walking stiffly between the two weights, the face of the child peering out from the shawl. Then the next time, as he stooped, she freed her arm and put it round his neck, clinging soft and warm, making all easier. (R 74)

One should first observe how the scene is built up from carefully observed and selected details: Tom's balancing act (Anna on one arm, the pan on the other), the grains and hay trickling to the floor, the rattling of the chains and the snuffing of the cattle, Tom's stiffness as he walks carrying his twin loads, the life-giving rain outside. Like Maurice Pervin's barn in "The Blind Man," this is a world of "sheer immediacy" and "rich positivity" (CSS 355). The identification between real things and what they symbolize is direct and complete.

The vivid and sympathetic evocation of the everyday life of the rural Midlands is evidence of Lawrence's debt to the George Eliot of *Adam Bede* and *The Mill on the Floss*. *The Rainbow* shares with these novels an elegiac glow and a strong sense of felt life: Lawrence would have been a great novelist even if he had never moved beyond this decidedly unrevolutionary aspect of his art. The cattle-feeding scene establishes the characters as part of a vanishing agricultural order. Tom Brangwen may be befuddled as regards his relations with his wife, but his identity as a man of the soil is sure and unquestioned. The rhythm of Tom's chore is part of the larger rhythm of farm life. He is part of a world in which human identity is still essentially secure, in which public and private man are still one.

But there is a larger resonance too, one that impressively demonstrates Lawrence's great blossoming in the few years since *The White Peacock*. The scene in *The Rainbow* connects not only with the pattern of agricultural life but also with what is coming to pass at the same time in the house: the entry of a new life into the world. The feeding of the cattle and the childbirth both make contact with the mystery and otherness at the source of life. Both are seen as part of one unified experience: the events of the everyday world are subsumed in the larger ordering of the great world. "They were in another world now."

Tom is reminded of his mother and feels "a boy at home" again: past and present also merge into the same unity, this "timeless stillness" (R 70). It is as if there has been a visitation of the divine into the arena of the commonplace; the ordinary routine of daily life is transfigured. The scene is permeated with a great calm, but that calm is charged to overflowing with the powerful energies at the core of Lawrence's vision of life. The "horns of the cows" that "pricked out of the obscurity" (R 74) are emblematic of these energies. The cattle are no longer symbolic, as they were in *The White Peacock*. Every detail in the scene is first and foremost persuasive on a mimetic level. The larger meanings, cosmic as well as social, of the scene arise naturally from the intensely realized mimetic surfaces.

Little Anna finally relaxes her "fixed, blind will' (R 72) and shares the experience with her father in the barn, at the same time assenting to the birth taking place in the house: "Then the next time, as he stooped, she freed her arm and put it round his neck, clinging soft and warm, making all easier" (R 74). The barn is radiant with stillness—and there is a radiant stillness at the heart of Tom's suffering in which he is able to shelter his distraught child. Anna stops her willful resistance to the life emergies embodied in the scene, instead giving herself over to their flow. Elsie Whiston does the same in "The White Stocking" when she abandons herself to the dance with Sam Adams, the young soldier Bachmann does the same in "The Thorn in the Flesh" when he burns out his shame through sensual fulfillment with his sweetheart. The dance and sexual energies are more intense than those found in the barn, but the relaxation of the will is the same.

The feeding of the cows is a "journey" that "had to be performed several times" (R 74): the experience becomes ritualized. This is one of several important ritual scenes in the novel that dramatize the relation of the "essential" man

or woman to the unknown. Exactly the same sort of ritualiza-
tion of experience is found in the corpse-washing scene in
"Odour of Chrysanthemums" and in the back-washing scene
in "Daughters of the Vicar"—in climactic moments of direct
contact with the unknown. The scene in *The Rainbow* was not
possible at the time of *The White Peacock:* Lawrence's vision
of the connectedness of the everyday world and the unknown
beyond it came into full focus and coherence only in 1914.

This vision was built on the bedrock of Lawrentian doctrine—what he called his metaphysic—and that emerging
doctrine plays an important role in the scene in *The Rainbow*.
Lawrence's exploration of his metaphysic in expository prose
dates from the brief Preface to *Sons and Lovers*—never intended
for publication—which was written in 1913 after the completion of the novel, and, as we shall see, after the composition
in the same year of the story called "The Prussian Officer."
The *Study of Thomas Hardy*, which antedates the 1914 revision
of *The Rainbow*, is the first major work of metaphysic, and it
develops in great detail the dualism Lawrence was working
toward.

Lawrentian metaphysic is generally idiosyncratic and
often opaque. Nevertheless, the doctrine was immensely
important to him, providing an essential underpinning for
his art: "Men live and see according to some gradually
developing and gradually withering vision. This vision exists
also as a dynamic idea or metaphysic—exists first as such. Then
it is unfolded into life and art."[21] There seems to be something
like an effect of oscillation between art and metaphysic. It's
impossible to say which comes first because both exist as part
of the same ongoing process: metaphysic unfolds into art,
but then in turn the "pseudo-philosophy . . . is deduced from

21. *Fantasia of the Unconscious,* quoted from *Psychoanalysis and the Unconscious*
and *Fantasia of the Unconscious,* pp. xiv–xv. Copyright 1921, 1922 by
Thomas Seltzer, Inc., renewed 1949, 1950 by Frieda Lawrence. Copyright 1960 by The Viking Press, Inc. Reprinted by permission of
Laurence Pollinger Ltd., the Estate of the late Mrs. Frieda Lawrence,
and The Viking Press, Inc.

the novels and poems."[22] Each work, whether expository or purely imaginative, as it succeeds its predecessor is an attempt to explore and annex new territory. Each new territory then provides a starting point for further exploration.

The Rainbow is a more coherent novel than *Sons and Lovers* partly because of the new role of doctrine in the Lawrentian aesthetic. It is only at the time of *The Rainbow* and the final revision of the *Prussian Officer* stories that doctrine became a crucial consideration of his art. The doctrine would change, often radically, even leading him into such blind alleys as the fascination with leadership in the first half of the twenties. Nevertheless, all his subsequent ventures into art would work at making such a reconciliation.

It is not necessary to be well-versed in Lawrentian metaphysic in order to understand the scene in the barn with Tom and the young Anna, and yet the full meaning depends on the emerging doctrine. Even the repeated interplay of light and dark, prefigured in the parallel scene in *The White Peacock*, is now based on dialectical premises. Lawrence's universe is radically dualistic. New creation comes out of the perfect polarity between antithetical principles: male-female, Love-Law. However, as Graham Hough puts it, the "intense polarity is never a fixed relation" but rather a "matter of momentary revelations."[23] The dialogue between dark and light in the scene helps produce the moment of harmony and stillness that can lead to such revelation.

As the scene progresses, it moves farther into the realm of doctrine:

The two sat very quiet. His mind, in a sort of trance, seemed to become more and more vague. He held the child close to him. A quivering little shudder, re-echoing from her sobbing, went down her limbs. He held her closer. Gradually she relaxed, the eyelids began to sink over her dark, watchful eyes. As she sank to sleep, his mind became blank.

22. *Fantasia*, p. xiv.
23. Graham Hough, *The Dark Sun: A Study of D. H. Lawrence* (New York, 1957), p. 228.

When he came to, as if from sleep, he seemed to be sitting in
a timeless stillness. What was he listening for? He seemed to be
listening for some sound a long way off, from beyond life. (R 75)

We are dealing here with a shift of consciousness into a more
primal level of awareness. The strange sleep signals an im-
minent change of being, and when Tom comes to, he realizes
that he is in the presence of the unknown.

He then carries the sleeping Anna back into the house
and goes upstairs to his wife. The sound of the owl and the
moaning of Lydia in labor are perceived by Tom as "not
human." Lydia "was beautiful to him—but it was not human.
He had a dread of her as she lay there. What had she to do
with him? She was other than himself." He recognizes and
even fears the otherness of his wife. In the grip of the intense
experience of this night, he once again is able to perceive
her, not as someone he knows personally and loves, but more
elementally, as a mysterious, ultimately unknowable focus
of life's energies. The birth of the child is an event that occurs
on a more basic level than that of human personality and
relationship. Lydia does not even "know him as himself. But
she knew him as the man. She looked at him as a woman in
childbirth looks at the man who begot the child in her: an
impersonal look, in the extreme hour, female to male" (R 76).
This language and these ideas are closely related to the famous
letter to Garnett about the "old stable ego—of the character,"
to be discussed more fully in Chapter II. The same sort of language is also found throughout the *Prussian Officer* volume. At
this point I wish only to underscore the strongly theoretical
orientation of the passage. Tom and Lydia, having gone
through the crucible of an intense "life" experience, have
been reduced down to male and female.

A "great, scalding peace" goes over Tom. He is never fully
comfortable in the presence of this Polish lady whom he never
comes to know and who seems a stranger. But he does understand intuitively that the polarity achieved between them—
and renewed in this scene—provides them with rich fulfillment and with connection with the unknown as well. Tom
goes outside, lifts his face to the rain and feels the darkness,

exulting in his contact with the mystery of life and over his own rebirth. When he turns to go indoors he does so "humbly," knowing that life has mysteriously bestowed its bounty on him. He has been "silenced" and "overcome": "There was the infinite world, eternal, unchanging, as well as the world of life" (R 76). The scene in the barn culminates in a moment of transfiguration. Such transfiguration is also the keynote of the best of the *Prussian Officer* volume.

Lawrentian metaphysic is nearly always crucial to his artistic accomplishment. Lawrence came into his own only when he decided that his writing would be founded on the interplay of art and metaphysic, only when he realized that he wanted to interpret the life around him in terms of a larger, even a cosmic, vision of human possibility. Some will argue that this decision was to prove immensely detrimental to his career, for it had the effect of legitimizing one of his worst artistic proclivities, his tendency toward preachiness. Finally, however, the important consideration is the great artistic advance made possible by the decision.

The best of the *Prussian Officer* tales belong to the same turning point in Lawrence's career. They are filled with similar moments of elemental stillness, moments in which the author strips away the surfaces of the everyday world and reveals the mystery at the heart of the nonhuman source of life. Like *The Rainbow*, the final versions of these stories dramatize individuals in the grip of the larger impersonal forces of the universe. Between *The White Peacock* and *The Rainbow* Lawrence worked his way toward a visionary art, and he also began to work out his metaphysic, aiming to produce an art with prophetic overtones. The same movement toward doctrine is discernible in the *Prussian Officer* stories. But even beyond such important similarities, a unity exists between the emergent tales and novels. This unity can be traced to Lawrence's vision of the "oneness of life; the separateness and irreducible otherness of lives; the supreme importance of 'fulfilment' in the individual."[24]

24. F. R. Leavis, *D. H. Lawrence: Novelist* (New York, 1956), p. 117.

My study of the evolution of the *Prussian Officer* stories
holds up a mirror to Lawrence's progress and artistic growth
during these years of crisis and emergence from crisis. Early
insubstantial tales like "A Sick Collier," "Goose Fair,"
"Second Best," and "A Fragment of Stained Glass" were
essentially dead ends and did not receive much revision.
Lawrence must have realized that they were beyond salvaging:
they exist in the volume as artistic fillers and as interesting
residue of a younger artist who had not yet found his true
medium. But when he revised such stories as "Odour of
Chrysanthemums," "Daughters of the Vicar," "The Shades
of Spring," "The White Stocking," and "The Thorn in the
Flesh," he radically transformed them, making them an
integral part of his newly emergent vision. The making of the
title story, "The Prussian Officer," is (as we shall see) a category unto itself. Yet it too has an important tale to tell in
Lawrence's search for a fiction that embodies both art and
doctrine.

Lawrence was to pursue his art and his vision for the rest of
his life. Some of the doctrine that was to evolve in later years
was less than beneficial to the creation of great fiction. Yet
never was he to abandon his belief that art and doctrine,
Love and Law, must be wedded. The very fragmentariness
of *Aaron's Rod* and *Kangaroo*, the shrillness of *The Plumed Serpent*,
are evidence that he was himself aware that the process of
reconciliation was not always easy or successful.

It was in 1914, the time of *The Rainbow*, the time of the
final *Prussian Officer* revisions, that Lawrence fully committed
himself to the visionary art that he would make his own for
the rest of his life. My study of the *Prussian Officer* stories aims
to cast new light on that apprenticeship—and on the great
writer of fiction who left the apprenticeship behind.

Chapter II

The Prussian Officer and Other Stories
A Working History

"I am drudging away revising the Stories"

The development and evolution of the *Prussian Officer* stories provide an interesting map of Lawrence's literary apprenticeship. In Lawrence's letters, throughout his career, most of the references to his stories are related to the ongoing effort to sell them. The progress toward Duckworth's publication of *The Prussian Officer and Other Stories* in December 1914 is clearly traceable. In this chapter I will indicate the key steps along this road up to June 1914 before focusing in greater detail on the last crucial revisions and the facts of publication. I will also take up the important question of the relationship between the final *Prussian Officer* revisions and *The Rainbow.*

In the autumn of 1907 the *Nottinghamshire Guardian* advertised a Christmas short story contest. As Jessie Chambers, the original of Miriam, recalled, Lawrence decided to enter it in a comprehensive fashion: "During his second autumn in College, Lawrence devised a plan for raising a little money. A local journal offered a prize of three guineas for the best Christmas story. Lawrence wrote three short stories, and suggested that I, a college friend, and he, should each submit one story to this journal."[1] The "college friend," toward whom Jessie was understandably somewhat diffident, was Louie Burrows, Jessie's successor as Lawrence's fiancée. In October 1907 Lawrence described the contest to Louie, declaring that he had written some stories "just for fun" and because Jessie and her brother "asked me why I didn't, & so put me upon doing it to show I could" (LL 6). It seems as if D. H. Lawrence wrote his first short stories on something like a dare.

1. Jessie Chambers ("E. T."), *D. H. Lawrence: A Personal Record* (London, 1965), p. 113. This book will hereafter be cited as ET.

Jessie submitted his story entitled "A Prelude" for the
"Enjoyable Christmas" category, and it won. It was published
in the *Guardian* in December, marking Lawrence's first
appearance in print. He realized the story's limitations and
never republished it in his lifetime; in fact, it wasn't redis-
covered until 1949. The other two stories Lawrence submitted
were early versions of two of the *Prussian Officer* stories. The
story he sent in under his own name for the "Legend" category—appropriately entitled "Legend"—later became "A
Fragment of Stained Glass." The "Amusing Adventure"
Louie submitted was an early form of "The White Stocking."
Thus, "A Fragment of Stained Glass" and "The White Stocking" are the *Prussian Officer* stories with the longest histories.
"A Prelude," the only innocuous story among the three
submitted, is the story that won, a fact that seems to prophesy
Lawrence's lifetime of difficulties with the reading public.

Lawrence the short story writer had set out with a bona
fide local success. His productivity was never to slacken. The
original version of "The Shadow in the Rose Garden," with
its echoed situation from *Jane Eyre*, is also early work, and the
minor "Second Best" dates from sometime in this period. By
October 1908 he was sending his blue-stocking friend
Blanche Jennings a self-conscious query about magazines
where he could place his stories: "Where could I send short
stories such as I write? . . . I will take to writing frivolously
and whimsically, if I can—if I could but write as I behave!
There, I've had twenty years' experience in dishing up my
strong-flavoured feelings in a nice smooth milk sauce with a
sprinkle of nutmeg or cinnamon; but I've only had a few
months of experience in making melted butter to be served
with my writing" (CL 30).

On 30 June 1909 Lawrence wrote Louie that he was
pleased she was writing stories: "I can't do 'em myself. Send
me them, please, & I'll see if I can put a bit of surface on them
& publish them for you. We'll collaborate, shall we?" (LL 38).
This is the first mention in the correspondence of Lawrence
and Louie working together on a story. The exact role she

played in the composition of "Goose Fair" will probably never be known, but it seems likely that she wrote the first draft.[2] At any rate "Goose Fair," which dates from the early summer of 1909, marked another step forward in the history of Lawrence's short story publication, for on 26 July 1909 he sent a story to the London and Provincial Press Agency to be placed with a publisher. A misunderstanding about the Agency's fee led to the decision to "send my tales direct to the mags now" (LL 42). He considered beginning with a new magazine called the *Tramp*, but at this point his literary fortunes were to improve dramatically.

Lawrence had first shown a copy of the *English Review* to the Chambers family at Christmas 1908. With Lawrence's permission, Jessie copied out some poems in June 1909 and sent them to the magazine. In August, Ford Madox Ford, the editor, wrote encouragingly and said he wanted to meet Lawrence. Lawrence visited Ford the next month, and on September 11 he revealed to Louie that some of his poetry would appear in the November *Review*. Ford would be "glad to read any of the work I like to send him" (LL 43). The young writer was quick to take him up on the offer.

Lawrence sent *The White Peacock* to Ford in October 1909 (and to Heinemann in the middle of December). He sent "Goose Fair" and an early version of "Odour of Chrysanthemums" to the magazine in early December, both of which were accepted. Eventually the magazine also published versions of "A Fragment of Stained Glass," "Second Best," "The Thorn in the Flesh," and "The Prussian Officer" (among the stories collected in *The Prussian Officer and Other Stories*), as well as such important later tales as "England, My England," "Samson and Delilah," "The Blind Man," and "The Horse Dealer's Daughter."

The *English Review* successfully launched the young short

---

2. In July 1909 he suggested that they "go whacks" (LL 39) on the costs and profits of the story. Subsequently, he referred to it as "your, my, story" (LL 43), and when he sent Louie the check he received from the *English Review*, he described it as "the first-fruits of your literary tree" (LL 50).

story writer into the world of magazine publication. The appearance of "Odour of Chrysanthemums" in June 1911 was a particular turning point, for this great story attracted much attention. Martin Secker—who was Lawrence's principal English publisher from the early twenties onward—was so impressed that he wrote immediately, offering to print a volume of short stories.[3] Lawrence, flabbergasted, replied on June 11 that he sat "in doubt and wonder" (CL 78) over the offer, for he had written only five or six stories at the time. Spurred by the good news of a "book of short stories . . . practically promised for the spring" (LL 112), he wrote a long short story, almost certainly "New Eve and Old Adam," two nights later. Chances are, the offer was also instrumental in Lawrence's beginning the first version of "Daughters of the Vicar" on 15 July.

At the end of August, Edward Garnett first came onto the scene. Garnett, an editor for Gerald Duckworth, Ltd., wrote Lawrence on behalf of the *Century*, an American magazine he was trying to find stories for. Undoubtedly a reading of "Odour of Chrysanthemums" in the June *Review* called Garnett's attention to the young writer. Lawrence met Garnett in October 1911, which was the beginning of the close association that lasted several years until the quarrel about *The Rainbow*. Lawrence had broken with Ford over *The Trespasser*; Garnett became his new mentor as well as his close friend. It also helped that Garnett could "introduce me to quite a lot of people. I am not keen on it, but he says my business is to get known" (LL 142).

Garnett was particularly helpful with the publication of *Sons and Lovers*. He brought it to Duckworth and made the final revision of the text. He also encouraged Lawrence to rewrite *The Trespasser*, which he did in January and February 1912. Most of the extant letters about the short fiction written before 1912 were addressed to Louie Burrows. From the beginning of 1912 until the publication of *The Prussian*

3. *Letters from D. H. Lawrence to Martin Secker, 1911–1930* (privately printed, 1970), p. 1.

Officer, Garnett, serving in the multiple role of friend, literary adviser, and informal agent, became the recipient of most of these letters.

The plans for the Secker volume of short fiction apparently fell through sometime early in 1912. Lawrence didn't have enough first-rate material ready, and he was having trouble trying to deal with too many publishers at the same time. On 20 October 1911 he wrote Garnett that Heinemann wanted to "publish the verses" and wanted him to "withhold the short stories from Martin Secker until autumn" (CL 83). He was trying to perform quite a juggling act: Heinemann, Duckworth, and Secker; poetry, a novel, and short fiction. He was still speaking about "The Secker volume" of stories in a letter to Garnett on 7 January 1912, a few weeks after the composition of the original version of "The Shades of Spring," but clearly he was beginning to have doubts. "What shall I say to Secker?" (AH 21).[4] Meanwhile in February or March "A Sick Collier" was one of four sketches of colliery life he wrote in connection with a national coal strike. Secker renewed his offer, but the project probably went a-glimmering before the elopement with Frieda on 3 May. Lawrence was also making progress as a novelist: the first version of *Sons and Lovers* was finished in April 1912, and Lawrence's final revisions were completed in Italy in November.

On 29 June Lawrence told Garnett that he had written three stories in Germany (including the early version of "The Christening") "under the influence of Frieda" with a "moral tone" that "would not agree" with his countrymen (CL 133). A little over a month later, his money was getting scarce, and short story publication became more urgent. He planned to "write six stories" because he had to

4. *The Letters of D. H. Lawrence,* edited by Aldous Huxley (London: William Heinemann Ltd., 1932; New York: Viking, 1932). Copyright 1932 by the Estate of D. H. Lawrence, copyright 1960 by Angelo Ravagli and C. Montague Weekley, Executors of the Estate of Frieda Lawrence Ravagli. Reprinted by permission of Laurence Pollinger Ltd., the Estate of the late Mrs. Frieda Lawrence, and The Viking Press, Inc.

"try and make running money" (CL 137). Lawrence counted on his tales to provide him with short-term money. For example, in September 1911 he wrote Louie that he would have some cash after he was "paid for the next story" (LL 139). In 1916 he wrote J. B. Pinker, who had become his agent in 1914, that when he finished *Women in Love* he would "*only* write stories *to sell*. I hate getting further into debt" (CL 469). These remarks in no way undermine the artistic seriousness with which Lawrence regarded his short fiction. They merely emphasize the hard facts of his financial situation. Money from the novels was scarce, a situation that became even more acute with the banning of *The Rainbow* and his inability to sell *Women in Love* during World War I. Obviously he could write and sell short stories more quickly than novels, and he relied on them to keep a little money at hand.

Lawrence began *The Insurrection of Miss Houghton*, the novel which ultimately became *The Lost Girl*, in late December 1912. He laid it aside in mid-April and did not complete it until after the war. He began *The Sisters*, which was to grow into *The Rainbow* and *Women in Love*, in March 1913 and finished it by early June. Following his characteristic pattern of alternating between work on novels and on short fiction, Lawrence spent the late spring and summer of 1913 engaged in a great flurry of activity with his short fiction.

By 10 June he had finished "Honour and Arms," the first version of "The Prussian Officer," and he probably finished "Vin Ordinaire," the original "Thorn in the Flesh," a few days later. He then embarked on a project that took most of the summer. By this time he had a considerable backlog of unpublished stories, dating all the way back to "The White Stocking." In the summer of 1913 he revised most of these tales and tried to get them into print. "Daughters of the Vicar," "The Christening," "The Shadow in the Rose Garden," "A Sick Collier," "New Eve and Old Adam," and "The Primrose Path" are among the stories he tried to sell during the summer, all of them almost certainly revised in one way or another.

Lawrence was back in England from mid-June until

early August of 1913, and it was obviously much easier to round up all his manuscripts there. This logistical fact plus his financial needs made the plan for the summer extremely sensible. Perhaps there was a hidden psychological undercurrent too. Lawrence was embarked on a new life; it was time to clear his desk of all the vestiges of the old.

The 1913 revisions required an intense burst of energy. In mid-July he wrote that he was "drudging away revising the Stories. How glad I shall be when I have cleared that mess up!" (CL 213). A few days later he wrote that he was "swotting away at the short stories—and shall be glad to get them done" (CL 214). By July 22 he was already thinking of his return to Europe—and to the rewriting of *The Sisters*: "I have been grubbing away among the short stories. God, I shall be glad when it is done. I shall begin my novel again in Germany" (CL 215).

The summer's work was profitable. Lawrence sold the early versions of both "The Prussian Officer" and "The Thorn in the Flesh" to the *English Review*. Among the earlier stories that ultimately appeared in the *Prussian Officer* collection, he sold "A Sick Collier," "The Christening," and "The Shadow in the Rose Garden" at this time. The latter two stories appeared in the *Smart Set* in February and March 1914. "The White Stocking," which was published in the October number of the same magazine, may have been purchased at the same time. Most of the stories subsequently collected in *The Prussian Officer* had come a long way from their original composition, but even so, in 1913 all the best of the stories except "The Prussian Officer" itself remained very much *in potentia*. It was the concentrated period of revision the following year that was to make all the difference. The final recasting of these stories is integrally a part of the process that produced Lawrence's great Brangwen saga. The relationship between short story collection and novel needs to be considered in fuller detail before I turn to the individual stories.

The letters to Garnett about the composition of the novel

that eventually evolved into *The Rainbow* and *Women in Love*
contain Lawrence's most impressive statements about a
work in progress. He experienced more difficulty wrestling
the materials into shape than he ever had before; all the
while he felt certain that he was creating a new kind of
novel. Since Garnett heartily disliked the early versions of
The Rainbow that he read, Lawrence was challenged to articulate his aims.

If the novel had begun as a "pot-boiler" (CL 197) in
March 1913, it soon had grown into a major statement of
what was to be his most important theme: "I can only write
what I feel pretty strongly about: and that, at present, is the
relation between men and women. After all, it is *the* problem
of today, the establishment of a new relation, or the read-
justment of the old one, between men and women" (CL
200). Apparently the first version of the novel, finished by
June 1913, was dominated by Frieda; Lawrence wrote that
he had tried to "depict Frieda's God Almightiness in all its
glory" (CL 208). He hadn't worked out the character of
Ursula even in the second version and conceded to Garnett the difficulty of "trying to graft on to the character of
Louie, the character, more or less, of Frieda" (CL 263). By
the third writing the experience of living with Frieda had
been better assimilated and appears only with the indirect-
ness of art.

A letter to his acquaintance Henry Savage in the autumn
of 1913, while Lawrence was working on the second version
of *The Rainbow*, is one of the first full statements of what he
was attempting:

There is something in the Greek sculpture that any soul is hungry
for—something of the eternal stillness that lies under all movement, under all life, like a source, incorruptible and inexhaustible.
It is deeper than change, and struggling. So long I have acknowl-
edged only the struggle, the stream, the change. And now I begin
to feel something of the source, the great impersonal which never
changes and out of which all change comes. (CL 241)

Lawrence had abandoned the Greek sculpture metaphor

by the time he was writing the more intense letters to Garnett in the spring of 1914, but although the descriptive terms changed, his purpose did not. The attempt to reach the stillness that lies beneath change is an attempt to create an art capable of discovering the deepest reality. "The great impersonal" reverberates throughout the prose and poetry of this greatest period of his creative life. In all the best stories in the *Prussian Officer* collection, the crucial moment arrives when characters find themselves in the grip of the charged, impersonal forces of the universe: Mrs. Bates's reverie over the corpse of her husband in "Odour of Chrysanthemums," the dance in "The White Stocking," the back-washing scene in "Daughters of the Vicar," the murder in "The Prussian Officer" itself, the restorative love-making in "The Thorn in the Flesh."

Garnett did not like the second version of the novel, and Lawrence began it a third time in February 1914. On 22 April "with only some 80 pages more to write" (CL 272) Lawrence replied to Garnett's suggestion that he was free to take the novel to another house besides Duckworth. His defense of the book in this famous letter, in which he describes himself as a "passionately religious man," is one of the most eloquent artistic credos he ever wrote. The same letter contains a significant statement of the reason Lawrence felt the third version of his novel finally achieved what he was setting out to accomplish: "I am sure of this now, this novel. It is a big and beautiful work. Before, I could not get my soul into it. That was because of the struggle and the resistance between Frieda and me. Now you will find her and me in the novel, I think, and the work is of both of us" (CL 272). In Lawrence's mind, his novel was not only an expression of the relationship he was building with Frieda but also an integral part of the working out of that relationship. Frieda was equally important in the revisions of the *Prussian Officer* stories he was about to undertake.[5]

5. Furthermore, when Lawrence tells Garnett he is "sure of . . . this novel," he is declaring that he has outgrown the need for a mentor. Less

By 5 June Garnett had read the entire novel and had written Lawrence about it. The vigor of Lawrence's reaction to Garnett's letter makes it clear that the criticism was sweeping. The familiar letter to Garnett of 5 June 1914 echoes throughout my discussion of the later revisions of the most important *Prussian Officer* tales. Bear in mind that Lawrence wrote this letter shortly before undertaking the sweeping revisions of the stories:

That which is physic—non-human, in humanity, is more interesting to me than the old-fashioned human element—which causes one to conceive a character in a certain moral scheme and make him consistent. . . . In Turgenev, and in Tolstoi, and in Dostoievsky, the moral scheme into which all the characters fit . . . is, whatever the extraordinariness of the characters themselves, dull, old, dead. . . . I don't so much care about what the woman *feels*—in the ordinary usage of the word. That presumes an *ego* to feel with. I only care about what the woman *is*—what she IS—inhumanly, physiologically, materially—according to the use of the word: but for me, what she *is* as a phenomenon (or as representing some greater, inhuman will), instead of what she feels according to the human conception. . . . You mustn't look in my novel for the old stable *ego*—of the character. There is another *ego*, according to whose action the individual is unrecognisable, and passes through, as it were, allotropic states which it needs a deeper sense than any we've been used to exercise, to discover are states of the same radically unchanged element. (Like as diamond and coal are the same pure single element of carbon. The ordinary novel would trace the history of the diamond—but I say, "Diamond, what! This is carbon." And my diamond might be coal or soot, and my theme is carbon.) (CL 281-82)

Lawrence's defense of his novel articulates a deep dissatisfaction with nineteenth-century modes of fiction. The world of 1914 included aircraft and radiotelegraphy, psychoanalysis, Postimpressionism, and an ominous arms race. New forces had been released, and new fictional forms were needed to express and contain them. Though the oddly

---

than a year before, he had told Garnett he would be glad to "re-write the book" (CL 204) after hearing his adviser's criticisms.

scientific language is somewhat opaque, the basic meaning is clear enough. The letter to Garnett describes an attempt to delve beneath the surface in the creation of character, to probe deeper than man in his human relationships. In focusing on man as a representation of "some greater, inhuman will," Lawrence seeks to understand him in terms of the elemental laws of matter and energy that govern the universe. The novelist is interested in what a character "*is* as a phenomenon," not in what he "*feels.*"

This letter is the key statement in the formulation of Lawrence's mature aesthetic. He had written his first novel, *The White Peacock,* with the pastoral tradition and George Eliot in mind. By June 1914 that vision had expanded immensely. Fortunately, he remained more interested in man the social animal than the letter indicates. The point is that his work had taken on a new perspective in which man would be perceived as one of the phenomena in a world of living and nonliving things. John Galsworthy could write about diamond, and Arnold Bennett could write about coal or soot. Lawrence's new theme was carbon.

This cosmic vision is discernible in Lawrence's fiction from the beginning, including such an early story as "A Fragment of Stained Glass" and aspects of his first three novels. However, in 1914 the achievement and artistic exploration and unfolding of this vision became the explicit purpose of Lawrence's career. He was now equipped with a style and, increasingly, with a theoretical vocabulary sufficient to his ambition to write about men and women from such a grandiose perspective.

We have already seen that Secker's offer to publish a volume of short stories had come to nothing. In the autumn of 1913 Lawrence hoped that "The Prussian Officer," "The Thorn in the Flesh," "Once," and perhaps another Prussian story (which may have been the projected "Mortal Coil") would make a little book after they had all been published in the *English Review.* This project also failed to materialize, partly because it was superseded by the contract with Duckworth to publish *The Prussian Officer and Other Stories.*

Lawrence returned to England in late June 1914[6] and made arrangements to sell *The Rainbow.* David Garnett's account of the sale of the book to Methuen illustrates the close relationship between that contract and the arrangement with Duckworth for the *Prussian Officer* collection: "Lawrence had finished *The Rainbow*, for which Methuen's offered him £300 advance. In spite of all Edward [Garnett] could do, Duckworth would not give so much, but agreed to publish a volume of short stories, which came out several months later under the title of The Prussian Officer."[7] It seems doubtful that Garnett tried to do as much to place the novel with Duckworth as his son David remembers. The sale of Lawrence's first book of short stories seems almost apologetic: Duckworth wouldn't risk much on the novel but would buy the short stories as a kind of consolation prize. It was Pinker who placed *The Rainbow* with Methuen. With this sale, Pinker became Lawrence's agent until 1921, replacing the informal arrangement with Garnett in much the same way Garnett had replaced Ford. The difference is that Ford and Garnett were also mentors, but Pinker was only an agent.

Lawrence put aside the novel at this point and devoted most of his time to revising his short stories and getting the collection into print. Early in July he started gathering up the magazine versions of the tales. Considering the extent of the revision of many of the stories, Lawrence worked at a phenomenal speed. Most of the work was completed between the return to England and the middle of July.

The key document here is the letter Lawrence wrote to Garnett on 14 July 1914, one day after his marriage to Frieda in the Register Office in South Kensington. With

6. Lawrence to Edward Marsh, 25[?] June 1914, unpublished letter in the Henry W. and Albert A. Berg Collection of the New York Public Library.
7. David Garnett, *The Golden Echo* (New York, 1954), p. 246. Of course as it turned out, *The Rainbow* was not finally completed until April 1915, and the proofs were heavily corrected that summer.

this letter he sent "another batch of the short stories"; the
first batch had been dispatched to Duckworth ten days
earlier. Lawrence had "gone over the stories very carefully"
(AH 201-2). As he wrote Edward Marsh the next day: "I
have just finished getting together a book of short stories.
Lord, how I've worked again at these stories—most of them—
forging them up" (CL 287). Only the magazine version of "The
Thorn in the Flesh" still needed to be revised, and he planned to
finish work on it in a day or two.

Lawrence asked Garnett to "go through the selection I
have sent in, and see if there is any you would leave out, and
any you would like putting in" (AH 201). He also proposed
an order for the twelve stories, beginning with "A Fragment
of Stained Glass" and "Goose Fair" and concluding with
"Vin Ordinaire" (the original title of "The Thorn in the
Flesh") and "Honour and Arms" (the original title of "The
Prussian Officer" itself). This order is worth remarking, since
it bears no resemblance to the order of the stories in
the published book. Lawrence also asked Garnett which
story should be used for the title story, suggesting "Goose
Fair" as a possibility.

The puzzle concerning the arrangement of the stories can
be explained by examining the first proofs of the book,
which Lawrence corrected in mid-October 1914 (CL 292).
Through a happy accident, a set of these first proofs is extant.
Lawrence promised his old Eastwood friend Willie Hopkin
a copy of his short story collection but apparently forgot to
send him one. In January 1915 he sent Hopkin a splendid
substitute: "I just remember I've got this set of duplicate
proofs of my stories, and perhaps you'll accept them in
lieu of a bound volume. If ever I rise to fame these will be
unique—because there are many differences between these
sheets and those revised and published . . ." (CL 307). These
proofs, marked "First Proofs" and dated 1-19 October
1914, are among the Hopkin papers in the collection of the
Local Studies Library of the Nottinghamshire County
Library.

The order of the stories in these proofs (hereafter referred to as the Hopkin proofs) is exactly that proposed by Lawrence in his letter to Garnett of 14 July. In the proof set, the Prussian stories are known by their magazine titles. The story that Lawrence calls "The Dead Rose" in his letter ("The Soiled Rose" in its magazine version, "The Shades of Spring" in *The Prussian Officer*) is indeed entitled "The Dead Rose." These proofs lack a title page, but one must conclude that they constitute an early, unpublished state of the short story collection.

Autograph revisions in Lawrence's hand are found on only twenty pages of the Hopkin proofs, mostly in the story called "The Dead Rose." More often than not, these alterations did not find their way into the *Prussian Officer* text—and frequently *The Prussian Officer* prints a reading that Lawrence had *eliminated* in the minimal revision of the Hopkin proofs. It is evident that Lawrence revised most of the stories again before publication, some of them rather extensively. Lawrence's own distinction between the Hopkin "sheets and those revised and published" is clear enough. The limited holograph revision of the Hopkin proofs was a false start of some sort.

The second set of first proofs that Lawrence must have revised and sent to the printer is not extant, and no second proofs exist. There can be no doubt that Lawrence was fully involved in the final preparation of his text. However, it was Edward Garnett who renamed the title story and gave the collection its name, hoping to capitalize on the war market. Lawrence didn't like the change—"Garnett was a devil to call my book of stories *The Prussian Officer*" (CL 296)—but he went along with it. My guess is that Garnett was also initially responsible for the revised order of stories, but this too is a matter Lawrence would have been consulted about. Once "The Prussian Officer" had become the title story, the decision to rearrange the order must have followed naturally. And after all, the order as printed is much stronger and more calculated than the order Lawrence had originally proposed.[8]

It is important to observe that all the 1914 revisions—the key recasting of July, the quite limited revision in the Hopkin proofs, and the revision in the lost final proof set—are very much of a piece. The July revision is the most important: the two revisions in proof simply follow up on the implications of the fundamental recasting that took place at midyear. The crucial "re-seeing" occurred during this concentrated period of intensive work.

However, just when Lawrence seemed to be hitting his stride, both artistically and professionally, he received a great setback. Early in August the lucrative contract with Methuen for *The Rainbow* was unexpectedly canceled, and the manuscript was returned. He was left without the financial security he had counted on, and the outbreak of World War I made it impossible for him and Frieda to return to Italy: "Here is a state of affairs—what is going to become of us?" (CL 289).

Lawrence understandably needed a breather from his novel, and he went forward with his plans for a book on Thomas Hardy, his great fictional precursor. The project was ultimately to become the *Study of Thomas Hardy*, unpublished in Lawrence's lifetime and probably never brought to final form. The *Study* is now recognized as having had a vital impact on the final shape of *The Rainbow*. H. M. Daleski in *The Forked Flame* was the first to point this out, but the classic account is contained in Mark Kinkead-Weekes's "The Marble and the Statue: The Exploratory Imagination of D. H. Lawrence."

Kinkead-Weekes illuminates *The Rainbow* and *Women in Love* by scrutinizing in detail the ongoing creative process

8. The published order leads with strength (the two Prussian stories and "Daughters of the Vicar"); it groups together six stories of conflict in love and marriage; it offers the comic relief of "The Christening" as the next-to-last story; and it concludes impressively with the powerfully elegiac "Odour of Chrysanthemums."

that brought the novels into being. This work is a model for studies of textual evolution, and we are also indebted to its author for his concept of Lawrence's "exploratory imagination." Nevertheless, Kinkead-Weekes's case is weakened by his treatment—or rather his nontreatment—of the *Prussian Officer* stories. "The Marble and the Statue" contains a chronological account of Lawrence's progress from the time of the beginning of *The Sisters* and culminating with the completion of *Women in Love*, but the sweeping revisions of the short stories in July 1914 slip by without so much as a mention.

The major 1914 revision of the best of the *Prussian Officer* stories (excepting the title story itself) was the last imporant piece of work Lawrence completed before receiving the bad news about *The Rainbow* in August. The *Study of Thomas Hardy* was the project that came between that news and the beginning of the fourth version of the novel, and Kinkead-Weeke's case for the impact of the expository work on the novel is compelling. However, many of the things that Kinkead-Weekes believes Lawrence learned through writing the *Study* had already been learned in the process of revising the best stories in *The Prussian Officer*.

Kinkead-Weekes argues that "through studying Hardy's art and Hardy's people Lawrence had found a language in which to conceive the impersonal forces he saw operating within and between human beings; involving a new clarification of what the novel he had been trying to write was really *about*; and the discovery of a 'structural skeleton' on which to refound it in a new dimension."[9] Kinkead-Weekes is correct in pointing to the "discovery of a 'structural skeleton' " that Lawrence derived from the writing of the *Study*, but his contention that "through studying Hardy's art and Hardy's people Lawrence had found a language in which to conceive the impersonal forces he saw operating within and

9. Mark Kinkead-Weekes, "The Marble and the Statue: The Exploratory Imagination of D. H. Lawrence," in *Imagined Worlds: Essays on Some English Novels and Novelists in Honour of John Butt*, ed. Ian Gregor and Maynard Mack (London, 1968), p. 380.

between human beings" is debatable. In fact, as the succeeding chapters will demonstrate, he had already found
most of the language and many of the ideas he needed when
he thoroughly recast the major *Prussian Officer* stories in the
summer of 1914. Kinkead-Weekes asserts that as Lawrence
"pondered Hardy's people, . . . his whole understanding of
the impersonal forces that operated within and between
men and women began to be clarified, extended, deep-
ened." [10] Rather, the beginning of that understanding had
already taken place in the 1914 *Prussian Officer* revisions; the
Study only added a fixed theoretical framework. The *Study*
was essential to *The Rainbow*, but so were the *Prussian Officer*
revisions.

The fourth and final version of *The Rainbow* was begun
after the last revision of the *Prussian Officer* stories was completed (CL 295), and it is only with this version that the
story of the first generation of Brangwens was grafted on.
The radiant vision of the novel is firmly grounded in the
everyday world at the same time that human existence is
seen in the perspective of the timeless rhythms of the universe. This integration of the daily and the cosmic is the
key to the achievement of *The Rainbow*; in fact, when this
integration breaks down in the second half, the novel tends
to break down with it. Eugene Goodheart is speaking about
the same aspect of Lawrence's art when he notes that Lawrence's "failure occurs when the imagination in its desire to
achieve transcendence wilfully ignores the resistances of the
world in which it has its life." [11]

The double vision of *The Rainbow* also characterizes the
best of the *Prussian Officer* stories. In the final versions of the
stories, as in *The Rainbow*, Lawrence achieves a rare artistic
poise. The young Lawrence's gift for the sympathetic
rendering of common life is a feature of these stories, but the
common life is charged with all the resonance of a vision of

10. Kinkead-Weekes, p. 381.
11. Eugene Goodheart, *The Utopian Vision of D. H. Lawrence* (Chicago,
1963), p. 88.

man's eternal place in the universe. Never again were these two aspects of Lawrence's imagination to be in such harmony, in such creative balance.

The 1914 revisions transformed the best of the *Prussian Officer* stories into products of Lawrence's mature imagination. These years of the first great blossoming of his maturity were the years when he created his best and most important novels. Bruised by the suppression of *The Rainbow* and his experience during the war, rejected by his countrymen, he went off to America in search of the artistic equilibrium he never fully regained. The first years with Frieda were years of deep personal fulfillment for Lawrence, and she was important to the attainment of this artistic balance. Lawrence felt that he had come into his own with her. She too is part of the key moment of artistic transition charted in the pages to follow.

It is easy enough to argue that Frieda did not solve any problems, just as *Sons and Lovers* did not really exorcise any ghosts. The most casual reading of the three "leadership" novels of the twenties demonstrates that the struggle for self-integration was to remain a continuing effort. Nevertheless, the point here is that in 1914 Lawrence *believed* that he had found himself and had grown beyond the problems of his young manhood. This abiding belief, even if it was only a sustaining myth, is integral to the fiction he wrote during this period.

Many of the insights of the revised *Prussian Officer* stories and *The Rainbow* would not have been possible without the deep and essential harmony of his life with Frieda at this time. Lawrence said as much in his letter to A. W. McLeod of 2 June 1914, written three days before the "carbon" letter to Garnett and a few weeks before the beginning of the recasting of the *Prussian Officer* tales:

I think the only re-sourcing of art, revivifying it, is to make it more the joint work of man and woman. I think the one thing to do, is for men to have courage to draw nearer to women, expose themselves to them, and be altered by them: and for women to accept and admit men. That is the start—by bringing themselves together, men and women—revealing themselves each to the other, gaining great blind knowledge and suffering and joy, which it will take a big further lapse of civilisation to exploit and work out. (CL 280)

It can be argued that Lawrence is simply attempting to inflate his current emotions into timeless philosophy. The deep fulfillment and confidence expressed in this letter were to prove transitory, but nevertheless these are precisely the qualities that inform the final versions of the *Prussian Officer* stories and *The Rainbow*. And the letter need only be compared with one he had written to Blanche Jennings six years earlier to measure the distance he had traveled. In 1908 he valued "the friendship of men more than that of women" and praised Jessie Chambers's brother Alan, "gentle as a woman to me." In contrast women "do not understand . . . in their souls" (CL 22-23).

Although something of the attitude expressed in the 1914 letter can be found in Lawrence's work from the beginning, it was not until 1914 that he attained the clarity and inner harmony that allowed such a radiant affirmation to be set forth. He and Frieda were "really very deeply happy" (CL 269), and this happiness had a direct bearing on the development of his art. As Keith Sagar has phrased it, the *Prussian Officer* "alterations . . . imply Lawrence's marriage and *The Rainbow* behind them."[12]

We have seen that *Goose Fair* was Lawrence's original title for the collection, and that Edward Garnett was responsible for the eventual name of the book. Lawrence often had difficulty settling on titles, and his first collection of short stories was no exception. He suggested *The Thorn in the Flesh* as the title when he revised and retitled "Vin Ordinaire" after the middle of July.[13] The most intriguing proposed

---

12. Keith Sagar, "The Genesis of *The Rainbow* and *Women in Love*," *D. H. Lawrence Review*, 1 (1968), 189.
13. Lawrence to Edward Garnett, 17[?] July 1914, unpublished letter in the Berg Collection of the New York Public Library.

title, however, came in a letter to Garnett in October when Lawrence was in the midst of revising the final proofs for publication: "And how good the stories are. . . . It really surprises me. Should they be called *The Fighting Line?* After all, this is the real fighting line, not where soldiers pull triggers" (CL 292).[14] Lawrence was obviously aware that he was writing for a war market. More significantly, however, the progress from the satiric-sounding *Goose Fair* to *The Fighting Line* shows his growing realization that the stories he had written were an attack against established beliefs and established modes of perception. The resounding title proposed in October shows how seriously he had come to take his tales—and his career.

Even though the road to *The Prussian Officer and Other Stories* was long and convoluted and even though the stories were originally written and revised independently of one another, the volume has a strong and unmistakable coherence. This is primarily because of what happened to the best of the stories when Lawrence recast them in July 1914. The same key insights appear over and over again, always couched in the same intense, passionate prose. This is not the place for me to set forth the particular nature of the revisions, for that is the point of the substantive chapters that follow. But with the publication of *The Prussian Officer*, the young Lawrence was no more. The mature Lawrence would be found on the fighting line for the rest of his life.

14. In the *Study of Thomas Hardy,* Lawrence remarks that "the aim of self-preservation" is to "carry us right out to the firing-line" (*Phoenix,* p. 409).

Chapter III

"Odour of Chrysanthemums"

"A story full of my childhood's atmosphere"

"Odour of Chrysanthemums," a story of colliery life, is rightly considered to be among Lawrence's finest tales. One of the most carefully wrought of the early stories, it exemplifies his art at its most dramatic, his vision at its most sympathetic. A moving statement about the human condition is made within the context of the world Lawrence knew as a child and young man. The collier's son was able to observe his own milieu with the eyes of an outsider; the domestic tragedy is rendered with what seems great detachment. A scholar lacking the biographical background of "Odour of Chrysanthemums" would be hard pressed to discover the author's deep personal involvement with its materials.

The story is bound together by the pervasive imagery of the flowers in its title. Chrysanthemums are associated with the cycle of birth, marriage, defeat and drunkenness, and death. This highly visible symbolic framework is perhaps a little overdone. Lawrence is here exploiting some of the formulas of late-nineteenth-century symbolic realism, working them up with an eye toward magazine publication. Indeed, "Odour of Chrysanthemums" was the story that first drew Lawrence to the attention of both Edward Garnett and Martin Secker.

The story has an austere simplicity and also shows the young writer experimenting with traditional tragic forms. The proud woman who is the central character is emotionally estranged from her collier husband. At the end of day she waits with her two children for her husband, overdue from the pit. She suspects that he has gone to the pub to drink, but as time passes her anger becomes deeply tinged with fear. In actuality the husband has been killed in a mine accident. The climax of the story—the bringing in of the collier's body, the washing of the corpse by the wife and the collier's mother, and the wife's realization of the years of estrangement between her husband and herself—is one of the most moving scenes in Lawrence's fiction.

The story's formal finish emerged only as the end product of a number of earlier, more tentative treatments of the same material. The climactic scene constitutes a Lawrentian archetype that remained central to his imagination all his life. He returned again and again, almost obsessively, to this emotion-charged tableau.[1] Because Lawrence was imaginatively so close to the story, the successive versions are one of the best available mirrors of his artistic and emotional growth during his first years as a writer.

Harry Moore tells us that the young Lawrence and his sisters often visited their three aunts who lived in Brinsley. One of these aunts, Aunt Polly, was the widow of his father's brother James. She had remarried some years after James Lawrence had been killed in a mining accident. According to Moore, "years later Lawrence used this aunt as the leading character in his story 'Odour of Chrysanthemums.' "[2]

There can be little doubt of the key role this bit of family history played in the original idea for the story, but Moore's formulation is too simple. The story probably was suggested by his uncle's death, but its basic materials are much closer to home. The great detachment of the narrative voice is all the more miraculous in light of the fact that his parents are the real prototypes of Walter and Elizabeth Bates. Despite its objectivity, the story is, as Lawrence himself put it, "full of [his] childhood's atmosphere" (CL 159). This is a revealing description of a story that ends with a collier's wife grieving over the dead body of her husband.

1. The poem "A Man Who Died," which exists in several versions, is an early example. Some obvious later variations are the scene over Gerald's body at the end of *Women in Love*, Kate's response to the wounded Don Ramón in *The Plumed Serpent*, and Mrs. Bolton's memory of the appearance of her dead collier husband in *Lady Chatterley's Lover*.
2. Harry T. Moore, *The Priest of Love: A Life of D. H. Lawrence* (New York, 1974), p. 18.

Walter and Elizabeth Bates are instantly recognizable as versions of Walter and Gertrude Morel, and the emotional link with Lawrence's own parents is self-evident. "Odour of Chrysanthemums," along with *The Widowing of Mrs. Holroyd*, makes use of his parents' marriage more directly than any other of his works except *Sons and Lovers*.

Lawrence's older brother Ernest died of pneumonia and erysipelas in London in October 1901. When the body was brought home to Eastwood, the huge coffin was placed across some chairs in the parlor.[3] The death of Ernest and Lawrence's response to it are rendered in the death of William in *Sons and Lovers*. The bringing in of the coffin in the novel is one of the most moving passages in the book:

> The coffin swayed, the men began to mount the three steps with their load. Annie's candle flickered, and she whimpered as the first men appeared, and the limbs and bowed heads of six men struggled to climb into the room, bearing the coffin that rode like sorrow on their living flesh.
>
> "Oh, my son—my son!" Mrs. Morel sang softly, and each time the coffin swung to the unequal climbing of the men: "Oh, my son—my son—my son!" (SL 139)[4]

This scene in his family's history found its way not only into *Sons and Lovers* but also into the climax of "Odour of Chrysanthemums," where the colliers carry in the dead Bates. Mrs. Morel cries, "Oh, my son—my son!" when the body is brought in. Mr. Bates's mother cries, "Oh, my boy, my boy!" (ER 427).[5]

Synge's *Riders to the Sea*, a play the young Lawrence called "the genuinest bit of dramatic tragedy, English, since Shakespeare" (CL 76), also influenced the composition of "Odour of Chrysanthemums." The carrying in and washing

---

3. Moore, *The Priest of Love*, p. 41.

4. *Sons and Lovers*. Copyright 1913 by Thomas Seltzer, Inc. Reprinted by permission of Laurence Pollinger Ltd., the Estate of the late Mrs. Frieda Lawrence, and The Viking Press, Inc.

5. The abbreviation ER indicates the version of the story published in the *English Review* in June 1911 (vol. 8, pp. 415–33).

of the drowned youngest son's body helped shape the end of the tale, and more than likely Lawrence modeled his wailing mother-in-law after Maurya in the play. Another grieving woman important to "Odour of Chrysanthemums" is the mother of Christ. Some of the emotional impact of the final tableau is unquestionably related to its associations with the pietà. Synge and the New Testament can both be felt in the story, but nevertheless the main creative impulse came from Lawrence's own experience.

Ford Madox Ford accepted "Odour of Chrysanthemums" and "Goose Fair" for the *English Review* in December 1909. Ford's account of his discovery of Lawrence is famous:

In the year when my eyes first fell on words written by Norman Douglas, G. H. Tomlinson, Wyndham Lewis, Ezra Pound, and others . . . —upon a day I received a letter from a young schoolteacher in Nottingham. I can still see the handwriting—as if drawn with sepia rather than written in ink, on grey-blue notepaper. It said that the writer knew a young man who wrote, as she thought, admirably but was too shy to send his work to editors. Would I care to see some of his writing?

In that way I came to read the first words of a new author:

The small locomotive engine, Number 4, came clanking, stumbling down from Selston with seven full waggons. It appeared round the corner with loud threats of speed but the colt that it startled from among the gorse which still flickered indistinctly in the raw afternoon, outdistanced it in a canter. A woman walking up the railway line to Underwood, held her basket aside and watched the footplate of the engine advancing.

I was reading in the twilight in the long eighteenth-century room that was at once the office of the *English Review* and my drawing-room. My eyes were tired; I had been reading all day so I did not go any further with the story. It was called *Odour of Chrysanthemums*. I laid it in the basket for accepted manuscripts. My secretary looked up and said:

"You've got another genius?"

I answered: "It's a big one this time," and went upstairs to dress.[6]

Some of Ford's best fiction is found in his various books of reminiscences, and much of his portrait of Lawrence fits this category. In writing about the literary men he had known, he was always apt to put strong emphasis on his own early awareness of their genius and on his decisive influence on their respective careers. Still, an impressive ring of truth penetrates through the complacent Fordian melodrama. The opening paragraph of the story is a brilliant, closely written descriptive set piece, carefully designed to establish the tone and mood of the story, to put the reader immediately into its imaginative world—and to produce a shock of recognition in an editor.

The young schoolteacher who wrote Ford was, of course, Jessie Chambers. In *D. H. Lawrence: A Personal Record*, she remembers a "beautiful June morning" in 1909 on which she copied some poems to be sent to Ford.[7] Ford insisted that Jessie sent him prose as well as poetry in her first Lawrence installment, "Odour of Chrysanthemums" and three schoolmaster poems. Consequently, June 1909 has always been accepted as the date for the composition of the story. However, the letters in the Louie Burrows papers at the University of Nottingham call for a revision of this date. In December 1909 Lawrence wrote Louie, the young woman who had replaced Jessie as his fiancée, that he had "sent the story, with another I have written, up to Ford Madox Hueffer on Thursday" (LL 47). "The story" is "Goose Fair," which Lawrence had been trying to place since the summer. The other story he had written was "Odour of Chrysanthemums," which thus dates from the late autumn of 1909 rather than from June of the same year.

Ford's account of his central role in discovering Lawrence's genius is thrown into at least partial disrepute because he never even published the story during his term

6. Ford Madox Ford, *Portraits from Life* (Boston, 1937), pp. 70–71.
7. ET, p. 157.

as editor. Austin Harrison had become editor of the *English Review* when the story appeared in June 1911, and by that time Lawrence had extensively revised the text that Ford had read. Ford accepted both stories and printed "Goose Fair" in the February 1910 issue of the *Review*. The first proofs of "Odour of Chrysanthemums," dated 10 March 1910, are among the Louie Burrows papers. However, this version was never printed. In late July, Lawrence reported that he had been asked to cut out five pages. In the early spring of 1911, Harrison, who had succeeded Ford, wanted further revisions. Lawrence had finished his revision of the March 1910 proofs by 2 April 1911. On that day he sent the manuscript to Louie Burrows to have a fair copy made. Louie's beautiful fair copy holograph can be found today in the collection of the Humanities Research Center at the University of Texas at Austin. This manuscript, which reached the *English Review* some time after the middle of April 1911, is virtually identical to the text published there in June 1911.

The story exists in two very different published versions and in two distinct unpublished proof versions: the early text the *English Review* set in type but never printed and the version found in the Hopkin proofs of *The Prussian Officer*.[8] In addition, Lawrence treated the same situation in three other works that fall between the years 1907 and 1915, the novels *The White Peacock* and *The Rainbow* and the play *The Widowing of Mrs. Holroyd*. I will be discussing the following texts:

1. "The Father": Part I, Chapter IV, of *The White Peacock*. Cyril and his mother rush to the bedside of the dying Mr. Beardsall but arrive too late. Completed by November 1908.

2. "Odour of Chrysanthemums." *English Review* proofs of the story Lawrence had completed by 9 December 1909, in

---

8. I will not be discussing the manuscript material owned by the University of Texas. The fair-copy holograph is very close to the June 1911 *English Review* text, and the brief holograph fragment at the end of the story in their collection is too hurried and sketchy to make analysis fruitful.

the collection of the University of Nottingham.[9] The proofs, which date from March 1910, are heavily revised, but I will be focusing on the text found beneath the revisions. Referred to as the *English Review* proofs and the 1910 proofs. The unrevised version of the proofs is now available in the 1969 number of *Renaissance and Modern Studies*.

3. "Odour of Chrysanthemums." Magazine text published in the *English Review*, June 1911. Lawrence revised the March 1910 proofs between 30 March and 2 April 1911. Referred to as the magazine text and the *English Review* text (ER).

4. *The Widowing of Mrs. Holroyd*, especially Act III. The play is a re-working of the same materials, and its conclusion is directly modeled on the story. Originally written some time before 13 December 1910. Revised in August and early September 1913.

5. "Odour of Chrysanthemums." Text found in the proof set Lawrence sent W. E. Hopkin, now in the collection of the Nottinghamshire County Library. Lawrence revised the magazine version in July 1914. Referred to as the Hopkin proofs.

6. "Odour of Chrysanthemums." Text included in *The Prussian Officer and Other Stories*, published in December 1914. Lawrence revised the Hopkin proof version in the autumn of the same year.

7. *The Rainbow*. Lydia and Anna confront the drowned body of Tom Brangwen in the "Marsh and the Flood" chapter. The final version of this scene was probably written after 4 December 1914, in Lawrence's fourth time through the novel.

Each successive text, from the *White Peacock* chapter through the different versions of "Odour of Chrysanthemums" to the passage in *The Rainbow*, reveals a different approach on Lawrence's part to the materials he was treating. Very often the progress from version to version reveals strikingly different conceptions of the confrontation with the dead father, the scene that is the crux of all the texts listed above.

---

9. An edition of the 1910 proofs, edited by James T. Boulton, was printed in the 1969 number of *Renaissance and Modern Studies* ("D. H. Lawrence's *Odour of Chrysanthemums:* An Early Version," 13:5–48).

Lawrence made a trial run with the materials in the scene from *The White Peacock*. Cyril Beardsall, the priggish young narrator, is an obvious self-projection. Lawrence's attitude at this time to the continuing battle between his parents is made clear when one realizes that his protagonist bears his mother's maiden name. Cyril's father has deserted the family long ago and has taken to drink. Early in the novel Cyril and a friend came upon him sleeping beneath a tree, although they do not realize who it is. There is no mistaking Lawrence's feelings toward his father: "The cap had fallen from his grizzled hair, and his head leaned back against a profusion of the little wild geraniums that decorated the dead bough so delicately. The man's clothing was good, but slovenly and neglected. His face was pale and worn with sickness and dissipation. As he slept, his grey beard wagged, and his loose unlovely mouth moved in indistinct speech" (WP 26). There is a brief exchange in which Cyril treats the man condescendingly, after which Mr. Beardsall walks away "feebly into the darkness" (WP 35).

In the next chapter Cyril's mother receives a note from his father. He is dying of a kidney disease, obviously induced by drink. Before she and Cyril set out for the cottage where he is staying, hoping to reach him before it is too late, Cyril tells the tale of his parents' marriage, devoting a total of one paragraph to it. The young Lawrence lays all the blame emphatically on his father:

The marriage had been unhappy. My father was of frivolous, rather vulgar character, but plausible, having a good deal of charm. He was a liar, without notion of honesty, and he had deceived my mother thoroughly. One after another she discovered his mean dishonesties and deceits, and her soul revolted from him, and because the illusion of him had broken into a thousand vulgar fragments, she turned away with the scorn of a woman who finds her romance has been a trumpery tale. When he had left for other pleasures—Lettie being a baby of three years, while I was five—she rejoiced bitterly. She had heard of him indirectly—and of him nothing good, although he prospered—but he had never come to see her or written in all the eighteen years. (WP 38)

The father is already dead when they reach him. The scene in which Cyril and his mother see the corpse of the dead father is clearly the first version of the climax of "Odour of Chrysanthemums." An old woman, the owner of the cottage where he lies dead, is on hand to wail, "Eh!—Eh! Dear—Lord, Dear—Heart. Dear—Heart!" (WP 43). She is the prefiguration of Mr. Bates's mother in the story. In this early version we get Cyril's response to the corpse rather than the mother figure's. This can of course be explained by the fact that Cyril is the narrator, but I feel it has deeper roots. The final tableau in "Odour of Chrysanthemums" is absolutely central in Lawrence's experience. The content of Mrs. Bates's reverie in successive versions of the tale is conditioned by Lawrence's own feelings about his parents as he grew older. Lawrence's attitude is implicit in the conclusion of all the versions of "Odour of Chrysanthemums," but in the early, immature form of the same materials in *The White Peacock*, Lawrence as Cyril is physically present as well.

Cyril's halting, imprecise response to the sight of his dead father is the embryonic form of Mrs. Bates's powerful inner monologue at the end of the *Prussian Officer* text of the story: "My heart was beating heavily, and I felt choked. I did not want to look—but I must. It was the man I had seen in the woods—with the puffiness gone from his face. I felt the great wild pity, and a sense of terror, and a sense of horror, and a sense of awful littleness and loneliness among a great empty space. I felt beyond myself as if I were a mere fleck drifting unconsciously through the dark" (WP 43). Mrs. Beardsall says only, "Oh, my son, my son!" (WP 57). This should have a familiar ring, but there is an essential difference between this lament and that of Mrs. Morel and of the old mother in "Odour of Chrysanthemums." Mrs. Beardsall, unlike the other women, has not lost a son. The sight of her dead husband affects her primarily by way of reconfirming her rejection of him in life and vindicating the bond she has formed with Cyril.

Cyril is not greatly upset either: "I shivered, and came back to myself. There were no tears in my mother's face, only a great pleading. 'Never mind, mother—never mind,' I said incoherently" (WP 43). Mr. Beardsall is dead by page forty of the novel, and life in Nethermere can proceed uninterrupted. In a novel in which Lawrence wanted to show young people growing more or less harmoniously to adulthood, the only way he could transform his own experience into art was by killing off his father. He did exactly the same thing in the earliest extant draft of *Sons and Lovers*, a version of the novel in which the father accidentally kills Paul's brother, is jailed, and dies after being released.[10] In his early twenties Lawrence felt that his father was responsible for the unhappiness he had experienced while growing up. In *The White Peacock*, his first novel, he makes his mother a widow without either hesitation or remorse.[11]

The version of "Odour of Chrysanthemums" that Ford Madox Ford accepted for the *English Review* in 1909 was first published in 1969, when James T. Boulton edited for *Renaissance and Modern Studies* the twenty-seven pages of proofs of the story now among the Louie Burrows papers. This edition of the unrevised text of the proofs also contains a useful critical apparatus that indicates the variations between the proofs, the revised proofs, and the version actually published in the *Review* in June 1911.

Lawrence recorded his intentions concerning his revision of the proofs in his correspondence with Louie Burrows in April 1911. On 2 April he wrote that "the desideratum is to shorten sufficiently the first part" (LL 90). On 6 April he said that he wanted the story to "work quicker to a climax" and that he had cut out "the kiddies share" (LL 93). These remarks are an accurate description of the revision he had undertaken.

10. Lawrence Clark Powell, *The Manuscripts of D. H. Lawrence: A Descriptive Catalogue* (Los Angeles, 1937), p. 3.
11. When Blanche Jennings criticized this scene, Lawrence vigorously defended it: "The 'father' scene is *not* ugly and superfluous. I will defend my construction throughout" (CL 36). Because he was unable to come to terms with his father, all he could do was remove him.

Even the most casual comparison of the 1910 proofs with the revised version published in the *English Review* in 1911 reveals that he followed through on these intentions.

As Boulton has noted, "the focus of the writer's attention has notably shifted from the beginning to the end; from, that is, the evolving situation in the Bates's house in which the circumstantial details of the mother and children awaiting Bates's return are central, to the adult emotions associated with the preparation of the dead man's body for burial."[12] The "children's games" material of the first half is fascinating, but Lawrence decided—probably with Austin Harrison's editorial prompting—that it was peripheral to the main thrust of the narrative and distracted the reader from the growing tension. The lengthy and elaborate passage in which the children play first at being gypsies and then at being colliers has such a self-sufficiency that it takes on a life of its own apart from the context of the story. The detail is lovely, but it distracts attention from the central situation. In his revision for the *English Review* of June 1911 Lawrence focuses on the absent collier and his wife's growing anger and concern. By the time the story reached its final form in 1914, the "kiddies share" had been fully and skillfully integrated into the story's central theme. For example, now young John is more subtly shown to be his father's son, and—like father, like son—he is champing at the bit of Mrs. Bates's authority.

The scene in the 1910 unrevised proofs in which the two women lay out and wash the body contains many elements that Lawrence retained in the version of the story that was finally printed in the *English Review*. There are slight, often interesting, differences in detail, but it is only in Mrs. Bates's reverie that the *English Review* version diverges radically from the conclusion of the 1910 proofs.

Mrs. Bates's reverie over the corpse of her husband is the emotional climax. In later versions of the story, the experience of seeing and washing her husband's beautiful body as it

12. Boulton, p. 8. Boulton's introduction contains an excellent discussion of Lawrence's revision of the 1910 proofs.

lies in the repose of death is a powerful epiphany, a shattering but illuminating experience that for the first time reveals to her the nature of her marriage. The brief version of the reverie at the end of the 1910 proofs is devoid of any such impact:

> Elizabeth, who had sobbed herself weary, looked up. Then she put her arms round him, and kissed him again on the smooth ripples below the breasts, and held him to her. She loved him very much now—so beautiful and gentle, and helpless. He must have suffered! What must he have suffered! Her tears started hot again. Ah, she was so sorry, sorrier than she could ever tell. She was sorry for him, that he had suffered so, and got lost in the dark place of death. But the poignancy of her grief was that she loved him again— ah, so much! She did not want him to wake up, she did not want him to speak. She had him again, now, and it was Death which had brought him. She kissed him, so that she might kiss Death which had taken the ugly things from him. Think how he might have come home—not white and beautiful, gently smiling . . . Ugly, befouled, with hateful words on an evil breath, reeking with disgust. She loved him so much now; her life was mended again, and her faith looked up with a smile; he had come home to her beautiful. How she had loathed him! It was strange he could have been such as he had been. How wise of death to be so silent! If he spoke, even now, her anger and her scorn would lift their heads like fire. He would not speak—no, just gently smile, with wide eyes. She was sorry to have to disturb him to put on his shirt—but she must, he could not lie like that. The shirt was aired by now. But it would be cruel hard work to get him into it. He was so heavy, and helpless, more helpless than a baby, poor dear!—and so beautiful. [13]

This version of the corpse-washing scene has no revelation to offer. The experience gives Mrs. Bates no new insights into her marriage; instead it fixes her in the attitudes she already has and further distances her from the truth. In Mrs. Bates's mind, the sight of her husband's body, "white and beautiful," cancels the years of ugliness in their marriage. She is "sorry for him," but, incredibly, her gladness seems almost to dominate. She does not "want him to wake up," and she kisses him, "so that she might kiss Death which had

13. Boulton, p. 44.

taken the ugly things from him." A strong undercurrent of the paragraph, whether or not Lawrence intended it, seems to be the happiness of a woman who is escaping from a bad marriage. This may seem rather shocking, but it is not so different from Lawrence's killing off of the father projection in *The White Peacock.*

Lawrence felt that this paragraph was a little inconclusive, for the revision contains two more sentences of dialogue between the women, and Bates is actually clothed at the end. As we shall see, he also added an extensive passage of authorial commentary that is outside the frame of the story and destroys the unity of tone he had worked so hard to maintain.

In the version of the corpse-washing scene found in the March 1910 *English Review* proofs, the collier's mother is counterpointed with Mrs. Bates. Her role of archetypal mother is part of the original conception of the story and remains a constant through the many revisions. The mother's raptures about her son's white skin and about his having made his peace before dying are incorporated, using much the same language, in all subsequent versions of the story and in the play too. Lawrence's archetype of maternity did not change, but his archetype of wifehood did. It is the recasting of Mrs. Bates's response to the tragedy and of her inner monologue that gives the story its changing meaning.

The ending of the version of the story published in the June 1911 issue of the *English Review* is badly overwritten. Lawrence was able to rise superbly to the occasion when a passage of carefully wrought descriptive prose was required, such as at the beginning of the story. But he did not come close to sustaining an extensive purple passage about life and death:

Life with its smoky burning gone from him, had left a purity and a candour like an adolescent's moulded upon his reverie. His intrinsic beauty was evident now. She had not been mistaken in him, as often she had bitterly confessed to herself she was. The beauty of his youth, of his eighteen years, of the time when life had settled on him, as in adolescence it settles on youth, bringing a mission to fulfill and equipment therefore, this beauty shone almost unstained again. (ER 432)

The key passage at the height of Mrs. Bates's reverie goes entirely awry:

It was this adolescent "he," the young man looking round to see which way, that Elizabeth had loved. He had come from the discipleship of youth, through the Pentecost of adolescence, pledged to keep with honour his own individuality, to be steadily and unquenchably himself, electing his own masters and serving them till the wages were won. He betrayed himself in his search for amusement. Let Education teach us to amuse ourselves, necessity will train us to work. Once out of the pit, there was nothing to interest this man. He sought the public-house, where, by paying the price of his own integrity, he found amusement: destroying the clamours for activity, because he knew not what form the activities might take. The miner turned miscreant to himself, easing the ache of dissatisfaction by destroying the part of him which ached. Little by little the recreant maimed and destroyed himself.

It was this recreant his wife had hated so bitterly, had fought against so strenuously. She had strove, all the years of his falling off, had strove with all her force to save the man she had known new-bucklered with beauty and strength. In a wild and bloody passion she fought the recreant. Now this lay killed, the clean young knight was brought home to her. (ER 432)

The diction is inflated throughout. In particular, such details as "the discipleship of youth," the uppercase "e" on "Education," and the man "new-bucklered with beauty and strength" call unfortunate attention to themselves. This is the sort of language Lawrence uses to undercut characters in such stories as "Goose Fair" and "A Modern Lover," but here there is no irony.

Even more curious is the sudden lapse into sociological disquisition on the fate of the poor collier. Lawrence is intent on explaining the hard lot of Mr. Bates in generalized terms. He mentioned his difficulty with the ending in the letter to Louie of 2 April 1911, just after he had finished revising the earlier proofs: "It has taken me such a long time to write these last two pages of the story. You have no idea how much delving it requires to get that deep into cause & effect" (LL 91). The decision to try to go "deep into cause & effect" is especially disastrous at the end of a story in which Lawrence had labored so valiantly to maintain unity of tone and mood and to keep himself out of the narrative. Perhaps he switched to the abstractness of this passage because of his closeness to its materials. Given Lawrence's ambiguous feelings toward the father contained in Mr. Bates, perhaps the easy way out was here the only way out. Instead of staying within the terms of the story, he goes outside it to preach a little sermon over the fate of the British collier. In an effort not to judge the father figure, he judges instead the system that produced him.

The sociological intrusion is not the only element contributing to the meaning of this version of the story. Sociology or no, the ending still sides with Mrs. Bates, who "had strove with all her force to save the man she had known." There is also a lesson to be learned in mother love:[14]

> When they arose, saw him lying in the reckless dignity of death, both women bowed in primeval awe, while the tears of motherhood rose in each. For a few moments they stood religiously silent. Then the mother-feeling prevailed. Elizabeth knelt down, put her arms round him, laid her cheek on his breast. He was still warm, for the mine was hot where he had died. His mother had his face between her hands, and was murmuring incoherently. (ER 430–31)

"Odour of Chrysanthemums" is a story about the basic relationships of mankind. This is one of the reasons the collier's mother plays such an important role. Unfortunately, Lawrence seems to be writing about the fundamental human relationships at a time when he has insufficient experience of some of them. The emphasis on Mrs. Bates's "mother-feeling" for the man who has been her husband and by whom she has had two children seems psychologically questionable. The passage I have quoted is Mrs. Bates's first reaction, coming immediately after she and the mother have stripped the body. Even if maternal feelings might be mixed into Mrs. Bates's

14. Mother love is also important in the 1910 proofs.

stunned response, one would expect them to be subordinate
to her feelings as a wife.

This psychological detail is by no means inexplicable
however. At this time Lawrence had been through the long,
painfully frustrating relationship with Jessie, which he had
broken off in November 1910, just before the death of his
mother. His relationship with Louie Burrows was at its height.
Louie, the prototype of Ursula in *The Rainbow*, was much
more passionate and full-blooded, but she too had a "churchy"
(CL 90) background and a strict "code of manners" (LL 146)
that caused him a great deal of frustration. In the spring of
1911 he had had no experience of a complete, continuing relationship with a woman. Indeed he was so within his mother's
grip that during her lifetime he was unable to establish a satis-
factory relationship with any other woman. As his mother
lay dying, Lawrence wrote Louie, then his fiancée: "So if I do
not seem happy with the thought of you—you will understand.
I must feel my mother's hand slip out of mine before I can
really take yours. She is my first, great love" (LL 56–57).
After his mother's death, Lawrence was seriously ill throughout most of 1911. He later spoke of the year as his "sick year":
"I was twenty-five, and from the death of my mother, the
world began to dissolve around me. . . ."[15]

Lawrence had finished the original version of "Odour of
Chrysanthemums" by December 1909. His mother died a
year later. When Lawrence revised the proofs of the story in
the early spring of 1911 to prepare the tale for magazine
publication, he had had no experience of conjugal love, but
he had experienced an excess of motherly love. Mrs. Bates
kneels to embrace her dead husband with the "mother-
feeling" prevailing.

The Widowing of Mrs. Holroyd, probably the best of Lawrence's
plays, is also fascinating as a case study of the way in which
Lawrence assimilated and transformed his experience into
art. The play uses not only the standard Lawrence mother-

15. Rejected preface to *Collected Poems*, in *Phoenix*, p. 253.

father materials but also the experience of his elopement with Frieda in 1912. The culminating act of the play is a reworking of "Odour of Chrysanthemums."

Elizabeth Holroyd is the Elizabeth Bates of the piece. The conflict with her husband is so intense that in Act I Mr. Holroyd brings home two tipsy tavern wenches. There is a gentle, young mine electrician in the play, though, and in Act II he proposes to Mrs. Holroyd that they run away together. When Mr. Holroyd comes home drunk, his wife locks him out at first—just as the drunken Morel locks out his wife in *Sons and Lovers*. When she lets him in, he passes out in a drunken stupor, and Blackmore and Mrs. Holroyd declare their love over his recumbent body. Blackmore proposes that they go to Spain—just as Lawrence took Frieda von Richthofen Weekley from England and went with her to Germany (and just as so many Lawrence stories and novels end with the lovers planning to set out for another country). Blackmore is twenty-seven and Mrs. Holroyd thirty-two: Lawrence was twenty-six and Frieda thirty-two when they eloped. Blackmore furthermore proposes that they take the children with them: Frieda's loss of her children was perhaps her greatest unhappiness and certainly one of the leading sources of friction in her marriage to Lawrence.

Act III of the play is essentially a dramatization of the story. Most of the characters and a good deal of the dialogue are borrowed. Nevertheless, the third act of *The Widowing of Mrs. Holroyd* is a remarkably transformed "Odour of Chrysanthemums." The translation from prose to drama would ensure this even if Lawrence's conception of the materials had remained the same. His sociological disquisition would have been difficult to dramatize, but we can be sure that he had no desire to retain this material from the *English Review* text of the story. The mother-feeling is another element that has disappeared. Lawrence had a new attitude toward his parents by the time he wrote *The Widowing of Mrs. Holroyd*, and the corpse-washing scene in the play receives an entirely different treatment.

In *The Widowing of Mrs. Holroyd* Lawrence believes that the
main character is guilty of having driven her husband to
drink and, in effect, of having destroyed him. Mrs. Holroyd
married her husband primarily because of his "muscles and
his good looks" (WMH 50),[16] a bond between them that
quickly became insufficient. Once again we have the collier
and the collier's wife who has married beneath herself, but
this time the wife must bear much of the blame for the failure
in marriage. Lawrence's sympathy has begun to swing deci-
sively to his father, which marks one of the great turning
points in his artistic growth. In *The Widowing of Mrs. Holroyd*
he confronts the dead body of his father and weeps over a man
destroyed by a woman who never tried to understand him.
Frieda mentions the shift in Lawrence's attitude toward his
parents in *Not I, but the Wind:* "In after years he said: 'I would
write a different "Sons and Lovers" now; my mother was
wrong, and I thought she was absolutely right.' "[17]

This shift in attitude is crucial to the meaning of the play.
Lawrence spells out the difference in class and education
of husband and wife, the main source of their deadly friction.
A typical exchange is found in Act i:

> H: You think you're something, since your uncle left
> you that money, an' Blackymore puttin' you up to it. I
> can see your little game. I'm not as daft as you imagine.
> I'm no fool, I tell you.
>
> Mrs. H: No, you're not. You're a drunken beast, that's all
> you are. (WMH 32)

At the beginning of Act iii, while Mrs. Holroyd and her mother-
in-law are waiting for the collier to come home, they have a
sharp exchange in which the mother-in-law accuses Mrs.
Holroyd of ruining her husband because of her overweening
pride. The old woman charges her daughter-in-law with having

---

16. *The Widowing of Mrs. Holroyd* (New York: Mitchell Kennerley, 1914).
Copyright 1914 by Mitchell Kennerley. All rights reserved. Reprinted
by permission of Laurence Pollinger Ltd., the Estate of the late Mrs.
Frieda Lawrence, and The Viking Press, Inc.
17. Frieda Lawrence, *Not I, but the Wind* (Toronto, 1934), p. 56.

a "stiff neck" and thinking herself "above him" and says that
the cause of the marital problem isn't "all on his side" (WMH
70, 71). "And what man wouldn't leave a woman that allowed
him to live on sufferance in the house with her, when
he was bringing the money home?" (WMH 72). Even the
six-year-old daughter suggests that "if you said something nice
to him, mother, he'd happen to go to bed and not shout" (WMH
64).

The bringing in of the corpse after these words from the
old woman and after the previous day's decision to escape to
the continent is a shattering experience to Mrs. Holroyd.
Lawrence makes it clear that she is feeling guilt rather than
mother love. There is no question about the source of
Mrs. Holroyd's grief in her speech to her dead husband,
the powerful climax of the play:

My dear, my dear—oh, my dear! I can't bear it, my dear—you
shouldn't have done it. Oh—I can't bear it, for you. Why couldn't
I do anything for you? The children's father—my dear—I wasn't
good to you. But you shouldn't have done this to me. Oh, dear, oh,
dear! Did it hurt you?—oh, my dear, it hurt you—oh, I can't bear
it. No, things aren't fair—we went wrong, my dear. I never loved
you enough—I never did. What a shame for you. It was a shame. But
you didn't—you didn't try. I *would* have loved you—I tried hard.
What a shame for you! It was so cruel for you. You couldn't help
it—my dear, my dear. You couldn't help it. And I can't do
anything for you, and it hurt you so! (*She weeps bitterly, so her
tears fall on the dead man's face; suddenly she kisses him*) My dear, my
dear, what can I do for you, what can I? (WMH 89–90)

"Well, I hope you'll be true to his children at least, Lizzie"
(WMH 92), says the collier's mother, returning with clothes to
bury him in, and the two women begin to undress the
corpse for washing as the curtain falls.

The demands of writing for the stage cannot account for
the radical reinterpretation of the "Odour of Chrysanthemums" materials. Lawrence had sent the completed *English
Review* text to Austin Harrison in April 1911, just four months
after the death of his mother. Lawrence met Frieda Weekley

in April 1912 and eloped with her to Germany on 3 May. During the rest of 1912, while he and Frieda grew into their relationship, Lawrence revised *Sons and Lovers* with Frieda's help. He always insisted that he had never read Freud before writing the novel. This is perfectly credible, for his own life had produced a more than adequate experience of the Oedipus complex. Frieda, however, *had* read Freud, and her help with the revisions probably focused the Freudian outlines of the work more sharply. More importantly, in reducing Lawrence's past to clinical terms, she must have aided him immeasurably in getting perspective on his relationship with his mother and thereby distancing it. By November 1912 he was expounding the novel in Freudian terms—the famous "split" theory—and generalizing Paul Morel's story into "the tragedy of thousands of young men in England" (CL 161).

From the beginning, Frieda helped Lawrence lay to rest the ghosts of his childhood. In doing so, she was also sure to be altering his attitude toward his parents. And if this attitude was altered, any reworking of a story like "Odour of Chrysanthemums" had to be significantly different.

Lawrence first wrote *The Widowing of Mrs. Holroyd* before the middle of December 1910. In August 1913 he wrote Edward Garnett about his need to revise it: "I have been very busy reading the play to Frieda. It wants a *lot* of altering. I have made it heaps better. . . . What a jolly fine play it is, too, when I have pulled it together" (CL 218). If a play including projections of his parents was first written in 1910, it is not surprising that Lawrence would feel it needed "a *lot* of altering" when he reread it in August of 1913.

The year 1912 was a busy one for Lawrence. In November of that year he completed *Sons and Lovers*, which he had first begun in October 1910. He also wrote most of the poems of *Look! We Have Come Through!* during this year. These poems chart the gradual progression of his relationship with Frieda in a frankly autobiographical way. By 1913 one would expect to find Frieda in Lawrence's more purely imaginative writing as well. This is precisely what happens in the revised, final version of *The Widowing of Mrs. Holroyd*. He grafted this new experience (in the form of the relationship between Blackmore and Mrs. Holroyd) onto a story he had already written and knew could be made into an effective play.[18] But in returning to "Odour of Chrysanthemums," he did much more than add this new experience. The relationship had changed him in such a way that he needed to reshape the entire story. Mrs. Holroyd feels guilty when she confronts the corpse of her husband because Lawrence was now able to take a more dispassionate view of his dead father. His father may have caused his mother to suffer, but her guilt was equal. Instead of siding entirely with the mother, he has grown to the point where he sees the relationship as a vicious spiral in which the misunderstanding and cruelty were mutual. This considerable advance is intrinsic to the ending of the play.

In June 1914 Duckworth agreed to publish a collection of twelve Lawrence short stories at the end of the year. "Odour of Chrysanthemums" is among the tales Lawrence recast most thoroughly early the following month. Further revision in proof took place sometime in the autumn of the same year. However, all the evidence demonstrates that Lawrence finally "discovered" his story while making the July revisions. A comparison between the version in the Hopkin proofs (the July revision) and the *Prussian Officer* text reveals a certain amount of minor verbal alteration, especially in the first ten pages, and some more significant changes in wording of the story's powerful conclusion. However, the *meaning* of the story— and the meaning Mrs. Bates finds in her marriage—is the same in both the July Hopkin proofs and the final text. At best a few of the revisions in proof intensify portions of the conclusion. Consequently, in an effort to avoid muddying the waters, I will devote most of my argument to the final

18. It can be argued that this was an unsuccessful grafting, for Mrs. Holroyd does not seem the sort of woman who would elope with two children and a man six years her junior.

version, with only a few glances at the text found in the Hopkin proofs.

E. W. Tedlock, Jr., has written that "the text published in *The Prussian Officer* bears frequent, but not severe, revision"[19] of the *English Review* version. This is an apt description of Lawrence's changes for most of the story, but it is evident that Tedlock did not actually compare the two published versions of the culmination of the story, the laying out and the corpse-washing. The sweeping transformation of the tale is not to be found in the spot revision, although, with some exceptions, this retouching did improve the story. The changes in the story's climax made it into an entirely different work of art.

The first part of the story, even after the last revisions, remains an example of the method of "accumulating objects in the light of a powerful emotion, and making a scene of them" (CL 263) that Lawrence said he no longer cared about in a letter to Garnett on 29 January 1914. The climax belongs to another mode entirely. By the time he revised the story, he had written three versions of *The Rainbow*. Lawrence wrote in January 1913 of his need to "have a woman at the back of me" (CL 179), and we have already observed how directly this relationship was incorporated into the revision of *The Widowing of Mrs. Holroyd* in the late summer of 1913. One year later, new attitudes about man and woman, about human existence, and about his art had crystallized to the point where he was now exceedingly sure of them and ready to use them to structure his fiction. The relationship between man and woman is at the center of Lawrence's mature vision; however, even in the most intimate relationship there is always an unbridgeable gulf. It is at this time that this basic assumption underlying his work throughout the remainder of his career emerged in its mature form. It is one of the beliefs that determine the shape and content of *The Rainbow*.

19. E. W. Tedlock, Jr., *The Frieda Lawrence Collection of D. H. Lawrence Manuscripts: A Descriptive Bibliography* (Albuquerque, N.M., 1948), p. 37.

By the time of *The Widowing of Mrs. Holroyd*, Lawrence was able to view the relationship of his parents with some detachment and equanimity. When he returned to "Odour of Chrysanthemums" in the early summer of 1914, he was able to go beyond the autobiographical mother-father aspect of the materials. He transcended the earlier terms of the story as he transformed the final confrontation scene one last time. In the *Prussian Officer* version of the story, Lawrence has passed beyond the personal question of his mother and father to express an insight into man's fate. In the Hopkin proof version of a few months earlier, Elizabeth exclaims, "What right had I to him!" (H 81). In the *Prussian Officer* text she asks, "Who am I?" (PO 308).[20]

The statement at the end of the story is powerful. Where the "women bowed in primeval awe, while the tears of motherhood rose in each" in the *English Review* text, we find the following in 1914:

... The women stood arrested in fear and respect. For a few moments they remained still, looking down, the old mother whimpering. Elizabeth felt countermanded. She saw him, how utterly inviolable he lay in himself. She had nothing to do with him. She could not accept it. Stooping, she laid her hand on him, in calm. . . . Elizabeth embraced the body of her husband, with cheek and lips. She seemed to be listening, inquiring, trying to get some connection. But she could not. She was driven away. He was impregnable. (PO 305)

A scene that was a lesson in personal guilt in the summer of 1913 has now become a lesson in human isolation. One of the failings of the *English Review* text was that the situation is so taut with emotion that it merits much more than a short sociological treatise at its culmination. The shock Mrs. Bates experiences would be overpowering, and the final version of the story, with its revelation of our irredeemable loneliness, has much more aesthetic aptness. Mrs. Bates's reflection in all

the early texts that death has restored her husband to beauty
and grandeur is now developed with full metaphysical
implications. As J. C. F. Littlewood has neatly put it, Lawrence
"discovered the meaning that had always been waiting to be
found in the story."[21]

When Lawrence wanted to make a point, he rarely resorted
to half measures. The last five pages of the story are filled with
the wife's realization of her husband's terrible apartness, in life
as well as in death. However, in moving beyond the personal
implications of the story, he did not neglect to give final justice
where justice was due. Where the magazine text speaks of "the
man she had known new-bucklered with beauty and strength,"
the final text contains an impressive statement of the full
dimensions of Mrs. Bates's guilt. Where in the *English Review*
version Mrs. Bates is glad that death has hidden the truth, in
the revision she is grateful for the lifesaving truth:

Her soul was torn from her body and stood apart. She looked at
his naked body and was ashamed, as if she had denied it. After
all, it was itself. It seemed awful to her. She looked at his face, and
she turned her own face to the wall. For his look was other than
hers, his way was not her way. She had denied him what he
was—she saw it now. She had refused him as himself.—And
this had been her life, and his life.—She was grateful to death,
which restored the truth. And she knew she was not dead. (PO 308)

In the Hopkin proofs Elizabeth is merely "coldly grateful"
to death, and astonishingly, "she knew—she was dead" (H 82).
Only in the final confrontation with his story does Lawrence
realize that the truth liberates and gives renewed life to his
heroine: "coldly" is deleted, "dead" becomes "not dead."

In the magazine text Mrs. Bates weeps "herself almost
in agony" (ER 432), but in the revision she has attained
to a knowledge beyond tears and is "rigid with agony" (PO
308). Only with her husband's death has she learned that they
have always been strangers. It is difficult for a man and a
woman to be anything more.

21. J. C. F. Littlewood, "D. H. Lawrence's Early Tales," *Cambridge
Quarterly*, 1 (1966), 123.

Life with its smoky burning gone from him, had left him apart
and utterly alien to her. And she knew what a stranger he was to her.
In her womb was ice of fear, because of this separate stranger
with whom she had been living as one flesh. (PO 307)

There were the children—but the children belonged to life. This dead
man had nothing to do with them. He and she were only channels
through which life had flowed to issue in the children. She was a
mother—but how awful she knew it now to have been a wife. And
he, dead now, how awful he must have felt it to be a husband.
She felt that in the next world he would be a stranger to her. If
they met there, in the beyond, they would only be ashamed of what
had been before. The children had come, for some mysterious
reason, out of both of them. (PO 309)

The passionate intensity and the accretiveness and repetitiveness of Lawrence's prose at the end of the story are characteristic of his mature work. In this particular context, the prose
cannot be quarreled with. Passages of such intensity in
Lawrence often seem overwritten. The climax of the *English
Review* text *is* badly overwritten, but at the time he lacked the
experience, both emotional and artistic, to rise to the challenge
of the task he had set himself. The passionate, onrushing
prose of the last pages of the story perfectly captures the inner
experience of the stunned wife as, almost instantly, she is
forced for the first time to come to grips with what her life has
been.

There is one other corpse-washing scene in Lawrence's early
fiction. It is found in the "Marsh and the Flood" chapter
of *The Rainbow*, one of the many passages in Lawrence that
shows his debt to *The Mill on the Floss*. Tom Brangwen has been
drowned. His wife Lydia and his daughter Anna confront
his dead body:

Almost in horror, she began to take the wet things from him,
to pull off him the incongruous market-clothes of a well-to-do
farmer. The children were sent away to the Vicarage, the dead body
lay on the parlour floor, Anna quickly began to undress him, laid his
fob and seals in a wet heap on the table. Her husband and the

woman helped her. They cleared [sic] and washed the body, and laid it on the bed.

There, it looked still and grand. He was perfectly calm in death, and, now he was laid in line, inviolable, unapproachable. To Anna, he was the majesty of the inaccessible male, the majesty of death. It made her still and awe-stricken, almost glad.

Lydia Brangwen, the mother, also came and saw the impressive, inviolable body of the dead man. She went pale, seeing death. He was beyond change or knowledge, absolute, laid in line with the infinite. What had she to do with him? He was a majestic Abstraction, made visible now for a moment, inviolate, absolute. And who could lay claim to him, who could speak of him, of the him who was revealed in the stripped moment of transit from life into death? Neither the living nor the dead could claim him, he was both the one and the other, inviolable, inaccessibly himself.

"I shared life with you, I belong in my own way to eternity," said Lydia Brangwen, her heart cold, knowing her own singleness.

"I did not know you in life. You are beyond me, supreme now in death," said Anna Brangwen, awe-stricken, almost glad. (R 247–48)

This version of the corpse-washing scene essentially duplicates the attitudes expressed in the conclusion of the final version of "Odour of Chrysanthemums." In death Tom is unapproachable, and his wife feels her own singleness. The short scene in *The Rainbow* is definitely inferior to the ending of the story. Its awkward diction and its brevity are part of the problem: such a confrontation should be highly charged emotionally, but Lawrence has not even bothered to polish or develop it. In fact most of the emotional content of the scene in the story is absent here, and instead we have the feelings of the women presented almost intellectually. The conceptualization of the passage in the novel is the same as that found in the ending of the tale, but in the novel there is too long a string of adjectives without relation to the feelings of the women. Tom is "inviolable," "inviolate," "unapproachable," "inaccessible," "inaccessibly himself," and "absolute." The dead Walter Bates is just as inviolable and absolute, but these qualities are rendered dramatically. The dead Tom is simply a "majestic Abstraction." The speeches (presumably interior monologues emanating from somewhere deeper than "the old stable ego—of the character") of the mother and daughter only serve to underscore the abstractness of the scene.

The story of Tom and Lydia was the last section to be added to *The Rainbow*.[22] It seems fairly obvious that the revised "Odour of Chrysanthemums" came before this little scene. The brevity of the scene and the stiffness and abstractness of its language suggest that Lawrence had already worked out the situation to his satisfaction when he revised "Odour of Chrysanthemums" for book publication and that he simply borrowed the same insights, written out sketchily, when he needed the same scene for his novel. The pressure of emotional urgency can be felt behind all the earlier renderings, but once he had at last gotten the scene "right" in the story, he was able to make almost casual use of it in the novel.

Of greater interest, however, is the closeness in feeling and concept between the first section of *The Rainbow* and the final version of "Odour of Chrysanthemums." The marriage of Tom and Lydia Brangwen, like that of Walter and Elizabeth Bates, is a study in human isolation. The basic insight of the final version of "Odour of Chrysanthemums" is closely related to a main theme of *The Rainbow*, and of course they share the same sort of narrative intensity. The final confrontation of the story presents a vision of human relationship very reminiscent of that depicted in the life of Tom Brangwen and the Polish lady he marries. Tom and Lydia's story has much in common with the revised version of the tale. Lawrence learned how to write about Tom and Lydia Brangwen by writing about Walter Bates and his proud wife.

Throughout their lives, the relationship between Tom and Lydia is marked by their separateness. Tom waits for something in his life to happen to him until one day he sees a strange

22. See Mark Kinkead-Weekes, "The Marble and the Statue: The Exploratory Imagination of D. H. Lawrence," in *Imagined Worlds: Essays on English Novels and Novelists in Honour of John Butt*, ed. Ian Gregor and Maynard Mack (London, 1968), p. 384.

woman passing. "Her face was pale and clear, she had thick
dark eyebrows and a wide mouth, curiously held. He saw her
face so distinctly, that he ceased to coil on himself, and was
suspended. 'That's her,' he said involuntarily" (R 23–24). Tom
does not know her. In marrying her he does not know
her. In their marriage he never comes to know her.

Mrs. Lensky's foreign origin serves to underscore her apartness. When Tom sees her in church, he is struck by "the
foreign woman with a foreign air about her, inviolate, and
the strange child, also foreign, jealously guarding something"
(R 28). After church "he became aware of the woman looking
at him, standing there isolated yet for him dominant in her
foreign existence" (R 28). As for Lydia, "she saw him fresh
and naive, uncouth, almost entirely beyond relationship
with her" (R 31). "She did not know him. He was a foreigner,
they had nothing to do with each other" (R 32).

When Tom goes on a windy March night to ask Lydia
to marry him, in one sense it is Lawrence replaying the
marriage of his father and mother all over again. Even
more deeply, however, he is acting out in fiction his marriage
to Frieda: "All these things were only words to him, the fact
of her superior birth, the fact that her husband had been a
brilliant doctor, the fact that he himself was her inferior
in almost every way of distinction" (R 36). It is no accident
that a single fictional situation has its roots in both the marriage
of Lawrence's parents and of Lawrence himself, for when the
collier's son eloped with the baron's daughter, he was reenacting
the marriage of his parents in an extreme form. With this in
mind, it is not surprising to learn the ages of Tom and Lydia
at marriage:

> "But I am much older than you," she said.
> "How old?" he asked.
> "I am thirty-four," she said.
> "I am twenty-eight," he said.
> "Six years." (R 41)

In the spring of 1914 Lawrence was twenty-eight and Frieda was
thirty-four. Apparently one of the lessons he was to learn in

their first years together was one of separateness. This is the lesson of the first section of *The Rainbow* as well as of "Odour of Chrysanthemums."

As Tom approaches the house of the woman he has come to court, he looks through the window and sees Lydia in a rocking chair before the fire, with her little daughter sitting on her knee. "Then he heard the low, monotonous murmur of a song in a foreign language" (R 38). He feels cut off from her: this haunting image of human isolation helps establish the framework for the meeting of Tom and Lydia. A highly charged, moving scene ends with the decision that they will marry. The language at the end of the chapter is curious language for the description of a betrothal, but it is in perfect accord with the level of emotional and artistic development that Lawrence had reached. It is also precisely the language of "Odour of Chrysanthemums": "They were such strangers, they must for ever be such strangers, that his passion was a clanging torment to him. Such intimacy of embrace, and such utter foreignness of contact! It was unbearable. He could not bear to be near her, and know the utter foreignness between them, know how entirely they were strangers to each other" (R 44).

Of course there is a crucial distinction to be drawn. The separateness in the Tom-Lydia relationship produces, at its best, a richly creative and fulfilling—though finally mysterious—harmony, whereas Elizabeth Bates's pride and willfulness break the male-female polarity and destroy her marriage. Tom doesn't know Lydia socially but "knows" her intimately in the unknown; Walter Bates doesn't know his wife at all. Nevertheless, my point holds: the emergent idea of separateness, expressed in remarkably similar language, is central to both novel and story.

This idea is not an isolated one in Lawrence's career. The "double measure" that George Ford finds in Lawrence—his impulse toward communion, his impulse toward isolation[23]— has its roots in the fiction from the beginning, but it comes to

23. George H. Ford, *Double Measure: A Study of the Novels and Stories of D. H. Lawrence* (New York, 1965).

fruition only with Frieda. Many of the characteristic Lawrentian beliefs crystallize in the late revisions of the *Prussian Officer*
stories and in the writing of *The Rainbow*.

Ursula must reject the mechanical Skrebensky in *The Rainbow*
because he is not able to lead her into the unknown,
even though she has no conception of the sort of relationship
she must wait for. Rupert Birkin arrives in *Women in Love*
in the midst of a crumbling civilization with his concept of
star-polarity, and he and Ursula leave for the Mediterranean at
the end of the novel. Star-polarity has as one of its bases
the knowledge and acceptance of man's essential isolation. With
the advent of Frieda, Lawrence was able to shake off the
incubus of his past. He gained an inner self-assurance and
achieved a rare emotional equilibrium. By May 1913 he was
writing that his marriage was "the best I have known, or
ever shall know" (CL 207). At the same time he quickly realized
that he and Frieda remained two separate individuals. Marriage was a sort of creative tension, and the moments of
stillness were rare.

Only with the concrete experience of a complete adult
relationship was Lawrence able to build a mature love ethic.
The cornerstone of star-polarity is the isolation intrinsic
in the human condition. Man *must* retain his own individuality
and separateness, says Birkin—knowing full well that man has
no choice. Man and woman must come together for renewal,
for in love they partake of, and are in harmony with, the vital
energies of the cosmos. But then they must separate and walk
proud in their own fierce isolation.

"Odour of Chrysanthemums" has long been considered one
of Lawrence's finest tales, but only a few critics have fully
appreciated its implications. A study of the successive revisions
of the original story—in connection with Lawrence's biography—
allows us to date with some precision the moment a central
Lawrentian belief assumed its mature form. The culmination
of the story is one of the starting points for the Lawrence of
The Rainbow, Women in Love, and the 1920s.

Chapter IV

"Daughters of the Vicar"

"Something sufficiently emotional, and moral"

Of the dozen stories collected in *The Prussian Officer and Other Stories* in December 1914, only "Daughters of the Vicar" had never previously been published. This fact is a comment on its length—over twice as long as the next longest stories in the volume—rather than its quality. Lawrence's letters testify that length was the main factor in magazine editors' reluctance to accept it. Indeed, it is considered a short story only because of an accident of publishing history: if "Daughters of the Vicar" had not first appeared in a collection of short stories, doubtless it would be thought of as the novella that it is. The shape of the story and many of its incidents point clearly toward *The Virgin and the Gipsy*, the novella Lawrence wrote in the mid-twenties.

"Daughters of the Vicar" seems to have grown out of a remark the young Lawrence made to Jessie Chambers when he told her that the usual plan for writing novels was to "take two couples and develop their relationships."[1] The story is Lawrence's first published work built around the two-sisters motif. The sisters in question are the down-to-earth Louisa, who rejects the stifling atmosphere of her father's household and ultimately marries a miner, and the beautiful Mary, who sells herself to financial security in marrying a willful, incompletely human clergyman. Louisa is endowed with the Lawrentian gift of life. Her love transforms the tormented

---

1. ET, p. 103. Martin Green thinks the story is a reflection of the von Richthofen sisters, Frieda and Else, and their respective marriages to Lawrence and Edgar Jaffe. He concedes, however, that he has "taken liberties of interpretation," notably in that Lawrence wrote the first two versions of "Daughters of the Vicar" before meeting Frieda or Else! He argues for an "imaginative connection" nevertheless. See *The von Richthofen Sisters: The Triumphant and the Tragic Modes of Love* (New York, 1974), pp. 25–27, 367, 383.

young Alfred Durant into a whole man, and she also self-lessly nurses his dying mother. "Daughters of the Vicar" is memorable for its radiant vision of human relatedness beyond the artificial barriers of class, and its exploration of Oedipal love counterpoints it neatly with *Sons and Lovers*. All in all, the components of the story should seem familiar to readers of Lawrence: "the passional versus the cerebral sisters, the destructive Christian middle-class milieu, the moralistic and unmanly intellectual lover versus the rebellious and virile outsider, along with such subordinate motifs as the obscene love of the mother, the satire on moral benevolence."[2] It goes without saying that the tale offers a background glance at the author's own origins.

"Daughters of the Vicar" is another of the *Prussian Officer* stories that was radically recast in 1914, a revision that added the new theoretical insights into human personality (and the language expressing these insights) that are part of this key moment in Lawrence's career. Even though the tale was never published before its inclusion in *The Prussian Officer*, its genesis and development are extremely complicated. Indeed the critic might legitimately complain that too many layers of composition are visible in this palimpsest. The profusion of intertwined materials is sometimes difficult to untangle and to talk about clearly. Two fascinating, complex manuscripts of the story in the collection of George Lazarus afford a unique opportunity to look over Lawrence's shoulder and observe one of his most ambitious pieces of short fiction as it emerges. I am indebted to Mr. Lazarus for permission to use these missing links between the rough, early "Two Marriages" and the glowing "Daughters of the Vicar," one of Lawrence's most joyous celebrations of the possibility of human contact.

I will be discussing the following versions of the story:

1. "Two Marriages." Twenty-three page holograph fragment in ink on copybook paper in the collection of George Lazarus. This fragment begins after the back-washing scene and runs

2. Kingsley Widmer, *The Art of Perversity: D. H. Lawrence's Shorter Fictions* (Seattle, 1962), p. 126.

continuously to the end of the story. There is also one loose page, numbered 23, from earlier in the story. The unrevised text is almost certainly the original draft, begun on 15 July 1911 and completed the next day. I will refer to the entire manuscript as manuscript *A* and to the unrevised text contained in it as the 1911 "Two Marriages" holograph. This text will not figure very prominently in my analysis, since it contains only the last part of the story.

2.   George Lazarus's manuscript *A* contains all that is left of the rough draft of the story. The revised and typed version dating from October 1911 is the first that Lawrence tried to sell. This version can essentially be reconstructed by combining two extant texts.

2a.   "Two Marriages." Part of the October 1911 rewriting of the story can be found in George Lazarus's *B* manuscript. Manuscript *B* exhibits two discrete stages of development: unrevised typescript that dates from 1911 (discussed here as item 2a) and the 1913 revision of that typescript (discussed as item 3). Lawrence extensively revised the July 1911 holograph of manuscript *A* (item 1) in October of the same year. The unrevised typescript portion of manuscript *B* was made from the revised 1911 holograph of *A* and is almost identical to it. The typescript text is not itself complete because in the summer of 1913 Lawrence revised it so thoroughly and added so much to the text that in many sections he wrote out long pages of 14-inch holograph fair copy to replace typescript text, which he then discarded. The typescript that remains commences at the point Louisa leaves to go visit the Durants (Section VIII in the *Prussian Officer* version) and runs continuously to the end (except for scattered pages of the new holograph, notably in the last few pages). I will refer to the unrevised typescript of manuscript *B* as the 1911 "Two Marriages" typescript.

2b.   "Two Marriages." The rest of the October 1911 text can be found in a long fragment published without any editorial details (not even the information that the text is incomplete) in *Time and Tide,* 24 March 1934. The fragment ends inexplicably after the back-washing scene. This fragment was published from a typescript now in the collection of the University of California at Berkeley.[3] I will refer to the *Time and Tide* text as the 1911 magazine "Two Marriages."

The text of version 2b is virtually identical to the 1911 typescript of manuscript *B* where the two overlap. The *Time and Tide* "Two Marriages" contains the seven opening sections missing from the 1911 typescript; the 1911 typescript continues past the point where the *Time and Tide* "Two Marriages" breaks off, up until the last two pages of the story. Thus, between these two texts a nearly complete version of the October 1911 "Two Marriages" can be reconstructed.

3.   "Daughters of the Vicar." Holograph revision of the 1911 typescript of the *B* manuscript of "Two Marriages." This revision took place in the summer of 1913, and involves extensive revision of the typescript in pencil and some revision in ink, plus holograph fair copy of the first seven sections and other scattered pages. It is highly likely that the pages of fair copy (which are themselves slightly revised) date from exactly the same time as the revision of the typescript. I will refer to the holograph revision of manuscript *B* as the 1913 text and the 1913 revised typescript.

4.   "Daughters of the Vicar." Text found in the Hopkin proofs dating from July 1914, now in the collection of the Nottinghamshire County Library. There is much verbal variation between this version and the final *Prussian Officer* text, which dates from October of the same year, but almost all of this variation is inconsequential. I will make only occasional and passing reference to the Hopkin proof version.

5.   "Daughters of the Vicar." October 1914 revision of the Hopkin proof text. Published in *The Prussian Officer*,

---

3. Lawrence's name and "Two Marriages" are written on a label of Curtis Brown, Ltd., which is pasted onto the front page of this typescript. Curtis Brown, acting for Frieda, sold the typescript to *Time and Tide* as an unpublished story after Lawrence's death, even though it is only an incomplete early version of a published tale. Similar typescripts exist for early forms of "A Fragment of Stained Glass," "The Shadow in the Rose Garden," and "Samson and Delilah." The *Time and Tide* "Two Marriages" (supplement of 24 March 1934, vol. 15, pp. 393–99) ends so abruptly because the Berkeley typescript breaks off at exactly the same point.

December 1914. Referred to as "Daughters of the Vicar" and the *Prussian Officer* version.

Although all this is a little confusing, it need not seem daunting. The five versions are all discrete and well-defined: the rough draft of July 1911, the extensive revision of October of the same year, the major revision of the summer of 1913 that first converted "Two Marriages" into "Daughters of the Vicar," the Hopkin proof text of July 1914, and the *Prussian Officer* version. Furthermore, for the sake of clarity I will be focusing, generally speaking, on two versions: "Two Marriages" as revised in 1911 (item 2a and 2b) and "Daughters of the Vicar," published in December 1914 (item 5). I will make reference to other versions, both earlier and intermediary, but I will organize my discussion of these materials in accordance with the way they illuminate the radical differences between "Two Marriages" and "Daughters of the Vicar."[4]

The gradual evolution of the story is well documented. A brief account of the making of the story should assist the reader in his effort to keep the various texts straight. Lawrence began the story on 15 July 1911, but the next day he reported that the finished product, called "Two Marriages," wasn't "worth sending by post" (LL 121). The next important date was 10 September, when he sent two stories to Edward Garnett, hoping that he could place them with the *Century*, an American magazine (CL 80). When Garnett returned the stories—the first Lawrence had ever sent to him—a few weeks later, Lawrence decided to have him try to place "Two Marriages": "I send you this, which I think would easily split up into three. It is only the first writing, rough, and not sufficiently selective. Bear with me if the first part is tedious—there are . . . good bits later on. I tried to do something sufficiently emotional, and moral, and—oh, American!" (CL 80). Garnett was encouraging about the manuscript. On 2 October Lawrence wrote Louie that he had sent Garnett "a long 3-part story which he thinks the

4. George Lazarus has recently acquired yet another holograph of "Two Marriages." This text in no way alters my basic conclusions about the evolution of the story.

Century may accept when I've had it typed out," adding that
he was "so busy revising 'Two Marriages' for the type-writer."
A luncheon with Garnett had also been arranged so that
Garnett could "see what sort of animal I am" (LL 138–39).
On 6 October, Lawrence wrote his new mentor that "the MS. of
the story is with the typewriter" (CL 81); about a month later
he complained that the typist was "devilish dilatory" (LL 146).
Lawrence's typist was a soldier acquaintance who proved unreliable when he tried his hand at professional typing, as
Lawrence explained to Garnett on 11 November: "This
morning I hear from a mate of the soldier that the latter
rascal went on drink when he got my p.o. of payment. He
never used to be like that. If marriage has driven him to
it already, it is a sad look-out. However, the pal will get the
thing done directly" (CL 85–86). However, the *Century* turned
the story down: "The Americans are just as stupid as we
expected" (CL 90). Garnett must have kept the typescript until
the summer of 1913, when Lawrence again tried to sell the
story.

The original text that Garnett saw, written in July 1911, is the
unrevised holograph of manuscript *A* (item 1, which survives
only in a fragment). Garnett's good opinion of the story encouraged Lawrence to rework it, and on 2 October he was busy
revising the story for the typist. These revisions are the holograph interlinear revisions of manuscript *A*. This text also
appears as the 1911 typescript of manuscript *B* (item 2a),
the version of "Two Marriages" that Lawrence submitted un-
successfully to the *Century*. Lawrence's tribulations with the
soldier and his "pal" are even visible. The story is badly
typed; Lawrence's typist was ignorant of the most fundamental
rules regarding the typing of punctuation. The switch in
typist is perhaps discernible too, for near the end of the typescript there is a sudden change of typewriter. The revised
holograph of manuscript *A* is almost identical to the 1911
typescript of manuscript *B* because this is the text Lawrence
sent to his unreliable soldier-typist.

Lawrence next picked up "Two Marriages" in the summer

of 1913, the summer he tried so hard to sell the stories he had written earlier but never published. *Sons and Lovers* had been published a few months before, and Lawrence was well into the composition of *The Sisters*, the original *Rainbow*. His creative energies were overflowing as he tried to get into print all the tales that predate his elopement. The revision of "Two Marriages" is not specifically mentioned, but it is obviously one of the unpublished tales that Lawrence reworked at this time. During this revision the story was transformed into the earliest form of "Daughters of the Vicar," as is made clear in a letter to Garnett of 24 August: "I enclose the letter from the Northern Syndicate. I think they might take 'Two Marriages'—now called 'Daughters of the Vicar'—which they might easily split up to a three-part serial" (AH 136). The revision of "Two Marriages" in the summer of 1913 is highly visible in the *B* manuscript. It is seen there both as revised typescript and as new holograph fair copy (item 3).

"Daughters of the Vicar" received another extensive revision in July 1914, when Lawrence was preparing his stories for publication in *The Prussian Officer* (item 4). The final revision took place in October of the same year (item 5). Many of the 1914 changes are particularly striking, involving a whole new attitude toward his materials. These changes, as we shall see, are closely related to the other important short story revisions of the same period. It is also true in this instance that the summer 1913 revision is clearly headed in the direction of the final version of the story.

I will focus on four major patterns of revision. Because of the great length of the story and the countless variations, I will take up each of four significant and traceable developments in turn, rather than going through the story sequentially.

1. Considerations of class are gradually subsumed in a vision of human relationship beyond class.
2. From the earliest version, the depiction of the mother-son relationship reflects the *Sons and Lovers* situation, but the final

revisions show a dramatic change in Lawrence's perspective on this material.

3. The characteristic Lawrentian intensity, especially in describing sexual passion, increases as the story develops, most notably in the final revisions.

4. The central dichotomy in the story, the body and human contact vs. the mind and "abstraction," is more and more sharply defined and articulated. This is especially true of the 1914 revisions, which make considerable use of the metaphysic and the theoretical vocabulary of this period.

Other patterns are discernible, and the four I have chosen contain unavoidable areas of overlap. Furthermore, the topical treatment I have chosen means that my discussion of the story will be somewhat selective rather than comprehensive. Nevertheless, the four patterns I concentrate on most directly reveal Lawrence's artistic growth during these years.

F. R. Leavis's analysis of "Daughters of the Vicar" in *D. H. Lawrence: Novelist* is also a refutation of one of T. S. Eliot's most damning assertions about Lawrence: "no man was ever more conscious of class-distinctions." Leavis accurately counters that the part played by class distinctions in the story "is a sinister one, and the theme is their defeat—the triumph over them of life."[5] However, this unmistakable triumph was somewhat equivocal until the final versions of the story. The evidence of the earlier versions suggests that Lawrence began with decidedly mixed feelings about the romance between the collier and the vicar's daughter.

Such feelings should not come as a surprise, and the Lawrence admirer should not be distressed to discover them. The first versions of "Daughters of the Vicar" date from a time when Lawrence's own attitude about the working class he sprang from was a divided one. He sensed in its vitality a positive value for his art: thus Louisa Lindley deserts her own class and marries a young collier. At the same time he was

5. F. R. Leavis, *D. H. Lawrence: Novelist* (New York, 1956), p. 78. The Eliot quotation originally appeared in the *Listener* for 13 August 1953.

perceiving his own career as an escape from the working class into the genteel world of letters. Consider his uneasiness about his social origin at the beginning of his literary career. When he told Jessie Chambers that he would write poetry, he wondered "what will the others say. That I'm a fool. A collier's son a poet!"[6] Lawrence's own equivocal feelings figure in the somewhat ambiguous treatment of class in the early versions of the story.

This is borne out fascinatingly by two early rejected endings. "Daughters of the Vicar" is quite open-ended—we are left with Alfred and Louisa planning to get married and start a new life in Canada. However, as late as the summer of 1913 the story was to have ended with the young couple married and settled down in Aldecross, and with rather curious consequences.

Especially intriguing is the ending found in the revised "Two Marriages" holograph of October 1911. This ending forms a kind of coda to the story, sketching in the married life of Alfred and Louisa. Lawrence seems to have some difficulty bringing his story to a conclusion, and this coda invokes the old-fashioned convention of following the lives of the characters beyond the confines of the completed action.

This revealing example of the young Lawrence at work deserves to be quoted at length. Bear in mind that it was written less than a year after his mother's death:

Durant was infinitely glad of his wife. He served her his life long. But he had sufficient reserve, so that she never wearied of him.

She found a good deal of humiliation in her life: she was, socially, neither fish, flesh, nor good red herring, as she laughingly said to her husband. She refused the association of the miners' wives, and elsewhere she was refused. But what woman is not able to live socially alone, if it please her. She lived close and beautifully with her husband.

. . . .

He had a passion for the house and the garden, working at them unremittingly, scheming, planning, carrying out little improvement

6. ET, p. 57.

after improvement, little conveniences for his wife, making one thing after another please her taste. Soon, wherever she looked about the house, she saw his spirit: she was always using things he had contrived to be handy to her, or taking pleasure in things he had planted for her.

"The house is fairly clothed round with his work," she said to herself once as sat [sic] waiting for him to come from pit. Then suddenly she saw that their home was a fabric made out of his energy of tenderness: he had woven it out of his spirit. She sat still and worshipped in reverence. And she thought of the vicarage, where she had lived. Her children would be born into a real home, whose very stuff would have in it some of their father's spirit—and their mother's—and of their forefathers' and foremothers'. It would be nearly like a living thing, of their own blood. It was indeed a home. She dreamed of the boy, like Alfred, who would have the home when she left it. He would be like Alfred, but she would educate him.

She had several children, and was not disappointed. (A 53–54)[7]

The ending of this early version reads like a fantasy played on the central themes of Lawrence's young manhood. Like the married Louisa, Mrs. Lawrence was "neither fish, flesh, nor good red herring," but this was not something she laughed about.[8] It is astonishing to discover that Louisa "refused the association of the miners' wives": in this version she turns out to be as motivated by considerations of class and social pretension as her parents. There is also unmistakable class condescension in Louisa's happiness with a husband who is

7. The abbreviation *A* refers to "Two Marriages" as it is found in George Lazarus's *A* manuscript. This coda was part of the October 1911 revision of the manuscript.

8. Lawrence used this traditional phrase in exactly the same way but referring to himself near the end of his career in "Red-Herring," a splendid bit of doggerel collected in *Pansies*. He is neither fish, flesh, nor good red herring because he is caught between a father who "was a working man" and a mother who was a "superior soul" (CP 490).

The Complete Poems of D. H. Lawrence, edited by Vivian de Sola Pinto and F. Warren Roberts. Coypright 1964, 1971 by Angelo Ravagli and C. M. Weekley, Executors of the Estate of Frieda Lawrence Ravagli. All rights reserved. Reprinted by permission of Laurence Pollinger Ltd., the Estate of the late Mrs. Frieda Lawrence, and The Viking Press, Inc.

always "using things he had contrived to be handy to her, or taking pleasure in things he had planted for her." There is no mistaking Alfred's relation to his superior wife: "He served her his life long."

The marriage has failed to liberate Alfred and Louisa from the sterile values of the vicarage. Their isolation does not come about because they have rejected these values for something better. Rather it seems a defensive posture, a response to the pressure of community judgment in much the same way Maggie Tulliver finds herself isolated after going up the river with Stephen. The bland assertion that any woman is "able to live socially alone, if it please her" sounds like whistling in the dark: Louisa has lost her social identity and in exchange has acquired only a husband who is not her equal. It is not likely that the lively and gregarious vicar's daughter would be content with such isolation. The happy marriage of Alfred and Louisa seems like a make-believe version of Lawrence's parents' marriage, endowed with a harmony that never existed. He seems to be trying—and failing—to convince himself that enduring happiness could grow out of such a union. The basic problem is that Louisa has married beneath herself.

And so Alfred and Louisa live happily ever after, in a world of their own, revering each other, building a home that will carry on the spirit of their forefathers and "foremothers." Revealingly, Louisa is already dreaming of the future. Her desire to educate an Alfred, Jr., "who would have the home when she left it" is striking proof of Lawrence's inner contradictions at this point in his career. Of course Louisa Durant will educate her son, for this is what Lydia Lawrence did for her son, enabling him to escape from the pit. And yet Louisa dreams both of educating her son and of passing on her house to him. Lawrence knew that the educated collier's son flees the colliery world at the earliest opportunity, for he had done so himself. But in his effort to paper over the class division—and imaginatively to reconcile his parents—he depicts an educated collier's son who will stay at home and presumably in the pit. The education to be provided for the next generation is also evidence in itself of Lawrence's uneasiness over the fate of his heroine.

The 1913 manuscript *B* revision of this passage is not quite so remarkable, but Lawrence remains ill at ease about having his vicar's daughter marry a collier. The story concludes with a rewriting and condensation of the manuscript *A* ending:

> "But mother," she said, when she had been married ten years, "I've less to regret than any of them, and I've plenty to be thankful for. I chose my man myself, mother—and he wanted me. I was no fool."
> She found she had a love that would wear. He did not always understand. But he was always hers, always there, always reliable. And they had some very happy times, at evening, talking and reading, for he was intelligent and straight forward [*sic*] in his mind, if not very profound. Moreover, when she thought she knew him altogether, she would find she had been too ready. Queer little things he said, or a few half articulate words he spoke in his sleep, showed her his feeling went much deeper than it seemed, and she was ashamed, for she had been tempted to draw a line under her estimate of him, and say, that was all.
> He was very happy, working all his life for her. She liked the house and garden, and therefore he spent most of his leisure planning out improvements, little conveniences. He was always busy, and she felt as if he were building his own little world round her. (B 56)[9]

This revision took place in the summer of 1913, but the tone of the passage is still primarily apologetic; condescension also remains a keynote. Alfred, happy in "working all his life for her," sounds more like a servant than a husband. The description of his intellectual capacities seems to veil disappointment: he does not "always understand," but he was "always hers, always there." The couple enjoys talking and reading together, for Alfred turns out to be "intelligent and straight forward in his mind, if not very profound." Louisa would still underestimate her husband if it weren't for those "few half articulate words" he says in his sleep. In the summer of 1913, a few months

---

9. The abbreviation *B* refers to "Daughters of the Vicar" as it is found in the 1913 holograph fair copy and the 1913 revised typescript of George Lazarus's *B* manuscript. I have used Mr. Lazarus's pagination, for Lawrence's own numbering is hopelessly tangled and incorrect.

after the publication of *Sons and Lovers*, Lawrence was still afraid that his heroine had married beneath herself.

The overt references to Louisa Durant's social position have been eliminated, but Lawrence is still very conscious of her uncertain status. Louisa feels in her life as if Alfred "were building his own little world round her." The social realities of the mining town would ensure that such a marriage would isolate her. The marriage could only flourish if they managed to create a "little world" of their own. This ending points directly to the conclusion of the next and final version of the story. In "Daughters of the Vicar" Lawrence faces the fact that the marriage could not thrive in such a hostile community and sends his lovers in flight to a vague Canada, an imaginary world elsewhere where their love will not be constricted by social pressures. In leaving the ending so open, he eliminated all the uncertainties of attitude found in the earlier conclusions. He was now able to affirm unequivocally the union of Alfred and Louisa, for in "Daughters of the Vicar" they come together on a plane much more basic than that of class identity.

A similar uncertainty about class can be observed at other points in the early versions of the story. For example, in the *Time and Tide* "Two Marriages," Louisa has reservations about Alfred even after the back-washing scene in which she feels an attraction to him that is purely and powerfully physical: " 'He is very keen-sighted, he can see a long way,' said Louisa, looking full at his eyes. 'But he can't see into things, he's not introspective' " (TT 399).[10] In "A Modern Lover," Cyril Mersham, the effete intellectual and *litterateur*, likewise sizes up his working-class rival, classifying him as one of the men "who are children in simplicity, who can add two and two, but never xy and yx" (CSS 13). Throughout "Two Marriages," a doubt that Alfred is good enough for Louisa seems to linger in Lawrence's mind. In "Daughters of the Vicar," however, there

10. The abbreviation TT refers to the October 1911 revision of "Two Marriages," which was published as a supplement to *Time and Tide*, 24 March 1934.

is no real quesion of Louisa marrying beneath herself. The marriage will be a good one if only Alfred can free himself from his mother. The physical attraction between the young man and the young woman has become sufficient unto itself.

In the same scene in the 1911 "Two Marriages" typescript, Alfred stares at Louisa and realizes that "she was far above him, she was beyond him in education, in thought as well" (B 38). The 1913 revised text retains this theme: Louisa is "above him. She had beautiful white plump hands—a lady's hands. . . . How beautiful to have a superior woman like her sitting near one" (B 38–39). No trace of this class element remains in the passage as published in *The Prussian Officer*. Alfred still feels apart from Louisa, but the reason is different: "She was all that was beyond him, of revelation and exquisiteness. All that was ideal and beyond him, she was that—and he was lost to himself in looking at her. She had no connection with him. He did not approach her. She was there like a wonderful distance" (PO 118). In "Daughters of the Vicar" Alfred suffers because of a divided image of woman: "the *idea* of women, with which he sometimes debauched himself, and real women, before whom he felt a deep uneasiness, and a need to draw away" (PO 105). This problem of bringing his ideal conception of woman down to earth, a problem caused by his Oedipal tie to his mother, here replaces material that had originally shown Alfred's feelings of working-class inferiority. This is in keeping with Lawrence's new confidence and clarity concerning the Alfred-Louisa relationship in "Daughters of the Vicar."

His earlier doubts surface with particular hilarity near the end of the betrothal scene in the 1913 revised typescript version. The social gulf between Alfred and Louisa here looms large and comically:

There was something he wanted to say, that he dared not. He followed her round, laughing uneasily, respectfully. . . .

"It doesn't matter—does it?" he asked.

"What?"

"As I did it."

He meant that he had kissed her. In spite of herself she winced at his bad English. (B 51)

Lawrence seems to share somewhat in Louisa's condescension here, and once more he suggests that this will be a marriage with unavoidable problems.

At the end of the story Alfred must go to the vicarage to receive Louisa's parents' grudging permission to marry their daughter. In the 1911 "Two Marriages" typescript Alfred hates the vicarage because it robs him of "his natural value and manliness" (B 53). In the 1913 revision of this passage he still knows that "there he was a collier, not a man" (B 53). These feelings based on class anxieties do not appear in "Daughters of the Vicar." Instead—much like the newly confident Bachmann at the end of "The Thorn in the Flesh"— he goes to the vicarage with the inner strength that will prevail over the sneers of the Lindleys and "filled with a blessed feeling of fatality. He was not responsible, neither had her people anything really to do with it" (PO 133). Salvation comes through submission to the fate that has reached Alfred from the unknown: one thinks immediately of the courtship of Tom Brangwen in *The Rainbow*. A world of class awareness has been replaced by a world of transfiguration. The same sort of evolution can be traced in the versions of the backwashing scene and of Louisa's reaction to Alfred immediately afterwards. However, in those passages what was added to the text is even more interesting, so I will reserve my analysis until the proper time later in the chapter.

One interesting detail in "Daughters of the Vicar" suggests Lawrence's continuing awareness that the social and cultural gulf between Alfred and Louisa won't be removed by marriage. Alfred Durant is singled out from his fellow workers not only by his skill as a piccolo player but also by his intellectual aspirations. In the revised typescript these intellectual interests are associated with Louisa, who seems intent on uplifting Alfred: "Sometimes Miss Louisa lent him books, and discussed them with him" (B 29). Alfred's aspirations survive into the *Prussian Officer* version, and indeed there he is even beginning to "hold fixed ideas which he got from the Fabians" (PO 106). This odd credential may be intended to give a kind of sanction to the marriage that is to take place at story's end. Or perhaps it indicates the lovers' insecurity with one another: he feels the need to improve himself, she feels the need to improve him. Even as Lawrence's myth of passional vitalization emerges, the story never loses its foundation in observed social reality.

The development of Lawrence's attitude toward class as embodied in the successive versions of "Daughters of the Vicar" reveals a significant transition. From the beginning, he invokes the myth of working-class vitality by imagining Louisa's escape from the cold and sterile gentility of her vicarage background via marriage to a young collier. Nevertheless, in the early versions Louisa is something of a woman between, unable to accept the life-denying behavior of her class and yet noticeably unhappy in her descent to a man her social and intellectual inferior. The early versions contain this element of confusion because the young author did not know exactly what to make of his own working-class background. Only with the final revisions of 1914 does the union of the collier and the vicar's daughter become unequivocally triumphant. Only in the *Prussian Officer* version, to use Leavis's terms, does "life" clearly prevail over class.

The Oedipal situation of *Sons and Lovers* also seems to resonate throughout the story that grew into "Daughters of the Vicar." Alfred Durant lives in an emotional nightmare, imprisoned within the bondage of mother love until Louisa Lindley brings him release. The basic difference in the treatment of the mother-son relationship between the 1911 "Two Marriages" text and "Daughters of the Vicar" can be expressed concisely. In the early forms of the story, Alfred never really frees himself: Louisa simply becomes his new mother. In the later versions— the 1913 revised typescript and the *Prussian Officer* text— Alfred's Oedipal agonies are heightened and intensified. This is part of a narrative strategy in which Lawrence wants to make the young collier's genuine liberation and finding of himself through Louisa seem all the more triumphant.

Mrs. Durant is quite familiar from very early in the October

1911 magazine "Two Marriages." She does not speak in "the vernacular; she came from Nottingham, was a burgher's daughter" (TT 393). This passage was cut out, but several details added in this part of the 1913 revised typescript and printed in "Daughters of the Vicar" underscore the *Sons and Lovers* nature of the mother-son relationship. In "Daughters of the Vicar" Mrs. Durant is characterized as a "woman who has brought up and ruled her sons" (PO 68). We learn that "she loved her youngest boy, because he was her last." She tells the vicar that Alfred is "the one lad as I wanted to keep by me" (PO 69), and when he replies that he is better off serving Queen and country, she says, "He is wanted to serve *me*." "Alfred was her baby, her last, whom she had allowed herself the luxury of spoiling" (PO 70). These additions prefigure the detailed discussion of the mother-son relationship in Section VIII of "Daughters of the Vicar," material that also was introduced into the story in the 1913 revision in manuscript *B*.

A three-paragraph description of the relationship between mother and son in "Two Marriages" is amplified and expanded to occupy nine long paragraphs in Section VIII of "Daughters of the Vicar." This change in emphasis transforms the thrust of the whole story. In the *Time and Tide* "Two Marriages," Mrs. Durant "had been fairly well educated" (TT 397). Alfred is familiar to readers of Lawrence too: dominated by the relationship with his mother, he is the typical young prig of the early fiction: "His love for his mother . . . became the strongest force in his life, which life had remained remarkably pure. Now for four years Alfred had kept his mother at home. He was thirty-one years old, and had never had a sweetheart: not because he was timid or a ninny, but because he had never turned his thoughts to a girl, being never in a position to marry whilst his mother needed and monopolized him" (TT 397). This is the basic history that is also found in the 1913 *B* text and "Daughter of the Vicar," but in both later texts it is greatly elaborated on.

The "Daughters of the Vicar" exposition of this relationship is based on that found in the 1913 revised typescript of manuscript *B*, but in many ways the texts are profoundly different. There is more tension in the mother-son relationship in "Daughters of the Vicar." In the revised typescript Alfred does not "care much for drink, nor for the public-house company," but in "Daughters of the Vicar" he has taken to drink. In the revised typescript Mrs. Durant is "proud of the little talks and arguments they had together" (B 29). In "Daughters of the Vicar" "there grew up a little hostility between them" because "at the bottom he did not satisfy her, he did not seem manly enough" (PO 104).

In the 1913 text Alfred returns "quite chaste" (B 29) from his service in the Navy, but in "Daughters of the Vicar" he returns "almost quite chaste" (PO 105). The following experience recounted in the *Prussian Officer* text comprises part of the difference:

In Genoa he went with an under officer to a drinking house where the cheaper sort of girl came in to look for lovers. He sat there with his glass, the girls looked at him, but they never came to him. He knew that if they did come he could only pay for food and drink for them, and was anxious lest they lacked good necessities. He could not have gone with one of them: he knew it, and was ashamed, looking with curious envy at the swaggering, easy-passionate Italian whose body went to a woman by instinctive impersonal attraction. They were men, he was not a man. (PO 105-6)

Alfred had also gone to a house of prostitution overseas where he had "felt as if he were, not physically, but spiritually impotent: not actually impotent, but intrinsically so" (PO 106). It is not surprising to find a Lawrentian hero repelled by this kind of sex, but two details are especially noteworthy because of their association with artistic ideas that were emerging in 1914. The distinction between the cold north and the passionate south was to become one of the shaping mythologies in Lawrence's subsequent fiction. He had already begun *The Lost Girl,* which is built on Alvina Hughton's attraction to a "swaggering, easy-passionate Italian," had written the early versions of the essays that became *Twilight in Italy,* and was also at work on the novel that was to evolve into *Women in Love,* which ends with Gerald Crich's death by ice. The "instinctive impersonal attraction" of the Italian also belongs unmistakably to the 1914 revision, as we shall' see in detail in the discussion of metaphysic in "Daughters of the Vicar" that concludes this chapter.

The end of Section x of the story, which includes the back-washing scene, further illustrates that the *Sons and Lovers* material became more dominant with the 1914 revision. At this point in the 1913 text, Alfred goes outside, brooding about the fatal illness of his mother: "Till he got out of the house. Then suddenly he began to pant with sobs, because the snow and the stars made him feel curious and small and lost, amid an immense dark unknown. He was afraid to think of his mother" (B 39). This is greatly expanded and intensified in "Daughters of the Vicar." The passage is directly reminiscent of Paul's agony in "the vastness and terror of the immense night" (SL 420) at the end of *Sons and Lovers*:

And, when he got out of the house, he was afraid. He saw the stars above ringing with fine brightness, the snow beneath just visible, and a new night was gathering round him. He was afraid almost with obliteration. What was this new night ringing about him, and what was he? He could not recognize himself nor any of his surroundings. He was afraid to think of his mother. And yet his chest was conscious of her, and of what was happening to her. He could not escape from her, she carried him with her into an unformed, unknown chaos. (PO 118–19)

The outline of "Daughters of the Vicar" is clearly drawn. Alfred, almost paralyzed by his agony, will be free to come to Louisa only when he can escape from his mother's dominion.

At first glance it seems puzzling that Lawrence so greatly amplified the Oedipal element; it seems more baffling that he intensified it even between the summer of 1913 and July 1914. The mother-son relationship was part of the original story because it was a projection of Lawrence's own relationship with his mother. This relationship was so dominant in 1911 and the years preceding that it is difficult to find a mother-son relationship in the early fiction that does not partake of Lawrence family history. *Sons and Lovers*, the work in which Lawrence attempted to come to terms with his past, was finished by November 1912 and had been published a few months before the 1913 revision of the typescript in manuscript *B*. The mother-son background in the 1913 text and "Daughters of the Vicar" is rendered with so much intensity that it cannot be argued that Lawrence was merely filling the story with material he had already worked out (which seems partly to be the case in such a later story as "The Lovely Lady"). The question remains: if he had successfully grappled with the mother-son situation in *Sons and Lovers*, why does it appear again in such an intense, full form?

Any explanation must be speculative, but I feel it can be found in the difference in tone between story and novel. The prose of "Daughters of the Vicar" displays little of the inner struggle present in *Sons and Lovers*, a work in which the process of writing was in part therapeutic, a concerted attempt by Lawrence to achieve emotional equilibrium. By the summer of 1913 he had arrived at a new vantage point about his personal history. After receiving the shock of reading the proofs of *Sons and Lovers* in March 1913, Jessie Chambers had commented to Helen Corke that Lawrence's attitude toward Mrs. Morel and Miriam, which seemed grossly unjust to her, was "evidently too deep-seated in David to be eradicated."[11] However, by the time Jessie read the proofs, Lawrence had been with Frieda for nearly a year, and a new perspective on his past was emerging. This new perspective can be discerned in the final text of "Daughters of the Vicar." Lawrence believed that his Oedipal problems had been fully and finally resolved through his experience with Frieda. In "Daughters of the Vicar" he uses the familiar mother-son materials, but now he is using them

11. Jessie Chambers to Helen Corke, March 1913, unpublished letter in the collection of the University of Nottingham Library. I am grateful to the University of Nottingham Library for permission to quote from this letter.

retrospectively. Alfred's emergence from the domination of his mother through the love of Louisa Lindley imaginatively celebrates Lawrence's own coming through.

In *Sons and Lovers* Paul Morel rejects both Miriam and Clara but retains his deep allegiance to his mother. Though he has the strength to walk toward the lighted city, he is at least temporarily cast adrift. His role as son has prevented him from mastering the role of lover, and at novel's end he is, as the final chapter title tells us, derelict. However, in "Daughters of the Vicar" Alfred must *extricate* himself from the relationship with his mother before he is free to participate in the more mature relationship with Louisa, and that is precisely what he does. Lawrence's deep fulfillment with Frieda—"a woman that I love . . . keeps me in direct communication with the unknown" (CL 179)—taught him the lesson found in the difference between the endings of the two works. Just as the elopement with Frieda enabled him to believe he had escaped from his past, the experience with Louisa helps Alfred free himself from his mother and grow toward manhood. The intensification of the mother-son relationship in the story allows Lawrence to express the triumph he felt at his own emergence from a similar situation into his first real experience of adult love. He does so by sharpening the contrast between Alfred Durant's tormenting mother love and the tender and radiant love between him and Louisa. Only in "Daughters of the Vicar" does Lawrence display a firm sense of how a character can emerge successfully from such emotional difficulties.

The various versions of the betrothal scene in which Alfred and Louisa decide to defy convention and get married are especially interesting in the context of the *Sons and Lovers* materials. The *Prussian Officer* text reveals an author who has achieved real perspective on his long-standing emotional problems; in contrast, the betrothal scene in the earlier version is hard to comprehend without some awareness of precisely those problems.

In "Daughters of the Vicar" the betrothal—in Section xiii— shows Alfred and Louisa yielding to the powerful and imper-

sonal forces of the universe. The experience of transfiguration
and the primal stillness of the scene call to mind the barn
scene in *The Rainbow*, analyzed in Chapter I. Alfred's
agonies in Section VIII give way to this celebration of the
mysterious otherness of his new beloved and of the powerful
energies radiating through the universe. However, in the 1911
"Two Marriages" typescript, Lawrence had only been able to
imagine the marriage between Alfred and Louisa as the
exchange of one mother for another. In a fascinating passage
Alfred talks awkwardly about getting married because "you've
got to marry somebody":

> This made her smile: what a child he was, after all his experience.
> Still, perhaps he only meant to say, that he didn't know of anyone
> he wanted to marry. "You've got to marry somebody—"
> "It is true," she smiled, in answer to him.
> "Well—!" He was at the end of his tether, and he could not give
> a jump and break it. His masculine modesty was worse than any
> maidenly.
> She was angry with him, very angry. Should she leave him, the
> jibbing, shying child. . . .
> "Do you *want* to marry?" she asked, firmly.
> He looked full at her, and trembled. "Oh these men!" she sighed.
> "Do you *definitely* want to marry?" she persisted, with an effort.
> She managed to look up at him. She was startled, almost shocked.
> He was biting his lip with his white teeth, and from his eyes the
> tears were just running over. (B 50-50A)

Alfred's "masculine modesty" reminds one of Cyril Beardsall
of *The White Peacock* and of Cyril Mersham, Edward
Severn, and Bernard Coutts, the priggish heroes of the early
short fiction. The roles dramatized in the exchange are
unmistakably those of mother and son. Alfred is still a sheepish
little boy, "very much ashamed of himself" (B 50A). After the
lovers embrace for "an hour," the clinch is broken and they
banter about their immediate future. They decide to get
married right away, and Alfred seems "grateful as a child" (B
50A)—a lost child who has found his mother again.

Though Alfred has found a surrogate mother in this early
version of the story, he never gets over his loss of the real

thing, as is made clear by the coda that concludes this
text:

Occasionally, after their marriage, he would sit and fall into an intense
brooding. If she spoke to him, she would see his eyes draw
away from her with a heavy, haunted look. Then she knew she
would have to leave him alone. At first, it was bitter to her. And
at first, when she heard him in his sleep talking inarticulately, and
evidently suffering again a little delirium of grief, she was tempted
to wake him, to comfort him. (A 53–54)

"Daughters of the Vicar" is a celebration of the possibility
of human contact and communion, but "Two Marriages"
seems instead a lesson in the primacy and persistence of mother
love. Not only does Alfred choose a new mother for
himself but he also spends a lifetime of brooding and bad
dreams over the loss of his own mother, seemingly doomed to
a permanent Oedipal sorrow. It is as if Lawrence has not
quite perceived the meaning of his story. He challenges the
assumption of class by bringing the collier and the vicar's
daughter together, but the love between Alfred and Louisa
seems limited in its efficacy, never emerging from the shadow
of his love for his mother. Only gradually did the Alfred-
Louisa marriage come to embody the human salvation
available through the dark mystery of the body.

The revision of 1913 goes a long way toward establishing this
more mature meaning. Alfred still looks at Louisa with
"curious, childish obstinacy" (B 50), but for the most part
there is little identification of Louisa with a mother figure.
Alfred is now a man in greater contact with the Lawrentian
unknown: "At last she wanted to see his eyes. She looked up.
They were strange and glowing. . . ." After being "silent
for a long time, too mixed up with passion and grief and
death to do anything but clasp each other in pain and kiss with
long, hurting kisses wherein death was transfigured into desire"
(B 50A), they separate. The writing is embarrassingly purple,
but the idea rings loud and clear. Those "long, hurting kisses"
signal that salvation is of the flesh. Louisa looks Alfred
"square in the eyes" (B 51) and tells him that she loves him.

Surely this is a love that has nothing to do with the love of mother for child.

"Daughters of the Vicar" intensifies Alfred's Oedipal problems with his mother, but nothing at all remains of the Oedipal overtones of his love for Louisa. Instead Lawrence probes once again beneath the old stable ego of the character as he dramatizes the coming together of his two young lovers. This meeting has become elemental, as we shall see in the discussion of metaphysic that closes this chapter. The bond will endure between Alfred and Louisa because it has been formed on a level so much deeper than class or everyday relationship— deeper even than the bond of mother love. Alfred's drift toward death is over; he has freed himself from his mother's tenacious grasp. His passional fulfillment with Louisa is really an experience of rebirth: "death was transfigured into desire."

As one would suspect, the physical nature of Louisa's attraction to Alfred is heightened in "Daughters of the Vicar." As Lawrence freed his hero from his stifling relationship with his mother, he also increased the emphasis on the power of warm-blooded physical attraction between the young lovers. Indeed this power is itself instrumental in Alfred's liberation. In the later versions—the revisions of 1913 and 1914—the characteristic Lawrentian rhetoric of sexual attraction came to play an important role. The passage detailing Louisa's feelings after her visit to the Durants early in the story, added only in the 1914 revision, is typical:

Her heart, her veins were possessed by the thought of Alfred Durant as he held his mother in his arms; then the break in his voice, as she remembered it again and again, was like a flame through her; and she wanted to see his face more distinctly in her mind, ruddy with the sun, and his golden-brown eyes, kind and careless, strained now with a natural fear, the fine nose tanned hard by the sun, the mouth that could not help smiling at her. And it went through her with pride, to think of his figure, a straight, fine jet of life. (PO 82–83) [12]

12. The young gamekeeper in "The Shades of Spring" stands "like the thick jet of a fountain balanced in itself" (PO 154).

Section x contains the back-washing scene, the emotional culmination of "Daughters of the Vicar" in very much the same way the corpse-washing and Mrs. Bates's inner monologue provide the climax for "Odour of Chrysanthemums." The physical intimacy of washing the coal dust from Alfred's back makes the relationship between Louisa and him irrevocable: at the end of the section she writes a note to the vicarage explaining that she is staying overnight at the Durants'. The main alteration of this material—as well as one of the major differences between the two stories—is the greatly heightened intensity of the final version. Much of this change took place in the revision of the summer of 1913 and can be seen in the revised *B* manuscript. The story continued to develop in this direction when Lawrence further revised the 1913 type-script for publication in *The Prussian Officer*. We have observed that such a heightening of narrative intensity was also charac-teristic of the later revisions of "Odour of Chrysanthemums."

Amusingly, Lawrence seems worried about Mrs. Grundy in the 1911 magazine version of the scene and feels the need to step in to apologize for what is about to happen: "It is so common for the men to wash themselves thus before the fire, that no one notices it, any more than if they were merely washing their hands. Even in the presence of strangers it seems as natural to a miner as it seems to some folk to dip their fingers in a finger-bowl after dinner" (TT 399). Obviously the impact of the scene is seriously blunted if the reader is to perceive it in these terms. We can be sure that Louisa would be denied her intense moment of revelation if Alfred were only washing his hands. Lawrence wisely deleted this absurd intrusion.

"Must I go and do it?" (TT 399) Louisa asks in the 1911 magazine "Two Marriages" when Mrs. Durant says that her son will need help washing his back. There is no such hesitation in "Daughters of the Vicar." The decision that Louisa will wash Alfred's back introduces the paragraph of greatest intensity—and perhaps importance—in all of "Daughters of the Vicar." The passage is greatly altered and expanded from the

1911 magazine "Two Marriages." In "Two Marriages" Alfred
takes the back-washing completely for granted because Louisa
is "so calm and official." She notices his "beautifully white and
unblemished" skin (TT 399), but this produces not a revelation
but a blush: "He was glad . . . because he knew he was so
perfectly developed and in such good condition. She knew
nothing about development or condition, only that he had a
beautiful skin. They were neither of them sorry when the
washing was done. She put down the flannel and fled upstairs,
flushing furiously" (TT 399). The passage's awkwardness
and curious matter-of-factness suggest that Lawrence wasn't
completely certain of what he wanted to accomplish. This
passage took on its central importance only with the 1914
revision.

In the "Daughters of the Vicar" text, many details from
the earlier version of this passage are closely echoed. However,
these surviving bits of the earlier text are now part of an altogether different shaping of the materials. In the revised
passage, Louisa's interior monologue begins at the social level:
"After all, there was a difference between her and the common
people." However, as she responds more and more passionately
to Alfred's body, Lawrence modulates her reverie beyond class
considerations until it embraces the question of human
identity. At first Alfred looks so strange with the frothy
soap on his back that she can "scarcely conceive him as human"
(PO 114). As his white skin emerges from the dirt, Louisa
is granted an intense new insight: "this also was what he was"
(PO 115).

It fascinated her. Her feeling of separateness passed away: she ceased
to draw back from contact with him and his mother. There
was this living centre. Her heart ran hot. She had reached
some goal in the beautiful, clear, male body. She loved him in
a white, impersonal heat. But the sun-burnt reddish neck and ears:
they were more personal, more curious. A tenderness rose in her,
she loved even his queer ears. A person—an intimate being he was
to her. (PO 115)

Louisa's class prejudices have been obliterated in the experience of intense, intimate contact with the physical being of another. Alfred's "beautiful, clear, male body" offers revelation of the radiant but impersonal mystery at the heart of life. It is a revelation that passes beyond class awareness, and it passes beyond human awareness as well. Louisa goes upstairs feeling "strange and pregnant" (PO 115): pregnant with the possibilities of life.

Unlikely as it may seem, in one important respect Louisa's experience as she washes Alfred's back is parallel to Paul Morel's experience in the garden just before he decides to break off with Miriam. Paul's perception of the flowers' fierce otherness, of their separate and independent existence, underscores in his own mind Miriam's refusal to let him be himself. Similarly, Alfred seems less a stranger to Louisa only after she has scrutinized some of the unique details of his physical being. His "beautiful white and unblemished" skin (PO 115), his "reddish neck," his "queer ears": such details are the external indices of Alfred's self-contained uniqueness. The "white, impersonal heat" signals that this relationship will take place on a deeper level than that of storybook romance. In the experience of washing his back, she comes into contact with his integral and inviolable self. Only in locating this primal identity can she anticipate relation to him in a way that will let each of them maintain his own individuality.

The insight granted to Louisa Lindley as she washes Alfred's back is identical to Elizabeth Bates's perception as she washes the body of her dead husband. Both scenes provide powerful revelations of impersonal maleness and the mystery of the unknown. Both women make contact with the energies of life by means of physical contact with a beautiful male body. The main difference is that in Louisa's case the insight has not come too late. In both stories this insight became part of the text only with the 1914 revision.

The betrothal scene in Section xiii of "Daughters of the Vicar" is the other passage in which Lawrence heightened the experience of passion. In both the 1911 and 1913 texts Louisa and Alfred at last make contact only because

she is so deeply moved by his obvious suffering, responding
to him as mother does to child. This is not at all the case in
"Daughters of the Vicar," where powerful physical attraction
draws them together:

He turned to her. Her face was pale and set. It looked heavy and
impassive, her hair shone richer as she grew white. She was to him
something steady and immovable and eternal presented to him.
His heart was hot in an anguish of suspense. Sharp twitches of
fear and pain were in his limbs. He turned his whole body away
from her. The silence was unendurable. He could not bear her to
sit there any more. It made his heart go hot and stifled in his
breast. (PO 127–28)

When Louisa seems "steady and immovable and eternal"
to Alfred, Lawrence is again trying to probe beneath human
personality to reach the impersonal beneath. Lawrence's
prose now strains to render verbally the passion that brings
them together:

Then suddenly a sharp pang, like lightning, seared her from
head to foot, and she was beyond herself.
. . . .
"Do you want me to go?" she repeated.
"Why?" he asked again.
"Because I want to stay with you," she said, suffocated, with her
lungs full of fire.
His face worked, he hung forward a little, suspended, staring
straight into her eyes, in torment, in an agony of chaos, unable to
collect himself. And as if he turned to stone, she looked back into
his eyes. Their souls were exposed bare for a few moments. It
was agony. They could not bear it. He dropped his head, whilst
his body jerked with little sharp twitchings. (PO 128–29)

Louisa's question breaks through convention, and the crisis
of passion has been reached. Caught up in the spell of
Alfred's eyes, she has "no will, no life any more." His eyes
hold her transfixed, and she stands "motionless, spellbound,
like a creature given up as prey." The expression of his face
is "strange and inhuman." He "cruelly, blindly" (PO 129)
takes her into his arms, in a passage of powerful intensity:
"Then, gradually, as he held her gripped, and his brain

reeled round, and he felt himself falling, falling from himself, and whilst she, yielded up, swooned to a kind of death of herself, a moment of utter darkness came over him, and they began to wake up again as if from a long sleep. He was himself' (PO 129). [13] The language of this passage suggests the scenes of passion in *The Rainbow*, three versions of which Lawrence had completed by July 1914. The closest parallel is found in the courtship of Tom Brangwen:

> He turned and looked for a chair, and keeping her still in his arms, sat down with her close to him, to his breast. Then for a few seconds, he went utterly to sleep, asleep and sealed in the darkest sleep, utter, extreme oblivion.
>
> From which he came to gradually, always holding her warm and close upon him, and she was utterly silent as he, involved in the same oblivion, the fecund darkness. (R 40–41)

Out of the sleep of oblivion comes radiant new life.

After they separate, Alfred seems "eternal" to Louisa too. Passion has produced transfiguration:

> And at last she drew back her face and looked up at him, her eyes wet, and shining with light. His heart, which saw, was silent with fear. He was with her. She saw his face all sombre and inscrutable, and he seemed eternal to her. And all the echo of pain came back into the rarity of bliss, and all her tears came up.
>
> "I love you," she said, her lips drawn to sobbing. He put down his head against her, unable to hear her, unable to bear the sudden coming of the peace and passion that almost broke his heart. They stood together in silence whilst the thing moved away a little. (PO 130)

The identity of the "thing" that moves away a little may be somewhat obscure, but this is recognizably the narrative voice of the mature Lawrence. In many ways Alfred and Louisa's experience and the language describing it prefigure

---

13. Bachmann, the young soldier in "The Thorn in the Flesh," makes contact with the eternal and emerges into his own being in very much the same language in another 1914 revision: "A curious silence, a blankness, like something eternal, possessed him. He remained true to himself" (PO 60).

the violent coming together of Jack Fergusson and Mabel Pervin in "The Horse Dealer's Daughter," a story Lawrence wrote in November 1916: "After the kiss, her eyes again slowly filled with tears. She sat still, away from him, with her face drooped aside, and her hands folded in her lap. The tears fell very slowly. There was complete silence. He too sat there motionless and silent on the hearth rug. The strange pain of his heart that was broken seemed to consume him" (CSS 455). In each story man and woman are drawn together by an irresistible force in a scene of intense, mysterious passion. The intensity is even greater in "The Horse Dealer's Daughter," for two years later Lawrence was writing a story in which the overflow of passion between the two main characters is absolutely unrelated to normal social modes of behavior. Nevertheless, the language of "The Horse Dealer's Daughter" is reminiscent of "Daughters of the Vicar," as is the declaration of love made under inner duress.

At the end of Section XIII Alfred and Louisa are "afraid of each other, afraid to talk." Surprised by the suddenness and intensity of passion, they have become shy. However, the section ends on a note of triumph. Louisa laughs "for joy" when Alfred says her parents will see her blouse is dirty, and he is "sharp with pride" (PO 131). Alfred and Louisa have tasted at the wellsprings of passion and have come through triumphantly. In the moment of passion with a woman, Alfred has been able to leave his grief behind and to take an enormous step toward manhood. "He was himself" (PO 129). Physical passion is liberating for both young lovers. Only through the intense experience of physical passion can the self be found. Lawrence fully discovered this meaning only in the final revisions.

Jessie Chambers commented on the last of the significant developments in the evolution of "Daughters of the Vicar" in a letter to Emile Delavenay written a few years after Lawrence's death, remarking that the *Time and Tide* "Two Marriages" "is *The Daughters of the Vicar* minus the theorising that comes out in the later writing. I prefer the earlier version."[14] The original title, "Two Marriages," makes it clear that from its inception Lawrence intended the story to progress in terms of contrast. This firm structural principle became even firmer, however, with the addition of a good deal of Lawrential metaphysic in the final revisions. Jessie believed that the metaphysic damaged the freshness and spontaneity of the tale. "Daughters of the Vicar" is thus an excellent text for the study of the interplay of Lawrentian art and metaphysic: what is gained by the introduction of metaphysic and what is lost?[15]

The development of Alfred's opposite number, Mr. Massy, the little clergyman who marries Louisa's sister Mary, is worth considering in this context. In the *Time and Tide* "Two Marriages," the description that introduces Massy is almost casual; in "Daughters of the Vicar" Massy becomes a rather programmatic composite of the story's negative values—physical, psychological, and intellectual:

He was very little, meagre to the last degree, silent, very nervous, looked about him in a vacant, goggling way from behind his spectacles, was apparently an idiot; he had the stoop and the rambling gestures and the vacant expression of one. Yet one soon felt he had

He had not normal powers of perception. They soon saw that he lacked the full range of human feelings, but had rather a strong, philosophical mind, from which he lived. His body was almost unthinkable, in intellect he was something definite. The conver-

14. Jessie Chambers to Emile Delavenay, 10 October 1934, quoted in Emile Delavenay, *D. H. Lawrence, l'homme et la genèse de son oeuvre: Les années de formation, 1885–1919* (Paris, 1969), II, 684. The letters from Jessie Chambers to Delavenay are not included in the English translation.
15. Delavenay seems not to notice the addition of the metaphysic. In *D. H. Lawrence, the Man and His Work: The Formative Years, 1885–1919* (tr. Katharine M. Delavenay [Carbondale, Ill., 1972], p. 205) he observes that in the final text "we get to know Alfred Durant better and to recognize beneath the layer of coal dust covering his face his real sensitivity and human potentialities." Actually Lawrence takes the reader far beyond "sensitivity and human potentialities" into that region deeper than the old stable ego of the character.

an indomitable little *"ego."* (TT 394)

sation at once took a balanced, abstract tone when he participated. There was no spontaneous exclamation, no violent assertion or expression of personal conviction, but all cold, reasonable assertions. (PO 76)

Mr. Massy is inspired by Mr. Casaubon in *Middlemarch*, but the two characters are fundamentally different. Casaubon is a three-dimensional character who arouses sympathy as well as laughter and contempt. Massy is a caricature made-to-order to embody Lawrence's satiric—and theoretical—needs. The "Daughters of the Vicar" passage is unmistakably the later description, for it catalogs with straightforward clarity everything Lawrence wants at the negative pole of his story. Massy, constructed according to an abstract schema—for example, in his attempts at charity "he only realized a kind of mathematical working out, . . . a calculated well-doing" (PO 78)—sometimes seems out of place among the more three-dimensional characters of "Daughters of the Vicar."

At the deathbed of Alfred's father early in the story, Mr. Massy's "non-human will dominated them all" (PO 80). This sentence was added only in the Hopkin proofs of July 1914, and the will became "non-human" only in the final revision the same autumn. The phrase seems to echo a familiar passage from the "carbon" letter written to Garnett in June 1914, in which Lawrence talks about his interest in a character as "a phenomenon . . . representing some greater, inhuman will" (CL 282). One is tempted to say that there are wills and wills, but there is no escaping the fact that it is precisely the radical theoretical language of this period of Lawrence's career that is associated with Massy. Lawrence may have intended Massy's "non-human will" to be an example of "some greater, inhuman will" as it operates in human personality, but Massy turned out a flat and extraordinarily unrevolutionary character. The ideas found in the letter to Garnett are useful in discussing what happens to Alfred and Louisa in their experience of passion, but when Lawrence seems to try to apply the same ideas to Mr. Massy, the effect is at best blurring. It's as if Lawrence is too eager to find cosmic significance. The danger always exists that in the excitement of his new ideas, he injected his stories with language that does not alway fit them. Great creative moments are not necessarily coherent or consistent.

The language of "will" does play a recurrent role in "Daughters of the Vicar," and generally it seems to signal Lawrence's new theoretical interests. For example, Section IV, a late addition to the story encapsulating Louisa's feelings about Alfred at the time of his father's death, is a good example of the story's analytic mode that dates from 1914. In the 1913 unrevised typescript Louisa visits Alfred, but he is stiff and treats her "not like a person, but as if she were some sort of mechanism and he a thing waiting in front of her" (B 15). In "Daughters of the Vicar" he is stiff and treats her "not like a person, but as if she were some sort of will in command and he a separate, distinct will waiting in front of her" (PO 84). "Will" also becomes the key word in the Massy-Mary marriage. Louisa reflects that the little clergyman "was a will that they could not controvert" (PO 87). Mary's own feelings about her marriage are in very much the same vein. In the 1911 typescript her motivation is expressed mostly in economic terms, but the *Prussian Officer* text offers an analytic passage that invokes the notion of will. The abstract rhetoric, obsessive cadences, and incremental repetition of her thoughts about her husband nicely embody the danger of suppressing the life of instinct:

> Mary, in marrying him, tried to become a pure reason such as he was, without feeling or impulse. She shut herself up, she shut herself rigid against the agonies of shame and the terror of violation which came at first. She *would* not feel, and she *would* not feel. She was a pure will acquiescing to him. She elected a certain kind of fate. She would be good and purely just, she would live in a higher freedom than she had ever known, she would be free of mundane care, she was a pure will towards right. (PO 88)

The final revision of this passage puts it squarely into align-
ment with the central dichotomy of the story: that between
the full life of human contact and the barren life of abstract
goodness.

In the story's structure the love between Alfred and
Louisa has all the spontaneity and uncertainty of human relationship as well as all the warmth of contact in the flesh. In
contrast the Massy-Mary marriage—the epitome of brittle,
sterile, cold-blooded living through the intellect—is presented as a battle of wills. The final version of the story
underscores this basic dichotomy so greatly that parts of the
tale become somewhat schematic. Mary's extended reflection on her baby, which entered the story only in the
autumn 1914 revision of the Hopkin proofs, is a case in
point: "She hated it because it made her live again in the
flesh, when she *could* not live in the flesh, she could not.
She wanted to trample her flesh down, down, extinct, to
live in the mind" (PO 90). Similarly where in the Hopkin
proofs Massy hears the "conviction" (H 116) in his wife's
voice as she does battle with him, in "Daughters of the
Vicar" it is the "will" (PO 93) in her voice that he hears. We
have already observed the late addition of "impersonal"
passion: the "instinctive impersonal attraction" (PO 106)
of the Italians and the "white, impersonal heat" (PO 115) of
Louisa's love of Alfred. The intellectual substratum is much
more visible—perhaps more obtrusive—in the *Prussian Officer*
version.

The late emergence of Lawrentian metaphysic in the
story is strikingly demonstrated in a passage that registers
Alfred's response to his mother's death. In the 1911 unrevised typescript, Lawrence offers a strangely cheerful catalogue of the young collier's former activities: "He was a
man whose life had been filled up with small activities: in
summer the garden, swimming, cycling; in winter shoe-
mending, soldering, making canny little contrivances for the
house-hold and then smoking and reading for an hour or
two, or practicing for an hour on the flute, or playing a game

of cards with his mother" (B 44). This passage is out of place in the midst of the agony Alfred is undergoing. Lawrence replaced it with an explanation, couched in his idiosyncratic psychological language, of the reason the death of his mother left Alfred so immobilized: "He was a man whose life had been filled up with small activities. Without knowing it, he had been centralized, polarized in his mother. It was she who had kept him. Even now, when the old housekeeper had left him, he might still have gone on in his old way. But the force and balance of his life was lacking" (PO 123). Lawrence had found the language for his metaphysic. The notion of "centralized, polarized" balance in this passage seems strongly theoretical.

The new theoretical underpinnings are especially noticeable in the passages most related to *The Rainbow*—especially those related to Tom Brangwen's courtship of the Polish lady, another story in which the mystery of human passion prevails over considerations of rank and status. For example, "Where shall I go?" (TT 396) Louisa asks herself in "Two Marriages," after she leaves the house and goes out into the snow—a journey that will take her to the Durants' and intimacy with Alfred. In "Daughters of the Vicar" the question is "Where am I going?" (PO 99). The question is modified because Louisa, like Tom, is walking towards her life, and her will has been replaced by the forces guiding human destiny.

Similarly, the theme of human separateness, so important to *The Rainbow* and *Prussian Officer* stories like "Odour of Chrysanthemums" and "The Shadow in the Rose Garden," plays a prominent part in the final version of "Daughters of the Vicar." In the 1911 magazine "Two Marriages," Louisa watches Alfred eating just before the back-washing scene: "His black face and arms were strange, his red mouth under the small, trimmed, but very coarse-fibred moustache, that looked like cocoanut fibre, only of a lighter brown, startled her. But in its dirt his face had a kind of nobility. . . ." Here the feeling of separateness that his appearance produces is related to class, for his dirty face and arms serve to remind her that he is a collier. She tries to get round this fact by discerning the "nobility" in his face beneath the working-class grime and by reflecting that the "coarseness" is only external and can be sponged off, leaving a man "so natural" (TT 399) that she can be attracted to him despite his social origins. However, in the *Prussian Officer* version the mature theme of human isolation comes through in all its intensity and emotional impact: "Her soul watched him, trying to see what he was. His black face and arms were uncouth, he was foreign. His face was masked black with coal-dust. She could not see him, she could not know him. The brown eyebrows, the steady eyes, the coarse, small moustache above the closed mouth—these were the only familiar indications. What was he, as he sat there in his pit-dirt? She could not see him, and it hurt her" (PO 112). Here Louisa is no longer concerned about Alfred's class. He sits "masked black with coal-dust," reminding her that we all wear masks when facing the world. She is no longer content with identifying him by means of "the brown eyebrows, the steady eyes, the coarse, small moustache," those external "familiar indications." She is now interested in the real man beneath the coal dust, the man she "could not see" and "could not know." In the 1911 "Two Marriages" (and the 1913 revised typescript as well) Louisa is trying to get deeper than Alfred's social class to find a basis of relationship with him. In "Daughters of the Vicar" she is trying to get deeper than the personality with which he faces the world every day to find the essential man beneath. Where Louisa watches Alfred in "Two Marriages," her "soul" watches him in "Daughters of the Vicar."

After the back-washing scene in "Daughters of the Vicar," Louisa becomes upset when she sees Alfred "clean, and in his shirt-sleeves," looking like a "workman": "Louisa felt that she and he were foreigners, moving in different lives. . . . Oh, if she could only find some fixed relations, something sure and abiding" (PO 115). She feels excluded because she and Alfred have returned to the world of merely social identity. She yearns to live in the world of pure human relation she had glimpsed during the back-washing, to recapture and never to lose that moment of transfiguration.

The tranfiguration returns in the betrothal scene, where once more the 1914 revisions introduced a more theoretical framework. As late as the October revision of the Hopkin proofs, the triumphant "He was himself" (PO 129) was added at the point where Alfred and Louisa are awaking from their mysterious, renewing sleep. The transcendent and radiant harmony of their coming-together is signaled by the silence that engulfs it. The hold each other, "helpless in speech" (PO 130)—another detail added in the October revision of the proofs—silent in the presence of life's mysterious and impersonal otherness. Similarly, where in the proofs Louisa sees Alfred's face "all wondering, and looked into his wide, good eyes" (H 153)—a rather sentimental construction—in the final text she sees his face "all sombre and inscrutable, and he seemed eternal to her" (PO 130). They have reached a deeper and more basic level of relationship.

As noted above, this scene between Alfred and Louisa has a good deal in common with the betrothal of Tom Brangwen and Lydia Lensky. Both scenes underscore the fact that characters have come into the presence of "the great impersonal." In the fullness of passion they are able to slough off their everyday personalities. They meet not as personalities but as essential selves, and Lawrence doesn't want them to seem like "characters" in their moment of meeting.

The scenes take place beyond the old stable ego of the character, and the lovers seem to be passively fulfilling a destiny ordained for them. Alfred's eyes are "like agate, expressionless" (PO 129), while Louisa is "to him something steady and immovable and eternal" (PO 128). Tom's eyes are "strangely impersonal" (R 39), while Lydia's are "steady and intent and eternal" (R 40). It is not easy to cast loose from one's moorings and give oneself over to the unknown. Both scenes illustrate the pain and difficulty of such an elemental encounter. Alfred's heart is "hot in an anguish of suspense"; he stares into Louisa's eyes "in torment, in an agony of chaos" (PO 128). Tom, spellbound by Lydia's eyes, "suffered"; her movement as she reaches toward him is "agony" (R 40).

The outlines of the Alfred–Mrs. Durant–Louisa action in the story became clear only with the final revisions of 1914. "Daughters of the Vicar" is a more doctrinaire tale than its predecessors because the crucial period in 1914 that found Lawrence nearing the end of the composition of *The Rainbow* and excitedly revising the *Prussian Officer* stories is a time of the emergence and crystallization of many of his ideas. The series of dichotomies underlying the story—mind vs. body, abstract virtue vs. human contact, "religion" vs. life—were put into sharper focus in the final version. The net result is a long story that, paradoxically, is at once more abstract and—because of the development of the central characters and their love—more radiantly abundant with life.

"Two Marriages" is very much the work of the young Lawrence, a story impressive for its convincing depiction of the social world—that of colliery and village vicarage—its author knew best. Although "Two Marriages" has a strong basis in social criticism, this aspect of the story is less important in later versions. In "Daughters of the Vicar" Lawrence seems much more intently interested in presenting and analyzing the nature of the relationship between his hero and heroine.

Thus the mode of "Daughters of the Vicar" is somewhat mixed: the social commentary is finally transcended by the exploration of passion between man and woman. It seems to me that much more is gained than lost by the story's new foundation in Lawrentian metaphysic. In the earlier versions Lawrence is sure about his rejection of middle-class gentility, but he has strongly mixed feelings about the collier his heroine escapes to. As we have seen, the curious codas to the early versions make it clear that this was indeed a problem he had difficulty with. Only in the final revision does he seem to achieve full confidence in the marriage between Alfred and Louisa. It is precisely his new vision— that in which everyday concerns are sloughed off as his characters come together in the presence of the mysterious nonhuman source of life—that enables him to solve the problem of a convincing basis for the marriage.

"I *will* have love," Louisa proclaims to herself after her sister marries Mr. Massy, "I *will* have it." Even as she stubbornly insists on the possibility and primacy of loving, Lawrence informs us that "she had her fixed will to love, to have the man she loved" (PO 92). Only the experience of physical attraction and contact melts away this willfulness and puts the vicar's daughter squarely in the camp of life. The worldly future of the young couple is uncertain at story's end, but the bond they have formed is deep and abiding, based on the dark mystery residing in the flesh.

CHAPTER V

"The Shades of Spring"

"After a while . . . I shall come back into the country"

As Julian Moynahan has observed, "The Shades of Spring" is "a kind of arch which ties together the erotic dilemma of *Sons and Lovers* and the final solution of the dilemma in *Lady Chatterley*."[1] The autobiographical Paul-Miriam relationship may be resolved in *Sons and Lovers*, but when Lawrence himself was first established in a faintly humming, glowing town, he had second thoughts about the abandonment of the countryside and the women he had loved there. The tension between London and Eastwood was a central fact of the apprentice years, one that he tried regularly to translate into fiction; Lawrence returned almost obsessively to this subject. "The Shades of Spring," with its introduction of the gamekeeper-lover, is the best and most interesting attempt in the early short fiction to come to terms with these unresolved autobiographical materials. The situation in which a young intellectual (a self-projection) has deserted his sweetheart, a farmer's daughter, and returns several years later to find himself replaced by a nonintellectual lover is archetypal in the first part of his career.

I will be dealing with "The Shades of Spring" and four earlier versions of the same fictional material. As with the discussion of "Odour of Chrysanthemums," other versions of the same story and entirely different treatments of the same material in other works of fiction are included. I will be discussing the following transmutations of the story:

1. Julian Moynahan, *The Deed of Life: The Novels and Tales of D. H. Lawrence* (Princeton, N.J., 1963), pp. 176–77. Emile Delavenay's "D. H. Lawrence and Sacher-Masoch" (*D. H. Lawrence Review,* 6 [1973], 119–48) uses "The Shades of Spring" as a central text, but the tendentious argument seems to have little to do with the story.

1. "The Scarp Slope": Book III, Chapter VI, of *The White Peacock*. Begun in 1906, completed in 1910. Cyril Beardsall returns from town to visit Emily and finds her affianced to Tom Renshaw, a young farmer.

2. "A Modern Lover." 1909. Cyril Mersham returns to visit Muriel and finds himself replaced by Tom Vickers, a young mine electrician.

3. "The Soiled Rose." Written in December 1911, revised by March 1912. John Adderley Syson returns to visit Hilda and finds that she is having sexual relations with a young gamekeeper. Published in the *Forum*, March 1913, and in the *Blue Review*, May 1913. Magazine version of "The Shades of Spring."

    The Berg Collection of the New York Public Library owns a revised typescript of this story. The revised typescript is very close to the magazine text, but I will make passing reference to some interesting relics of an earlier version that can be found beneath the cancellations.

4. "The Dead Rose." Revision of "The Soiled Rose," text found in the Hopkin proofs, July 1914. "The Dead Rose" is the only story in these proofs that shows considerable revision in Lawrence's hand. This revision is found through-out the first ⅔ of the text, and then it stops completely.

    The relationship between this revised text and "The Shades of Spring" is a curious one. Lawrence seems to have had second thoughts about the holograph revision when he revised the story a final time in October 1914. Sometimes he did use the revisions, but more often he ignored them, either replacing a word or phrase he had canceled in the proofs or substituting an entirely new word or phrase. With a few exceptions, "The Shades of Spring" text differs only in incidentals from both "The Dead Rose" and the holograph revision of "The Dead Rose"; "The Shades of Spring" is in no way a significant reshaping. Consequently, I will once again be making only passing use of the Hopkin proof materials.

5. "The Shades of Spring." Revision of "The Dead Rose," October 1914. Published in *The Prussian Officer and Other Stories*.

I am indebted to Keith Sagar's "'The Best I Have Known':
D. H. Lawrence's 'A Modern Lover' and 'The Shades of
Spring,'"[2] a fine brief discussion of the progress of this story
from *The White Peacock* to "The Shades of Spring." Most of
Sagar's conclusions are unimpeachable, though he seems to
me to underplay some of the negative aspects of Hilda's
new self-assurance. Limitations of space also prevented him
from giving the texts all the attention they merit, and he was
further handicapped because his work antedates the avail-
ability of the Louie Burrows letters.

The issues raised by the development of this story merit
close consideration. The progression of the title—"The
Soiled Rose," "The Dead Rose," "The Shades of Spring"—
is remarkable and revealing in its own right. Lawrence continually recast the materials of the story as he tried to come
to terms with one of the central problems of his young manhood—and the changes are striking.

The young Lawrence may have been novice enough to
make such a mawkish self-projection as Cyril Beardsall, the
narrator and protagonist of *The White Peacock*, but at least
he knew what he was doing wrong. In the summer of 1908
he wrote Blanche Jennings about the novel: "I will write
the thing again, and stop up the mouth of Cyril—I will kick
him out—I hate the fellow" (CL 25). Subsequent revisions,
however, were unable to solve the problem of Cyril, and the
novel is crippled as a result. Cyril survives indomitable
because his sensibility is so close to Lawrence's own.[3] The
lushness and immaturity of the novel are registered through
Cyril's consciousness. Awkwardness of expression and crude-
ness of insight are integrally related to the first-person focus.

The failure of the first-person point-of-view is apparent
in the "Scarp Slope" chapter, as it is everywhere. Each

2. Keith Sagar, "'The Best I Have Known': D. H. Lawrence's 'A
Modern Lover' and 'The Shades of Spring,'" *Studies in Short Fiction*, 4
(1967), 143–51.

3. In describing the novel to Blanche Jennings on 1 November 1909, he
refers to Cyril as "myself" (CL 57).

fictional version of the imaginary return begins with the protagonist walking through a vivid landscape, having left the city for the countryside of his youth. In *The White Peacock* the spring landscape is rendered in this language:

> I wandered around Nethermere, which had now forgotten me. The daffodils under the boat-house continued their golden laughter, and nodded to one another in gossip, as I watched them, never for a moment pausing to notice me. The yellow reflection of daffodils among the shadows of grey willow in the water trembled faintly as they told haunted tales in the gloom. I felt like a child left out of the group of my playmates. . . .
> . . . I was a stranger, an intruder. Among the bushes a twitter of lively birds exclaimed upon me. Finches went leaping past in bright flashes, and a robin sat and asked rudely: "Hello! Who are you?"
> . . . .
> The trees caught the wind in their tall netted twigs, and the young morning wind moaned at its captivity. As I trod the discarded oak-leaves and the bracken they uttered their last sharp gasps, pressed into oblivion. The wood was roofed with a wide young sobbing sound, and floored with a faint hiss like the intaking of the last breath. Between, was all the glad out-peeping of buds and anemone flowers and the rush of birds. I, wandering alone, felt them all, the anguish of the bracken fallen face-down in defeat, the careless dash of the birds, the sobbing of the young wind arrested in its haste, the trembling, expanding delight of the buds. I alone among them could hear the whole succession of chords. (WP 334)

The failings of this prose are obvious. The precious talking flowers and birds bring to mind the garden of live flowers in *Through the Looking-Glass* except that here no parody is intended. The "succession of chords" can be heard by Cyril alone because he is playing them himself (and hitting many false notes). This is the work of a very young novelist who has set himself the task of "doing" a landscape. The young man who wrote the passage believed that when a reader came to a beautifully written passage, he should know it without a doubt. As Lawrence realized, the style is "cloyed with metaphoric fancy" (CL 36) and grievously calls attention to itself.

The scene in *The White Peacock* between Cyril, Emily, and her new lover Tom Renshaw is only briefly developed. After a few pages, Cyril leaves Tom and Emily to visit with George and his wife, but his—and Lawrence's—attitude toward them is unmistakable. Tom is distinguished for his physical presence and his lack of subtlety:

> Tom was a well-built fair man, smoothly, almost delicately tanned. There was something soldierly in his bearing, something self-conscious in the way he bent his head and pulled his moustache, something charming and fresh in the way he laughed at Emily's last preposterous speech.
>
> . . . .
>
> He looked at me with his young blue eyes, eyes so bright, so naively inquisitive, so winsomely meditative. He did not know quite what to say. . . . (WP 336)

These are not qualities Cyril is prepared to value highly. He is frankly condescending:

> He was twenty-nine years old; had been a soldier in China for five years, was now farming his father's farm at Papplewick. . . . I liked Tom for his handsome bearing, and his fresh, winsome way. He was exceedingly manly: that is to say he did not dream of questioning or analysing anything. . . . He did not imagine that anything could be other than just what it appeared to be:—and with this appearance, he was quite content. (WP 336–37)

Cyril does not seem terribly upset about encountering his former sweetheart with her new fiancé, but he enjoys playing the scorned lover and toying with the unintellectual Tom:

> "Mr. Renshaw," I said. "You have out-manoeuvred me all unawares, quite indecently."
>
> "I am very sorry," he said. . . .
>
> "Do you really feel cross?" said Emily to me, knitting her brows and smiling quaintly.
>
> "I do!" I replied, with truthful emphasis.
>
> She laughed and laughed again, very much amused.

"It is such a joke," she said. "To think you should feel cross, now, when it is—how long is it ago—?

"I will not count up," said I.

"Are you not sorry for me?" I asked of Tom Renshaw. (WP 336)

Lawrence makes it clear that Emily has settled for a second best. Tom's physical vitality is not consciously a positive. She has had to accept him because she has lost her first choice. Given the opportunity, she would probably come racing back to the more cosmopolitan and exhilarating Cyril:

"And you love him for his youth?" I asked.

"Yes," she replied. "For that and—he is wonderfully sagacious—and so gentle."

"And I was never gentle, was I?" I said.

"No! As restless and as urgent as the wind," she said, and I saw a last flicker of the old terror. (WP 337)

The chapter is called "The Scarp Slope" primarily because the rest of it deals with George Saxton, who, disappointed by Lettie, has begun to brutalize himself with drink. However, the title's overtones refer to Emily too. After being disappointed by Cyril, she has had to descend sharply to someone beneath her. Cyril responds to her engagement with smugness and patronization. The situation is handled almost in passing because it has not occurred to Lawrence that there is more than one possible interpretation of his unsatisfactory relationship with Jessie. He treats the materials so hastily and with such self-assurance because he has not yet felt the need to think them through.

In March 1912 Lawrence wrote Garnett to report that the *Forum* had accepted "The Soiled Rose." In the same letter he enclosed an earlier story treating the same subject, clearly "A Modern Lover": "I enclose a story I wrote three years back, and had forgotten. It is on the same theme, and I thought it might interest you—it is really curious. But before it was ever submitted to a publisher I would like thoroughly to revise it" (CL 102). It is likely that he did

revise the story, but it was never published during his lifetime. "A Modern Lover" appeared in *Life and Letters* in 1933
and then was collected as the title story of the posthumous
volume of short stories published the next year. "A Modern
Lover" replays the homecoming situation of "The Scarp
Slope" with the addition of a generous supply of irony.

Cyril Beardsall has become Cyril Mersham (mere sham?)
and the narrative is now in the third person. The young
Lawrence and Beardsall are in many ways inseparable. "A
Modern Lover"[4] is in the third person partly because
Lawrence wants expressly to dissociate himself from Mersham. He exposes the falseness of Mersham's sensibility by
recording his thoughts as he walks down the road through
a wintry landscape, in search of an idealized past. The "old
places that had seemed so ordinary" now seem "very
wonderful and glamorous," but Mersham's response is con-
tradicted by the "road . . . heavy with mud," which is
"labour to move along" (CSS 1). The description of Mersham's return is filled with inflated language that, if found
in *The White Peacock*, would be unqualified by irony. In "A
Modern Lover" the overblown rhetoric and purple prose
undercut the protagonist's literary view of life:

Here, on the farther shore of the sunset, with the flushed tide at
his feet, and the large star flashing with strange laughter, did he
himself naked walk with lifted arms into the quiet flood of life.

What was it he wanted, sought in the slowly-lapsing tide of
days? Two years he had been in the large city in the south. There
always his soul had moved among the faces that swayed on the
thousand currents in that node of tides, hovering and wheeling
and flying low over the faces of the multitude like a sea-gull over
the waters, stooping now and again, and taking a fragment of life—
a look, a contour, a movement—to feed upon. Of many people, his
friends, he had asked that they would kindle again the smoulder-
ing embers of their experience. . . .

Surely, surely somebody could give him enough of the philtre
of life to stop the craving which tortured him hither and thither,

4. Lawrence borrowed the name of this story from the title of George
Moore's first novel (*A Modern Lover* [London, 1883]).

enough to satisfy for a while, to intoxicate him till he could laugh the crystalline laughter of the star, and bathe in the retreating flood of twilight like a naked boy in the surf, clasping the waves and beating them and answering their wild clawings with laughter sometimes, and sometimes gasps of pain. (CSS 2–3)

Lawrence relentlessly exposes the hollowness of this rhapsodic product of Mersham's sensibility. "Orion had strode into the sky," but Mersham "shivered, stumbled down the path" before coming into the "exceedingly, painfully muddy" yard with "a disgust of his own feet, which were cold, and numbed, and heavy" (CSS 3).

Cyril's soul is "open like a foolhardy flower to the night" (CSS 3), expecting a "fine broad glow of welcome" from Muriel and her family, but he is in for a disappointment. In two years in London he has grown away from them. They ask only for his "news" rather than for "the timorous buds of his hopes, and the unknown fruits of his experiences, full of the taste of tears and what sunshine of gladness had gone to their ripening" (CSS 4). When they sit down at table, he uses "English that was exquisitely accurate, pronounced with the Southern accent, very different from the heavily-sounded speech of the home folk," keeps up "a brilliant tea-talk that they failed to appreciate," and takes delight in the "irony of the situation." When Muriel's brothers kneel on the hearth-rug to wash their backs, Cyril, imprisoned in his aesthetic frame of reference, can only watch "them, as he had watched the peewits and the sunsets" (CSS 5). His photograph on the mantelpiece seems to him to be "radiant" and "subtle," even though it "had been called the portrait of an intellectual prig" (CSS 8).

After two years in the city, Mersham finds himself at loose ends. He returns to Muriel, unaware that he has been replaced. He acknowledges that their relationship had been a failure, and he wants to make a fresh start. He brings with him not a proposal but a proposition:

"You see," he said, "life's no good but to live—and you can't live your life by yourself. You must have a flint and a steel, both, to make the spark fly. Supposing you be my flint, my white flint, to spurt out red fire for me?"

"But how do you mean?" she asked breathlessly.

"You see," he continued, thinking aloud as usual: "thought—that's not life. It's like washing and combing and carding and weaving the fleece that the year of life has produced. Now I think—we've carded and woven to the end of our bundle—nearly. We've got to begin again—you and me—living together, see? Not speculating and poetising together—see?"

She did not cease to gaze absorbedly at him.

"Yes?" she whispered, urging him on.

"You see—I've come back to you—to you—" He waited for her. (CSS 9–10)

Mersham "used to shrink from the thought of having to kiss" Muriel (CSS 10), but he has changed. The halting pseudo-Paterian language in which Mersham couches his proposition makes the scene comic. The high-flown language only calls attention to the essential baseness of his overture as Lawrence explodes the fraudulence and hypocrisy of Mersham's sensibility.

The rival, Tom Vickers, is a working electrician in the mine, a profession that signals a partial escape from the working class. Tom is a "handsome man, well set-up, rather shorter than Mersham," who "[crushes] Mersham's hand" (CSS 12) when Muriel introduces them. Cyril Mersham's patronization of Tom Vickers is more thoroughgoing than Cyril Beardsall's patronization of Tom Renshaw in *The White Peacock*:

"We're always a public meeting, Muriel and I. Aren't we, Miel? We're discussing affinities, that ancient topic. You'll do for an audience. We agree so beastly well, we two. We always did. It's her fault. Does she treat you so badly?"

The other was rather bewildered. (CSS 12–13)

Mersham's classification of his rival is even more revealing:

Mersham noted the fine limbs, the solid, large thighs, and the thick wrists. He was classifying his rival among the men of handsome, healthy animalism, and good intelligence, who are children in simplicity, who can add two and two, but never xy and yx. His contours, his movements, his repose were, strictly, lovable. "But," said Mersham to himself, "if I were blind, or sorrowful, or very tired, I should not want him. He is one of the men, as George Moore says, whom his wife would hate after a few years for the very way he walked across the floor."

. . . .

Mersham sprawled his length in the chair, his eyelids almost shut, his fine white hands hanging over the arms of the chair like dead-white stoats from a bough. (CSS 13)

The conversation ends with Mersham referring to his own "virgin modesty." Ever the artist, he has "now developed the situation to the climax he desired" (CSS 15). After Tom sings "some of the old songs" (CSS 16) to Muriel's accompaniment—songs that Mersham had taught her—he decides to leave. The description of Tom lighting his bicycle lamp is clearly the first version of the scene in *The Lost Girl* in which Alvina looks down at Ciccio as he squats mending his bicycle tire at the beginning of their odd courtship. Both scenes are images of male vitality:

Vickers carefully struck a match, bowing over the ruddy core of light and illuminating himself like some beautiful lantern in the midst of the high darkness of the barn. For some moments he bent over his bicycle-lamp, trimming and adjusting the wick, and his face, gathering all the light on its ruddy beauty, seemed luminous and wonderful. Mersham could see the down on his cheeks above the razor-line, and the full lips in shadow beneath the moustache, and the brush of the eyebrows between the light. (CSS 18)[5]

5. Compare this with *The Lost Girl,* pp. 185–86:

Ciccio was crouching mending a tire, crouching balanced on his toes, near the earth. He turned like a quick-eared animal glancing up as she approached, but did not rise.

. . . .

"Yes, I will come," he said, still watching his bicycle tube, which sprawled nakedly on the floor. The forward drop of his head was curiously beautiful to her, the straight, powerful nape of the neck, the delicate shape of the back of the head, the black hair.

After Tom leaves, Mersham and Muriel go walking in the strange fairy-tale world of "the trees, the many stars, the dark spaces, and the mysterious waters," although Mersham goes "ankle-deep in mud" (CSS 19) on the way. No question exists about where Muriel's first allegiance still lies. She is even more worried about settling for second best than is Emily in *The White Peacock*:

> She came down from the wood-fence into his arms, and he kissed her, and they laughed low together. Then they went on across the wild meadows where there was no path.
> "Why don't you like him?" he asked playfully.
> "Need you ask?" she said, simply. (CSS 19)

In the language of the flower-picking scenes in *Sons and Lovers*, Mersham apologizes for his self-consciousness and inability to fall in love. "If you pull flowers to pieces, and find how they pollinate, and where are the ovaries, you don't go in blind ecstasies over to them." He praises Tom's lack of self-consciousness, but the kind words are devious: Mersham is about to repeat his proposition, this time in a low-key way. After criticizing Muriel for wearing corsets—"I like to see you move inside your dress" (CSS 20)—he once more makes his case for illicit love, trying to wheedle her into consent:

> "You see—we would marry to-morrow—but I can't keep myself. I am in debt—"
> She came close to him, and took his arm.
> "—And what's the good of letting the years go, and the beauty of one's youth—?"
> "No," she admitted, very slowly and softly, shaking her head.
> "So—well!—you understand, don't you? And if you're willing—you'll come to me, won't you?—just naturally, as you used to come and go to church with me?—and it won't be—it won't be me coaxing you—reluctant? Will it?" (CSS 20–21)

Muriel is not prepared for such an arrangement, and for Mersham "the glamour went out of life" (CSS 21). They part wearily. He does not kiss her. She does not even say good-bye.

In *Sons and Lovers* Lawrence lays much of the blame for the failure of the relationship between Paul and Miriam on Miriam's sexual fears. Jessie Chambers's *Personal Record* insists that this is a distortion of the way it actually happened and argues that in the novel he held over her "a doom of negation and futility," falsifying their relationship because "his mother had to be supreme, and for the sake of that supremacy every disloyalty was permissible."[6] In "A Modern Lover" it would appear that the timidity of both characters contributed to the stalemating of the old relationship. There had been plenty of "Carlyle and Ruskin, Schopenhauer and Darwin and Huxley" (CSS 6), but the relationship had never descended from the realm of pure intellect. However tarnished Mersham's motives are, he does want to try again with Muriel on a more mature basis. She is as frightened as ever.

The title of the story is ironic and so is its prevailing tone. However, at this stage Lawrence is not ready to seize upon the positives in the story embodied in the figures of the brothers and Tom Vickers. Mersham's dismissal of Vickers as a man who can't add "xy and yx" is meant to undercut Mersham, but when he classifies Vickers as a man "whom his wife would hate after a few years for the very way he walked across the floor," the irony seems to have disappeared. "Vickers was an old-fasioned, inarticulate lover; such as had been found the brief joy and the unending disappointment of a woman's life" (CSS 17). Such passages recall Walter Morel and remind us of Lawrence's emotional closeness to his theme of second best. No manuscript material is available for this story, but it seems obvious that the bicycle tableau was added in a revision Lawrence made after his March 1912 letter to Garnett; it is unlikely that it could have been written as early as 1909. Even in the version of the story we have, Lawrence is far from being able to make Tom Vickers the positive pole. As he sees the situation in 1909, Muriel would be marrying fatally beneath herself.

6. ET, pp. 213, 201.

After *The White Peacock* and "A Modern Lover," the homecoming situation reappears in "The Soiled Rose," completed in
March 1912, in "The Dead Rose" of the Hopkin proofs (July
1914), and in the final version of the story published as "The
Shades of Spring" in *The Prussian Officer*. The titles are
different, but the texts are all variations of the same story.

A letter to Garnett on 30 December 1911 dates the original
composition of "The Soiled Rose," which Lawrence had
written while convalescing: "My sense of beauty and of interest comes back very strong. I wrote this story last week, in
bed—before I could sit up much. You'll find it, perhaps, thin—
maladif. I can't judge it at all . . . " (CL 90). "The Soiled Rose"—
"a sickly title, but not a bad story" (CL 181)—did not appear
in the *Forum* until March 1913.

The protagonist of "The Soiled Rose"/"The Dead Rose"/
"The Shades of Spring" is John Adderley Syson (sigh son?), a
name with obvious, rather incriminating echoes of John
Addington Symonds. Like his predecessors, Syson has gone
away to London and has become cultivated. Recently married,
he returns for a visit in spring to the country of his past.
Unlike Mersham, this "trespasser" knows he has changed a
great deal and does not expect to be welcomed. He heads
through the wood, taking the shortcut to Willey Water Farm,
the home of Hilda Millership, his abandoned sweetheart.
(Miriam lives on Willey Farm in *Sons and Lovers*.) The
shortcut is not a public way, and Syson's path is blocked
by a handsome young gamekeeper, Arthur Pilbeam. Pilbeam
announces that he is courting Hilda and criticizes Syson
for continuing to correspond with her and to send her poetry
books.

At the farmhouse Syson is impressed by the "womanly"
Hilda. She takes him for a walk, demonstrating how much her
own she has made the countryside she and Syson had shared.
(The nests she shows him are of course reminiscent of scenes
between Paul and Miriam in *Sons and Lovers*.) Then she
reveals that the keeper had become her lover on the night Syson
was married. They arrive at the keeper's hut, pheasant coops

strewn before it, animal furs and carpenter's tools inside. (The hut is the first version of the hut where Mellors makes love to Constance Chatterley.) Hilda and Syson quarrel about their past until the keeper enters; Syson leaves shortly afterwards.

Stunned by Hilda's revelation, Syson, instead of going straight to the road, lies down on a hillside surrounded by flowers and tries to collect his thoughts. (In *Women in Love* Rupert Birkin—more literally stunned after Hermione has smashed him on the head with the paperweight—runs out of the house into the countryside, undresses, lies down among the flowers on a hillside, and reflects about Hermione and about his vision of mankind.) Syson overhears a conversation between Hilda and Pilbeam about marriage plans and looks through the bushes to see what is happening. The keeper unconsciously catches bees that settle on the bramble flowers and crushes them in his palm. When one crawls up his sleeve and stings him, Hilda picks out the sting and sucks away the poison. Noticing the mark her mouth has made, she says, "That is the reddest kiss you will ever have" (SR 340,[7] PO 174). Syson does not leave the hillside until they are gone.

"The Soiled Rose" and its revisions as "The Dead Rose" and "The Shades of Spring" are Lawrence's richest treatments of the homecoming material. I will be concentrating on "The Soiled Rose" and "The Shades of Spring"—the two most strikingly distinct versions—though I will also devote brief attention to a revised typescript of "The Soiled Rose" and to the Hopkin proof "Dead Rose." However, I would first like to discuss the special background and sources of the story. It is fascinating to see Lawrence's imagination at work, plucking details from a remembered experience, from a medieval German poem recently encountered while writing a book review, from a favorite painting, from a scene in a second-line Hardy novel. Out of such materials, such intellectual and emotional residue, a splendid short story was created.

7. The abbreviation SR refers to the text of "The Soiled Rose" that appeared in the *Forum*, March 1913 (vol. 49, pp. 324–40). Also cf. the blood on Martha's mouth when the serf kisses her in "A Fragment of Stained Glass."

The gamekeeper is obviously of particular interest. Arthur Pilbeam is not the most famous representative of his profession in Lawrence's fiction, nor is he the first. The latter distinction belongs to Annable, the rather squalid keeper in *The White Peacock*, with his philosophy of "Do as th' animals do" (WP 145). Apparently the gamekeeper figure goes back to a personal experience Lawrence had at the age of seventeen, recorded by Jessie Chambers:

A party of us, including my three brothers and Lawrence's sister, penetrated unwittingly into a private portion of the Annesley woods. There we found a spot that looked like fairyland—a stream flowing between smooth green banks starred with primroses, which are rare in our woods. We were enchanted; we gathered the flowers and sang and made plenty of noise. Suddenly a burly, red-haired keep with a youth close on his heels burst through the trees. He took my eldest brother and Lawrence aside and made them give their names. Then he told us all that these "pimroses" were private property and made us leave our bunches on the ground. We trooped home crestfallen, Lawrence white-faced and still.[8]

Lawrence introduces this experience bodily into *The White Peacock*. In Part II, Chapter I, Cyril, Emily, Leslie, and Lettie go for a walk in the woods. They walk along a brook, "never looking once at the primroses that were glimmering all along its banks" (WP 141). They realize that they are trespassing but proceed anyway until their idyll is interrupted by the rude appearance of Annable, a "malicious Pan." Not recognizing Leslie, he thinks they are two couples who have come to use the woods as a "bridal bed" (WP 143) and asks for their names. Annable apologizes when he realizes his mistake but regales the young people with some of his philosophy before he leaves.

Oliver Mellors is a Lawrentian self-projection; Annable is not. When Jessie expressed her dismay at Annable, Lawrence responded, "He *has* to be there. . . . He makes a sort of balance. Otherwise it's too much one thing, too much *me*."[9]

8. ET, pp. 117–18.
9. ET, p. 117.

Annable, a rather undiluted embodiment of man's animal nature, is somewhat overwhelming in the midst of the precious young people of Nethermere. Notwithstanding Lawrence's insistence that Annable remain in the novel, he did not yet know exactly what to make of such a character. Annable is killed off in an accident midway through the book. Perhaps his main significance is as a fascinating promise of things to come.

Annable is a much older man than Arthur Pilbeam, the young gamekeeper in the story. There is a tantalizing suggestion that Pilbeam may have been inspired by the fiction of Louie Burrows, who, like Jessie, had literary aspirations of her own. In the letter Lawrence wrote Louie on 7 October 1908, he comments on a story she had written: "Bonnie & the girl are good, but the young keeper is not well defined . . ." (LL 19). It is possible that Lawrence remembered that young keeper when he lay in bed and wrote "The Soiled Rose" three years later.

Arthur Pilbeam in "The Soiled Rose" takes the role of Tom Renshaw and Tom Vickers in the earlier renderings of the same material, and as such is a legitimate prefiguration of Mellors. Pilbeam is "taut with life, like the thick jet of a fountain balanced at ease" (SR 325), but the vitality is never really dramatized, and he is left the most anomalous of Lawrence's three gamekeepers. In the story John Adderley Syson, not Pilbeam, is the self-projection.

One detail in "The Soiled Rose" (canceled only when Lawrence transformed the story into "The Shades of Spring" in the fall) throws especially interesting light on the intricacies of the creative process. In the magazine text of "The Soiled Rose" Hilda's revelation that she has taken the keeper as a lover is met with Syson's mocking "Tandaradeï" (SR 333), the refrain from "Unter der Linden" by Walter von der Vogelweide, the medieval German lyric poet. On 6 December Lawrence wrote May Chambers Holbrook that he had "a book of German poetry and a book of Minnesinger translations" (CL 87) to be reviewed for the *English Review*. He had "done the reviews and sent them off" (LL 154) when he wrote Louie on

13 December and they appeared in the January 1912 issue
(vol. 10) of the magazine. In his review of Jethro Bithell's
book of translations from the Minnesingers Lawrence quotes
a stanza from "Unter der Linden":

Then take the first stanza of Walter von der Vogelweide's well-known
"Tantaradei" [*sic*], or "Unter den [*sic*] Linden."

On the heather-lea,
In the lime-tree bower,
There of us twain was made the bed:
There you may see
Grass-blade and flower
Sweetly crushed and shed.
By the forest, in a dale,
Tantaradei!
Sweetly sang the nightingale."

The translation certainly seems to have been easy, and in
making it the author will have made enemies of all who remember
the original.[10]

Two weeks after finishing the review, Lawrence wrote a story
in which the central male character has the refrain from
"Unter der Linden" on the tip of his tongue.

E. W. Tedlock, Jr., has suggested that the climactic scene
of the story may have been suggested by a painting Lawrence
copied in his youth, Maurice Greiffenhagen's "An Idyll."[11]

10. *Phoenix II: Uncollected, Unpublished, and Other Prose Works of D. H.
Lawrence,* edited by Warren Roberts and Harry T. Moore, p. 272. Copy-
right 1959, 1963, 1968 by the Estate of Frieda Lawrence Ravagli. Copy-
right 1920, renewed 1948 by Frieda Lawrence. Copyright 1925 by
Centaur Press, renewed 1953 by Frieda Lawrence. Copyright 1925 by
Alfred A. Knopf, Inc., renewed 1953 by Frieda Lawrence Ravagli.
Copyright 1928 by Forum Pub. Co., renewed 1956 by Frieda Lawrence
Ravagli. Copyright 1934 by Frieda Lawrence, renewed 1962 by Angelo
Ravagli and C. Montague Weekley, Executors of the Estate of Frieda
Lawrence Ravagli. Copyright 1940 by the Estate of Frieda Lawrence
Ravagli, renewed 1968 by Angelo Ravagli and C. Montague Weekley,
Executors of the Estate of Frieda Lawrence Ravagli. All rights reserved.
Reprinted by permission of Laurence Pollinger Ltd., the Estate of the
late Mrs. Frieda Lawrence, and The Viking Press, Inc.
11. E. W. Tedlock, Jr., *D. H. Lawrence, Artist and Rebel* (Albuquerque,
N.M., 1963), p. 15.

The evidence that the painting did influence the ending of the story, which seems to me to be definitive, has never been presented systematically. Greiffenhagen was a painter and illustrator of German origin who worked in London. He illustrated several of H. Rider Haggard's books, including *She*. "An Idyll" was exhibited in the Royal Academy in 1891 and is now in the collection of the Walker Art Gallery in Liverpool. The painting, which would be an excellent frontispiece for any study of Lawrence, contains obvious links with the ending of "The Soiled Rose." In a forest setting, a muscular young man dressed in animal skins passionately embraces and kisses a fair, full-bodied, passive Victorian maiden. The flowers that surround the two figures suggest virginity, which may or may not be ironic in the painting. The woman's passiveness is the only detail in "An Idyll" that does not have an echo in the story.

The young Lawrence was haunted by the painting. He probably never saw the original but became acquainted with the painting from a reproduction he was given by his friend Blanche Jennings. A letter he wrote to her on 31 December 1908 contains a long passage about the painting which begins:

> As for Greiffenhagen's "Idyll," it moves me almost as much as if I were fallen in love myself. Under its intoxication, I have flirted madly this Christmas; I have flirted myself half in love; I have flirted somebody else further, till two solicitous persons have begun to take me to task; it is largely the effect of your "Idyll" that has made me kiss a certain girl till she hid her head in my shoulder. . . . (CL 44)

Inspired by the painting, Lawrence goes on to philosophize about self-consciousness, passion, and passiveness in love. He promptly introduced the painting into *The White Peacock*, where Lettie and George discuss it for two pages.

Even more startling is the fact that Lawrence began making a copy of the painting on the night his mother died (CL 75). Nothing could demonstrate his deep involvement with it more than this desperate affirmation of life in the very teeth of death. In fact he copied the painting twice at this

time, a small one for his sister Ada and a large one for Louie
Burrows that he described as a "love picture" (LL 83) to her.
"An Idyll" is obviously the painting mentioned in the last
chapter of *Sons and Lovers*: "Everything seemed to have gone
smash for the young man. He could not paint. The picture he
finished on the day of his mother's death—one that satisfied
him—was the last thing he did" (SL 479).[12] It seems clear that
this painting contributes to the ending of the story.

Thomas Hardy also shares in this ending. The specific debt
is to a charming scene in *Under the Greenwood Tree*: Part IV,
Chapter 2, "Honey-Taking, and Afterwards." While Dick
Dewy and Frederick Shiner, rivals for the hand of Fancy Day,
stand by, Fancy's father, Geoffrey Day (an affluent steward
who doubles as a gamekeeper), suffocates the bees in two
hives so he can get their honey:

> "Have the craters stung ye?" said Enoch to Geoffrey.
> "No, not much—on'y a little here and there," he said with
> leisurely solemnity, shaking one bee out of his shirt sleeve, pulling
> another from among his hair, and two or three more from his
> neck. . . .
> "Are those all of them, father?" said Fancy, when Geoffrey had
> pulled away five.
> "Almost all,—though I feel one or two more sticking into my
> shoulder and side. Ah! there's another just begun again upon my
> backbone."

Fancy herself gets stung when she bites into a piece of honey-
comb that conceals a bee:

> Suddenly a faint cry from Fancy caused them to gaze at her.
> "What's the matter, dear?" said Dick.

12. Nor is this Lawrence's last reference to the painting. In December
1912 he wrote A. W. McLeod that he had "done 4 pictures. . . . But if you
can get a copy of the 'Idyll,' I'll do that as well" (CL 168). And in the
summer of 1916, in the midst of the bitterness of the war years, he wrote
Catherine Carswell: "Greiffenhagen seems to be slipping back and back.
I suppose it has to be. Let the dead bury their dead. Let the past smoulder
out" (CL 461). It was natural for Lawrence to describe the changes the
years had brought by measuring the distance he had traveled from
Greiffenhagen's "Idyll."

"It is nothing, but—Oo-o!—a bee has stung the inside of my lip! He was in one of the cells I was eating!"

"We must keep down the swelling or it may be serious!" said Shiner, stepping up and kneeling beside her. "Let me see it."

"No, no!"

"Just let *me* see it," said Dick kneeling on the other side; and after some hesitation she pressed down her lip with one finger to show the place. "O, I hope 'twill soon be better! I don't mind a sting in ordinary places, but it is so bad upon your lip," she added with tears in her eyes, and writhing a little from the pain.[13]

The rivals continue to compete in their efforts to minister to Fancy's swelling lip in this little version of pastoral.

In both Lawrence and Hardy a stung gamekeeper shakes bees from his clothes before a decisive shift of focus to the heroine's mouth. Of course Hilda's lips are rather less innocent than Fancy's, and the female vampire motif at the end of "The Shades of Spring" is also a characteristic Lawrentian addition. Although the *Study of Thomas Hardy*, produced later in 1914, makes clear Lawrence's great general debt to his artistic forebear, he also continually seems on the verge of rewriting the Wessex novels to align them with his own more radical vision. In a minor way, his use of the beekeeping episode from *Under the Greenwood Tree* for the conclusion of "The Soiled Rose"/"The Shades of Spring" seems such a rewriting. Much of the substance is similar, but pastoral has been left behind.

The revised typescript of "The Soiled Rose" in the Berg Collection is clearly the copy of the story that was sent to the *Forum* for publication. The typescript shows much interlinear revision in Lawrence's hand. Except for a few unimportant changes attributable to the printer, this typescript, including the revisions, constitutes the *Forum* text of "The Soiled Rose." Only one generalization of interest can be made about the canceled passages. Several emendations tend to make

13. *Under the Greenwood Tree*, Mellstock Edition (London, 1920), pp. 164, 168.

Syson less a fop and an aesthete and more a human being, although he is left with a long way yet to travel. This pattern is of significance, for the process of humanizing John Addington Syson was accelerated when Lawrence subsequently revised the *Forum* text of "The Soiled Rose."

One emendation in the Berg Collection typescript is particularly fascinating as an encapsulation of Lawrence's growth to maturity. In the keeper's hut Syson asks Hilda how her new lover is a disappointment. In a canceled passage in the typescript she says she misses the Syson who could "make rogues of the forget-me-nots." In the revision she says that Syson could make "the forget-me-nots come up at me like phosphorescence."[14] The earlier phrase smacks of the schoolgirl sensibility found throughout *The White Peacock* and could be a quotation from Cyril's return to Nethermere in "The Scarp Slope." In the revised text, the flowers are now a living part of the vital, dynamic universe of Lawrence's mature vision.

The published version of "The Soiled Rose" is much more sharply focused than "A Modern Lover." As Keith Sagar has observed, "the very name of Hilda Millership evokes an altogether more robust woman than Miriam, Muriel, or Emily."[15] "What a woman she is!" (SR 330) Syson exclaims to himself when he sees Hilda again. He is overwhelmed by her new self-assurance as she points out the local wildlife like "a brilliant hostess entertaining him in her wood." She is "brilliant as he had not known her" (SR 332), and her changed personality is vividly reflected in her changed appearance: "He noticed the fine, fair down on her cheek and her upper lip, and her soft, white neck, like the throat of a nettle flower, and her forearms, bright as newly blanched kernels. She was being discovered afresh to him, who thought he knew her so thoroughly" (SR 331). This sort of physical description

14. Revised typescript of "The Soiled Rose" in the Henry W. and Albert A. Berg Collection of the New York Public Library, p. 18. The revised version of the passage is also found on p. 335 of the *Forum* text.
15. Sagar, " 'The Best I Have Known,' " p. 148.

is present partly because Lawrence's attitudes have changed since "A Modern Lover." At the same time, it may also reflect that there was a different woman in his life. He had broken off with Jessie over a year before the composition of the story. He had been engaged to the more full-blooded Louie Burrows—"big, and swarthy, and passionate as a gipsy" (CL 90)—for nearly the same period. He copied Greiffenhagen's "Idyll" and sent it to Louie as a "love picture"—and used the same painting in the story's final tableau.

The revisions in the typescript had humanized Syson slightly, but in the magazine text he is still at a great ironic distance from his creator. He enters "dressed in stylish tweeds" (SR 324), introduces himself foppishly as "John Adderley Syson, late of Cordy Lane," and responds to the keeper's statement of his courtship of Hilda "with incredulous irony" (SR 326). The voices of the Millership sons rouse "the ironic spirit" in him when he appears at the farmhouse. "Smiling brilliantly at [Hilda]," he bows and introduces himself: "Myself—in all humility" (SR 328). Hilda's revelation of her relationship with the keeper produces the effete but absolutely appropriate allusion to "Unter der Linden."

However, the abandoned sweetheart of "The Soiled Rose" is a woman to be reckoned with. Growing impatient with Syson, she tells him "in very cutting tones" that he is "too glib." She is "speaking in cold tones" by the time they have finished their "duel" (SR 336). As Hilda and the keeper accompany Syson on his way back to the road, Syson begins, "half-sincere, half-mocking" (SR 337), to recite the last lines of Verlaine's "Colloque Sentimental," an appropriate dialogue between the ghosts of two dead lovers. Hilda interrupts to comment pointedly on the difference between the ghosts' relationship in life (they are able to walk *dans les avoines folles*) and their own past: " 'I never liked farce,' she replied, cuttingly. 'Besides, *we* cannot walk in *our* wild oats. You were too modest and good to sow any at that time.' " (SR 337).

Surely Lawrence intends to account for the changed Hilda—her self-assurance, her proud demeanor, her new womanliness—

in terms of her relationship with the gamekeeper. In Pilbeam's
hut she puts on a "cloak of rabbit-skin edged with white fur
and with a hood, apparently of the skins of stoats" and
laughs at Syson "from out of this barbaric mantle" (SR 334).
Nevertheless, Lawrence stops short of sanctioning unequivocally such a relationship. Part of the difficulty is in the
character of Pilbeam, who is outlined only roughly and who is
capable of worrying whether he and Hilda will be "married at
church, or chapel" (SR 340). Hilda meanwhile is not fully
reconciled to marrying the keeper. She intensely regrets the loss
of Syson's artistic vision, which brought stars and forget-me-
nots to life. The "expressionless composure of her face" conceals
"bitterness" and "calm acceptance of sorrow" (SR 330).
She weeps when Syson has left and regains her composure
only after Pilbeam is stung by a bee. Clearly the keeper is
a second best:

> "No," the woman answered. "I am not upset because he's gone.
> You won't understand. . . . "
> Syson could not distinguish what the man said. Hilda replied,
> clear and distinct:
> "You know I love you. He has gone quite out of my life—I don't
> know what I should do without you. . . . " She ended plaintively. (SR
> 340)

She consents to marry Pilbeam but in a "slightly
bitter" voice. She does not watch her new fiancé when
he departs, instead standing and "looking south over the sunny
counties toward London, far away" (SR 340). In 1912 Lawrence—still close to the version of the London literary life
he had made his vocation—does not reject Syson entirely, and he
does not seem prepared to give unqualified sanction to
a lifesaving figure of male vitality. The meaning of "The Shades
of Spring" is almost present in the *Forum* text of "The
Soiled Rose" but does not quite materialize. In contrast, the
attitudes embodied in "The Shades of Spring" are unequivocal.
When Lawrence revised "The Soiled Rose" in 1914, he was
able to do so with finality.

The title "The Soiled Rose" is a further indication that

Lawrence was not ready to see the story as the vindication of a
redeemed Hilda, and "The Dead Rose," the title of the Hopkin
proof version, is even harsher. ("One keeps a dead rose to look
at" [H 210], Syson tells Hilda in a passage cut from the
proofs.) "The Shades of Spring"[16] suggests quite a different
emphasis and a very different attitude: in the final treatment of
the homecoming material, Lawrence is laying at rest the ghosts
of his past. (At that, as a ghost, Hilda in the final version of the
story is notably corporeal.)

In May 1913 Lawrence wrote his close friend Helen Corke a
letter about "The Soiled Rose" that points the way toward
its transformation into "The Shades of Spring":

> Perhaps you are a little bit mistaken about "The Soiled
> Rose." I wrote it while I was still in Croydon—still in bed after the
> last illness. Don't you think it a bit affected? It is a bit stiff, like
> sick man's work.—So that the philosophy which is in "The Soiled
> Rose" didn't hold good for me long after the writing of the story. . . .
> You see, I have been married for this past year. . . . I cannot
> talk about it because it involves too much. . . . And *meine Frau* . . . is
> never very far from me, in any sense of the word. You would be
> surprised, how I am married—or how married I am. And this is
> the best I have known, or ever shall know. (CL 206–7)

In May 1913 Lawrence was already at work on the novel that
was to become *The Rainbow* and *Women in Love*. By the
time he revised "The Soiled Rose" for the *Prussian Officer*
collection, he had written Garnett that he was "sure" of
the novel because "the struggle and the resistance" between
Frieda and him was over: "Now you will find her and me in the
novel, I think, and the work is of both of us" (CL 272). It is
not surprising that the "philosophy which is in 'The Soiled
Rose'" no longer held good for Lawrence when he revised the
story. He felt he had become a different person, and a
different person would necessarily write a different story.

16. Book II, Chapter II, of *The White Peacock* is called "A Shadow in
Spring"; here the shadow in question is Annable. The final title was
probably suggested by the specters of Verlaine's poem.

The self-confident aesthete of "The Soiled Rose" has vanished from "The Shades of Spring." No longer "self-assured" or "dressed in stylish tweeds" (SR 324), Syson returns "like an uneasy spirit" (PO 153) rather than "like an emigrant" (SR 324). In the magazine text after leaving Pilbeam, "everything seemed to him ironic" (SR 328). In "The Shades of Spring" "everything irritated him" (PO 158). The voices of Hilda's brothers arouse a "tormented" (PO 159) rather than an "ironic" (SR 328) spirit in him. Where Hilda and Syson "mocked each other with irony" (SR 330) in the magazine version, they "hurt each other" (PO 161) in the revision, and Syson's "Tandaradeï" is eliminated. In the magazine text, in the hut Syson's "black eyes were playing a polite game with her, and his face . . . was flickering with polite irony" (SR 335). In the revision, "his black eyes were watching her, and his face . . . was flickering" (PO 169). The self-assurance is gone. As late as the autumn revision of the Hopkin proofs, Syson's "brilliant, quick" laugh (H 197) becomes a "brilliant, unhappy" laugh (PO 156). "What a fool he was! What godforsaken folly it all was!" (PO 158) Syson is converted from foppish caricature to human being.

At the same time, Hilda's new self-confidence and pride of bearing are further emphasized. In an addition to the *Prussian Officer* text, Syson feels "foolish, almost unreal, beside her. She was so static" (PO 160): once again the new theoretical language of this period is introduced. Significantly, where in the *Forum* text Hilda's composure conceals "bitterness" and "calm acceptance of sorrow" (SR 330), in the revision it reflects "calm acceptance of herself, and triumph over him" (PO 161).

In the *Forum* text, a reference is made to Hilda's "seeming assurance" (SR 333); "seeming" is deleted from the *Prussian Officer* text. Her assurance can no longer be questioned, nor can her great transformation. "You are very different" (SR 335), Hilda says in the magazine text. "We are very different" (PO 169), she says in the revision. They have both changed, and now Hilda is confident that she is on the right path while Syson has gone wrong.

The final version of Hilda's revelation is one of the key statements in "The Shades of Spring" of the emergent Lawrentian attitudes:

"They did well," she said at length, "to have various altars to various gods, in old days."
"Ah yes!" he agreed. "To whom is the new one?"
"There are no old ones," she said. "I was always looking for this."
"And whose is it?" he asked.
"I don't know," she said, looking full at him.
"I'm very glad, for your sake," he said, "that you are satisfied."
"Aye—but the man doesn't matter so much," she said. There was a pause.
"No!" he exclaimed, astonished, yet recognizing her as her real self.
"It is one's self that matters," she said. "Whether one is being one's own self and serving one's own God." (PO 165)

In "The Soiled Rose," Hilda questions Syson "pathetically" and admits "in a low husky tone, averting her face from him" (SR 333), that she has turned away from the old gods. In "The Dead Rose" of July, Syson asks her if she's "certain" about herself and her situation, and she can only muster a doubtful "Oh yes—I think so" (H 205) in response. In "The Shades of Spring," however, there is no question of apostasy. Hilda has simply found what she was "always looking for": Pilbeam represents the end of her quest as Syson never could. It is Syson, not Hilda, who remarks in the *Forum* text that "the man doesn't matter so much" (SR 333). There he is simply saying that woman, the torchbearer of civilization, is more obliged to strive after the ideal than man. When Lawrence gives the same words to Hilda in the revision, he has in mind his ideas about impersonality, ideas implicit in the beautiful Paul-Clara scenes in *Sons and Lovers* and so crucial to both *The Rainbow* and *Women in Love*. The man doesn't matter so much except as a way to find one's own self. "It is one's self that matters": this too is an addition to the story, and only in the autumn revision of "The Dead Rose" does Hilda add "serving one's own God" to "being one's own self." Hilda no longer grieves because Syson is not on hand to bring the stars and the flowers to life. "I have them all for myself, now" (PO 168), she says. When Syson asks what her new understanding amounts to, she replies emphatically (in another October addition), "One is free" (PO 166).

Syson is to blame for their failure in relationship because he refused to recognize her own individuality and tried to make her into something she was not, tried to saturate her with his own personality. The nonintellectual Pilbeam is content to let her be herself. In "The Dead Rose" Hilda accuses Syson of "always putting me where I was not myself" (H 206), but his violation of her identity is made even clearer in "The Shades of Spring": "You were always making me to be not myself" (PO 166), she exclaims. He had "considered her all spirit," but actually she is "like a plant" growing in "[her] own soil" (PO 167). Free at last from Syson's domination, she has come into her own.

When Syson returns, it is as if she were a stranger. "She was a different person to him. He did not know her. But he could regard her objectively now" (PO 163). We can never really "know" another person, and in mature Lawrentian terms one of the worst sins is to try to do so. The revised version of "The Shades of Spring" contains an emphatic statement of the same insight about human separateness that we discovered in the final text of "Odour of Chrysanthemums" and the Tom-Lydia relationship in *The Rainbow*. A comparison of the most important passage treating this theme in "The Shades of Spring" with the corresponding passage in the magazine text of "The Soiled Rose" is particularly fascinating, for this central insight replaces a piece of awkward ironic claptrap:

Forum text of "The Soiled Rose"	"The Shades of Spring"
"I disapprove of what you are becoming," she said.	"I disapprove of what you have become," she said.
"But you have still hopes of me! Then what must I do to be—" he checked himself—"to avoid this calamity?"	"You think we might"—he glanced at the hut—"have been like this—you and I?"
She saw that he was always laughing at her.	She shook her head.
	"You! no; never! You plucked a thing and looked at it till you

"If your own soul doesn't tell you, I cannot."

"I say," he cried, mock-serious, "where have I heard that before—? Besides," he continued politely, "one cannot live in Rome without being Romanized—unless one is fantastically patriotic—and really you know, I am of no country."

"No—?" she said bitterly.

"Unless I have been adopted unaware." That, he felt, was insulting, and his spirit turned in shame.

"You are a Roman of the Romans," she said sarcastically.

"Of the emasculated period," he laughed. "But 'twas you would have it so."

"I!" she exclaimed. (SR 335–36)

had found out all you wanted to know about it, then you threw it away," she said.

"Did I?" he asked. "And could your way never have been my way? I suppose not."

"Why should it?" she said. "I am a separate being."

"But surely two people sometimes go the same way," he said.

"You took me away from myself," she said.

He knew he had mistaken her, had taken her for something she was not. That was his fault, not hers.

"And did you always know?" he asked.

"No—you never let me know. You bullied me. I couldn't help myself. I was glad when you left me, really."

"I know you were," he said. But his face went paler, almost deathly luminous.

"Yet," he said, "it was you who sent me the way I have gone."

"I!" she exclaimed, in pride. (PO 169)

The exchange in the magazine version is on the superficial level of personal insult. The implications of the revised passage have bearing on one of Lawrence's central beliefs: the individual must above all be free to be himself. Syson's crime was to violate Hilda's "separate being." In "The Shades of Spring" Syson comes to the full realization of what strangers they have always been: "Syson looked at her. He was startled to see his young love, his nun, his Botticelli angel, so revealed. It was he who had been the fool. He and she were more separate than any two strangers could be" (PO 172). Interestingly, in "The Dead Rose" of July, Hilda and Syson are only "separate as any two strangers could be" (H 212). The split between them is greatest in the final version of the story.

As Syson climbs the bank to the gorse bushes in the magazine text, he is "extraordinarily wretched" (SR 338)—because he has been defeated. At the same moment in the revised story, he is "extraordinarily moved" (PO 172)—because he has learned the truth. In the magazine version he "lay quite still, feeling a kind of death" (SR 339). In the revised text, surrounded by the flowers, he marvels at "what a wonderful world it was—marvellous, for ever new" (PO 172). Confrontation of the truth has brought not death but renewal. In the *Forum* text his reflection on the hillside is absurdly abstract and inflated, clearly intended by Lawrence to undercut his protagonist. Syson has "destroyed Myself in her, and I am alone, my star is gone out. I have destroyed the beautiful 'Me' who was always ahead of me, nearer the realities. And I have struck the topmost flower from off her faith. And yet it was the only thing to do . . . " (SR 339). When "The Soiled Rose" became "The Dead Rose" in July 1914, Lawrence replaced Syson's awkward self-apology with a passage that seems overtly autobiographical. John Adderley Syson has a wife, but only in "The Dead Rose" do we learn about her:

> He thought of his own wife, and she seemed to him like a flower standing up, amongst other flowers. What had he to complain of? That which was between him and his wife was an unknown permanent thing, that he need not bother himself about. And now he was free of this old illusion, this painful feeling of connection with his old love, his ideal whom he had forsaken. He had forsaken her for the sake of physical satisfaction, and now he saw that the whole affair with her had been a bluff on both sides. He had bluffed himself that she was the woman of his soul, she had bluffed herself that he was the man of her soul, and they had fought to make their illusion true. (H 213)

The "unknown permanent thing" between Syson and his wife is immediately reminiscent of the "permanent surety" (PO 246) Ted Whiston feels at the beginning of his marriage to Elsie in "The White Stocking." It should also bring to mind Lawrence's expressed attitudes about Frieda during this period, for that is where these feelings come from. However, he must have felt that this version of Syson's meditation struck rather too close to home, especially the sentence about forsaking his sweetheart "for the sake of physical satisfaction." This passage is one of the most fascinating in the Hopkin proofs, but it's no surprise that Lawrence canceled it.

A literary allusion is injected into the final revision of the passage, but it is appropriate and not self-indulgent. It fits into the harmony and calm that Syson feels as he lies on the hillside reconciling himself to the truth:

> He felt as if it were underground, like the fields of monotone hell. . . . Inside his breast was a pain like a wound. He remembered the poem of William Morris, where in the Chapel of Lyonesse a knight lay wounded, with the truncheon of a spear deep in his breast, lying always as dead, yet did not die. . . . He knew now it never had been true, that which was between him and her, not for a moment. The truth had stood apart all the time. (PO 173)[17]

In the final version Syson is able to "see her as she [is]" (PO 163) and will "give her her due" (PO 164). Like Mrs. Bates in "Odour of Chrysanthemums," he has discovered that the truth is liberating.

The Greiffenhagen tableau that ends the story is also transformed. Hilda's tears are excised, for she has no reason to be weeping. When she agrees to marry the keeper, her voice is still "indulgent" (PO 174), but it is no longer "slightly bitter" (SR 340). However, in "The Shades of Spring" Hilda does not want to get married "just yet" (PO 174). "It is most beautiful as it is" (PO 175), she says, a remark that expresses a central meaning of the story at the same time it seems to reflect the two years Lawrence and Frieda lived together before they were legally able to marry. In both "The Soiled Rose" and "The Dead Rose," Hilda looks "south over the sunny counties toward London" (SR 340, H 215). Only in "The Shades of Spring" does she simply look "over the sunny country" (PO 175). She is content.

17. The Morris poem is "The Chapel in Lyoness." In August 1911 Lawrence wrote Louie Burrows that he was "rather fond of Morris," whom he was reading at the time (LL 130).

In "The Shades of Spring" the keeper remains a sketchy figure, but here and there we find retouching that attempts to make him a more obviously suitable man for the spring awakening of Hilda Millership. His body is now "self-sufficient" (PO 154), and the revision also equips him with a "wild animal's cunning" (PO 167). At the conclusion he no longer worries about where he and Hilda will be married. Perhaps the story would have been strengthened if the keeper were more sharply defined, but Lawrence seems intent on having him dominated by his sweetheart.

In fact there is no mistaking the aggressive edge of the new Hilda Millership. She has "a certain hardness like arrogance hidden under her humility," and her eyes go "hard" (PO 163) and she is "always dominant" (PO 164) as she gives Syson her guided tour of the countryside. Some of this language was softened when "The Dead Rose" became "The Shades of Spring" in the autumn of 1914: Syson is no longer "afraid of" her, her "proud, hard bearing" is modulated into a "distant bearing," and "her set mouth" and "the expressionless composure of her face" are deleted altogether (H 201, PO 161). Nevertheless, the "reddest kiss" vampire tableau at the story's conclusion must be reckoned with. Self-assurance has the potential to become something rather worse. Syson has learned the truth about his past and has been reconciled to it. Hilda has come into her own—but the young gamekeeper is in for some hard times.

Still, despite these nasty overtones, "The Shades of Spring" firmly endorses the validity of Hilda's transformation. The sketchiness of the keeper's character does not really matter because there is something else in the story that verifies the rightness of her new personality. The overflowing fecundity of nature is everywhere, forever changing but at the same time eternal. "Like a stream the path opened into azure shallows at the levels, and there were pools of bluebells, with still the green thread winding through, like a thin current of ice-water through blue lakes. And from under the twig-purple of the bushes swam the shadowed blue, as if the flowers lay in flood water over the woodland" (SR 327, PO 157). This bright natural world offers redemption in a way the gray city cannot. When Syson marvels at "what a wonderful world it was" as he lies on the hillside, he is unknowingly making his first progress toward Hilda's new insights.

Lawrence now had "a woman at the back of me" (CL 179), and he was confident of his new vision of human relationship. He was at last able to shape into a final harmony the materials that had been with him since the "Scarp Slope" chapter in his first novel. The progression from the *White Peacock* chapter to "The Shades of Spring" is a study in Lawrence's growth to maturity, of his ultimate acceptance of his past and of himself. The special radiance of "The Shades of Spring" also speaks clearly and directly to the fact that it is part of the emergent moment of *The Rainbow*. He had at last transformed something of a personal archetype into a first-rate work of short fiction.

Chapter VI

"The White Stocking"

"I feel I've got a mate and I'll fight tooth and claw to keep her"

Two of the stories collected in *The Prussian Officer* were originally written for the Christmas short story contest of the *Nottinghamshire Guardian* in 1907. Both "A Fragment of Stained Glass" and "The White Stocking" survived and evolved over the years leading up to Lawrence's first short story collection. Lawrence left the third story, "A Prelude," uncollected in his lifetime.

"A Fragment of Stained Glass" is by any measure less successful than "The White Stocking." Its medievalism tends to be stagey and melodramatic, and its effects seem labored. Perhaps the main interest of the story is as Lawrence's first foray into the demonic. Lawrence disliked the literariness of "A Fragment of Stained Glass" even before it appeared in the *English Review* of September 1911. That version is essentially the story that was published in the *Prussian Officer* collection. In 1914 he was working hard to discover new ways to express his feelings of hope and urgency concerning modern life. "A Fragment of Stained Glass," with its self-conscious fifteenth-century setting, its Browningesque vicar, and its awkward literary frame, no longer held much interest for him.

In contrast, "The White Stocking," a minor masterpiece, deals directly with the central issues of modern love and marriage. Lawrence evokes the life of the urban middle class with ease and assurance. The characterization, especially of the heroine, is subtle, and an unusual tripartite structure proves successful. Lawrence felt with good reason that this story was much more worth taking the time to get right. The final version is a skillful depiction of the psychology of marriage—and the psychological complexity was one of the last elements to be grafted on. The late revision reveals the advances, both artistic and personal, Lawrence had made during the first years with Frieda.

The development of "A Fragment of Stained Glass" is not sufficiently interesting to warrant treatment here, so I will concentrate on "The White Stocking." The young Lawrence may have called himself a "priest of love" (CL 173), but more often than not Lawrentian love is an activity that seems appropriate to a battlefield. The final version of "The White Stocking" is striking for its revelation of the turbulence beneath the surface of middle-class marriage.

The following versions of "The White Stocking" are extant:

1. "The White Stocking." Unpublished holograph in the collection of W. H. Clarke, Lawrence's nephew. I was unable to make use of this early text, which I suspect is the version submitted to the Christmas contest in 1907.

2. "The White Stocking." The magazine text of this story, probably completed in April 1911. Published in the *Smart Set* in October 1914.

3. "The White Stocking." Magazine text revised in July 1914, producing the version found in the Hopkin proofs. Revised *before* it had appeared in the *Smart Set* in magazine form.

4. "The White Stocking." Hopkin proof version revised in October 1914 for inclusion in *The Prussian Officer and Other Stories,* December 1914.

There is considerable revision in minor detail between the Hopkin proofs and the final text. In general this revision, most interesting in the dance scene in Section II, adds up to a slight intensification. For reasons of space and clarity, I will focus most of my discussion on a comparison of the *Smart Set* and the final versions, though I will glance occasionally at the intervening text in the Hopkin proofs.

Jessie Chambers remembered the version originally submitted to the *Nottinghamshire Guardian* Christmas contest in 1907 as "an idealized picture of his mother as a young girl going to a ball at the Castle and drawing out a long white stocking in mistake for a pocket handkerchief."[1] This incident must have been Lawrence's initial inspiration, but the story of Elsie Whiston is far removed from any family history. The local newspaper did not accept the first "White Stocking." By January 1910 Lawrence had rewritten the story (LL 49), and in the early spring of 1911 he revised it again (LL 98). This spring 1911 version is probably very close to the version published in the *Smart Set* in October 1914.

Lawrence was back in England in the summer of 1913, and he made a strenuous effort to place all his unpublished short fiction. "The Christening" and "The Shadow in the Rose Garden," which were published in the *Smart Set* in February and March 1914, were among the stories he sold that summer. "The White Stocking," which was published in the October 1914 number of the same magazine, may well have been purchased at the same time. He revised the story for the *Prussian Officer* collection in June or July of 1914 and again sometime in the autumn. Although the original "White Stocking" is one of Lawrence's earliest apprentice pieces, its final revisions date from the time of *The Rainbow*.

Perhaps as important in the summer of 1914 was Lawrence's marriage to Frieda on 13 July, two years after their elopement and a month and a half after Frieda was granted her divorce from Weekley. Frieda had played an essential role in the emergence of the mature Lawrence. In the summer of 1912 he wrote that "I feel I've got a mate and I'll fight tooth and claw to keep her. She says I'm reverting, but I'm not—I'm only coming out wholesome and myself. . . . I loathe Paul Morel" (CL 135). Six months later he wrote that "it is hopeless for me to try to do anything without I have a woman at the back of me. . . . A woman that I love sort of keeps me in direct communication with the unknown, in which otherwise I am a bit lost" (CL 179). On 2 June 1914, three days before he sent Garnett the revolutionary

1. ET, p. 114.

letter about character in *The Rainbow*[2] and a few weeks
before beginning the most important revision of "The White
Stocking," he wrote A. W. McLeod that "the only re-
sourcing of art . . . is to make it more the joint work of man
and woman." It was essential "for men to have courage to
draw nearer to women, expose themselves to them, and be
altered by them: and for women to accept and admit men"
(CL 280). We can trace something of these attitudes in
Lawrence's work from the beginning, and yet the evidence
suggests that it was only in the spring of 1914
that these ideas crystallized.

"The White Stocking" is a domestic comedy with serious
overtones about marriage. He had written the original version long before he had had any concrete experience of
marriage. The final version was written after he had been
with Frieda for over two years. It is not surprising that his
attitude was clearer and more complex in 1914.

In general the final text closely follows the *Smart Set* version, even though the revisions are extensive. The 1914 revisions of the story comprised a rewriting as much as a
retouching, and yet Lawrence never completely abandoned
the magazine text. Several events are transposed and a few
are deleted, but nevertheless he clearly had the earlier version before him when he produced the text he published in
The Prussian Officer. One version is closely modeled on the
other, and throughout there is a profusion of verbal echoes
between the two texts. The marvel is that the two texts, so
similar, are so radically different.

"The White Stocking" has always been admired for its
sense of life. F. R. Leavis is typical when he remarks that to
Lawrence the materials of the story were "without qualifica-
tion human life."[3] This quality is impressively present,

2. The futurists are mentioned in both letters, a fact that further asso-
ciates Lawrence's unprecedented emotional equilibrium with his literary
theorizing.
3. F. R. Leavis, *D. H. Lawrence: Novelist* (New York, 1956), pp. 309–10.

but the power of the story cannot be accounted for in terms of its evocation of marriage among the urban middle class. Any adequate appraisal of the tale must emphasize the emotional extremity and the irrational passion just beneath its surface.

Elsie Whiston—girlish, flirtatious, attractive, and rather careless—is married to a commercial traveler who is shaped by middle-class notions of work and morality. The first section of the story takes place on Valentine's Day, two years after the Whistons' marriage. Sam Adams, the florid, forty-year-old factory owner who had employed Elsie and Whiston before their marriage, has sent her earrings, a handkerchief, and a white stocking. Elsie tells her husband that the stocking is a valentine from Adams and admits that he had sent another the year before. They quarrel until Whiston, filled with rage and anxiety, leaves for work.

The second section is a flashback to a Christmas party at Adams's house two years earlier. Whiston is a wallflower, but Elsie is intoxicated by the marvelous dancing and male warmth of Adams. Whiston plays cards and grows more and more jealous. Before a final dance with Adams, Elsie reaches for her pocket handkerchief and finds to her horrified embarrassment that she has brought a white stocking instead. Adams picks up and keeps the dropped stocking. Elsie's behavior provokes an angry quarrel between her and Whiston. In its aftermath they are married soon afterwards.

The final section brings us back to the Valentine's Day with which the story began. Whiston returns from work and his quarrel with his wife recommences. Elsie puts on both of the stockings Adams has sent and dances round the room, taunting her husband; he responds abusively. When she admits that Adams had sent not only the stockings but also the earrings and an amethyst brooch, Whiston hits her across the mouth. The story ends with the jewelry on its way back to Adams and with Elsie sobbing in her husband's arms.

At any rate, these are the outlines of the story published in the *Prussian Officer and Other Stories* in December 1914. However, the text of the story published in the *Smart Set* is drastically different from that included in *The Prussian Officer* just two months later. A comparison of these versions of "The White Stocking"—with a few glances at the Hopkin proof version that came in between—demonstrates how Lawrence added some of his most characteristic concerns to the richly complex evocation of ordinary middle-class life with which he began.

The final version of the opening paragraphs introduces the reader to a much livelier heroine. Elsie replies "animatedly" in the final text where in the magazine text she simply replies. Phrases like "flicking her small, delightful limbs" and "her careless abandon made his spirit glow" (PO 223) are additions. Such details put Elsie's sexuality into sharper focus. In general, the sexuality is more overt in the final text. This fundamental change is important to the more complex story that emerges.

The description of her husband is altered in much the same way. The belt Whiston fastens round his "waist" (SS 97)[4] in the magazine text and as late as the Hopkin proofs of July 1914 (H 217) is fastened round his "loins" (PO 224) in the revision. "A well made young fellow of about twenty-eight" (SS 97) in the magazine version, he becomes "a shapely young fellow of about twenty-eight, sleepy now and easy with well-being" (PO 224). In the magazine text the rip in Elsie's kimono exposes "a delightful little arm," and Whiston suffers, thinking that "that round arm might be cold" (SS 97). In the revision the rip reveals "some delightful pink upper-arm," and Whiston suffers "from the sight of the exposed soft flesh" (PO 224).

The battle lines of marriage are drawn more sharply in the revised text, and Whiston becomes angrier with his flighty little wife. In the magazine version his "heavy mouth" is

4. I will use the abbreviation SS for all page citations of the October 1914 *Smart Set* text (vol. 44, pp. 97–108). The late introduction of "loins" definitely seems to point toward *Women in Love*.

"pushed out sulkily" and "the lower part of his face" displays a "rather bestial anger" (SS 100). In the revision Whiston's jaw is "set rather sullenly," the blood comes "up into his neck and face," he stands "motionless, dangerous," and he speaks "in anger and contempt, and some bitterness" (PO 230–31). At the height of his rage in the magazine version he calls Elsie "a damned little good-for-nowt" (SS 100). His anger is more brutal in the revision, and he says she would "go off with a nigger for a packet of chocolate" (PO 231). The stronger scene between them in the revised version prepares the reader for the violence that is to come.

The opening paragraphs of the revision of Section II, the flashback to Sam Adams's Christmas party, are further evidence of the heightened sexuality of the final version. Sam Adams acquires "a good presence, and some Irish blood in his veins" along with "a real warm feeling for giving pleasure." Elsie becomes "a great attraction for him" (PO 232–33). At the same time, Whiston is courting her. Lawrence's revision ironically undercuts the budding Elsie-Whiston relationship when he describes Elsie as she makes "splendid little gestures, before her bedroom mirror, of the constant-and-true sort. 'True, true till death——.' That was her song. Whiston was made that way, so there was no need to take thought for him" (PO 233).

Elsie and Whiston meet Sam Adams when they arrive at the dance. The "constant red laugh on his face" is an addition, as is a sentence with strikingly sexual overtones: "He opened his mouth wide when he spoke, and the effect of the warm, dark opening behind the brown whiskers was disturbing" (PO 234). The small talk between Adams and Elsie also becomes more sexual: "I should have to be pretty small to get in your mouth" (PO 235), Elsie says.

Sam Adams dances with Elsie three times in the second section of the final text of the story, twice more than in the magazine text. Lawrence took special pains over these passages, for he saw in the dance a metaphor for the power of human sexuality.[5] The deeper implications of the revised "White Stocking" are found most revealingly in the passages relating to the dance. In the magazine text Sam Adams is a rather gross old roué. In the revision he becomes a Pan figure, and his invitation to Elsie to dance with him unleashes powerful, dangerous forces that can easily submerge the humdrum of her middle-class existence.

A comparison of the magazine and the final versions of the first dance illustrates this vast difference in the conception of the scene. In the magazine version, Adams "gave her such support":

His hand held her firmly in the small of her back, and seemed to speak to her, holding her, carrying her, telling her what to do, and a thousand other things. He was a man who knew what he was about.

At the end, flushed, she looked straight at him, quickly, saying: "It was lovely."

He laughed with a queer little laugh, pleased throughout the whole of him. And he paid her attentions. (SS 102)

This is the only Elsie-Adams dance in the magazine version, and there is not very much to it.[6] The first dance in the revision is another matter altogether:

Catching the eye of the band, he nodded. In a moment, the music began. He seemed to relax, giving himself up.

"Now then, Elsie," he said, with a curious caress in his voice that seemed to lap the outside of her body in a warm glow, delicious. She gave herself to it. She liked it.

He was an excellent dancer. He seemed to draw her close in to him by some male warmth of attraction, so that she became all soft

5. See Langdon Elsbree, "D. H. Lawrence, *Homo Ludens,* and the Dance" (*D. H. Lawrence Review,* 1 [1968], 1–30) for a general discussion of the dance in Lawrence.

6. Amazingly, in the magazine version *both* Adams and Whiston are described in identical words as "a man who knew what he was about" (SS 101, 102). This is a shockingly careless bit of characterization, but Lawrence left absolutely no doubt about the differences between Adams and Whiston when he revised the story.

and pliant to him, flowing to his form, whilst he united her with him and they lapsed in one movement. She was just carried in a kind of strong, warm flood, her feet moved of themselves, and only the music threw her away from him, threw her back to him, to his clasp, in his strong form moving against her, rhythmically, deliciously.

When it was over, he was pleased and his eyes had a curious gleam which thrilled her and yet had nothing to do with her. Yet it held her. He did not speak to her. He only looked straight into her eyes with a curious, gleaming look that disturbed her fearfully and deliciously. (PO 235-36)

The *Prussian Officer* version of the dance could easily be a description of sexual intercourse. Interestingly, as late as the Hopkin proofs, the "curious caress" in Adams' voice "did not move her inside" (H 228)—an antisexual detail that Lawrence finally dropped. Adams does not speak to Elsie, and his eyes have "nothing to do with her": this detail reflects the impersonality that is a central feature of the mature love ethic. In the dance Adams and Elsie have celebrated the cosmic energies of the universe together—but they have not attempted to know each other.

The heightened intensity, repetitiveness, and accretiveness of the dancing passages in the revised "White Stocking" are closely associated with the language of *The Rainbow*. In fact there is a passage in the novel in which the dance is used in the same way. The description of Ursula dancing with Skrebensky at the wedding of Fred Brangwen is highly charged and erotic:

At the touch of her hand on his arm, his consciousness melted away from him. He took her into his arms, as if into the sure, subtle power of his will, and they became one movement, one dual movement, dancing on the slippery grass. It would be endless, this movement, it would continue for ever. It was his will and her will locked in a trance of motion, two wills locked in one motion, yet never fusing, never yielding one to the other.

. . . .

There was a wonderful rocking of the darkness, slowly, a great slow swinging of the whole night, with the music playing lightly on the surface, making the strange, ecstatic, rippling on the surface of the dance, but underneath only one great flood heaving slowly backwards to the verge of oblivion, slowly forward to the other verge, the heart sweeping along each time, and tightening with anguish as the limit was reached, and the movement, at crises, turned and swept back. (R 316–17)

Elsie is carried by "a kind of strong, warm flood," Ursula by "one great flood." In *The Rainbow,* as in the revised "White Stocking," the dance liberates the powerful sexual energies of Lawrence's young heroine.

The second dance in the revised text of "The White Stocking" replaces a good deal of material that Lawrence wisely excised in July 1914. One character, Sam Adams's nephew Harry, is completely eliminated. Harry is rather whimsically associated with the devil, but these allusions are confusing and have no apparent function. The revised version of the story has a clear, uncluttered structure in accordance with a sharpened perception of what the story is about.

Another scene that is cut is the incident of the spilled coffee. In both versions Whiston, after playing cards (his name is taken rather crudely from whist), attends to the "plain" ladies. In the magazine version Adams, "getting more and more affected by wine and heat," is telling Elsie some of his adventures when he accidentally knocks a coffee cup out of Whiston's hand and burns himself. Adams jumps around "with a ridiculously exaggerated gesture," rebukes Whiston with "his face purple," and goes off "in a towering passion." Admittedly the spilled coffee has sexual implications, but Adams comes off as a buffoon in the episode, and Elsie has to giggle "in spite of herself" (SS 103–4). The scene is meant to function as a contest between Elsie's two rivals, but it is handled clumsily. At the same time, Lawrence does add some overt sexual innuendo to the revised version of the scene. The game is cribbage in both texts, but only in the revision does Whiston take "the little red peg away from her and [stick] it in its hole" (PO 237).

The last thing Lawrence wanted to do in the revised story

was to deflate Sam Adams. In the *Prussian Officer* text an "opposite, heavier impulse" takes Elsie briefly to Whiston in the card room, but he does not know how to dance. Soon Adams is "holding her near him, in a delicious embrace" when the time comes to dance with him again. "Gratified" by the "gleam" in Adams's eyes, she is under his spell: "She was getting warmed right through, the glow was penetrating into her, driving away everything else. Only in her heart was a little tightness, like conscience" (PO 236). The "curious, impersonal light" that gleams in his eyes as he takes her out to the dance floor emphasizes once again the cosmic nature of the energies that are being generated. He speaks "with a kind of intimate, animal call to her" (PO 238). The second dance is an even more intensely sexual experience than the first:

> The dance was an intoxication to her. After the first few steps, she felt herself slipping away from herself. She almost knew she was going, she did not even want to go. She lay in the arm of the steady, close man with whom she was dancing, and she seemed to swim away out of contact with the room, into him. She had passed into another, denser element of him, an essential privacy. The room was all vague around her, like an atmosphere, like under sea, with a flow of ghostly, dumb movements. But she herself was held against her partner, and it seemed she was connected with him, as if the movements of his body and limbs were her own movements, yet not her own movements—and oh, delicious! He also was given up, oblivious, concentrated, into the dance. His eye was unseeing. Only his large voluptuous body gave off a subtle activity. His fingers seemed to search into her flesh. Every moment, and every moment, she felt she would give way utterly, and sink molten: the fusion point was coming when she would fuse down into perfect unconsciousness at his feet and knees. But he bore her round the room in the dance, and he seemed to sustain all her body with his limbs, his body, and his warmth seemed to come closer into her, nearer, till it would fuse right through her, and she would be as liquid to him, as an intoxication only.
>
> It was exquisite. When it was over, she was dazed, and was scarcely breathing. (PO 238–39)

This dance became a sexual experience in the July revisions, but as late as the succeeding autumn a few details further sexualized it. In the Hopkin proofs Elsie swims "out of contact with the room" (H 231); only in the very last revision did Lawrence add "into him." Similarly, Elsie "swam" (H 231) with him in the proofs, but she "was connected" with him in the *Prussian Officer* text. Adams's first words to Elsie, " 'Twas good, wasn't it, my darling?" (PO 239) are the language of sexual detumescence. Again this is more fully erotic than "All right, eh, my darling?" (H 232)—the formulation in the Hopkin proofs.

The eroticism of this dance passage did not go unnoticed: in February 1915 there was a rumor that *The Prussian Officer* had been withdrawn from circulation by order of the police (CL 316). The addition of all this sexuality reflects Lawrence's changing attitudes. After two years with Frieda, Lawrence wanted to say something about the darkly powerful forces found just beneath the surface of the marriage compact. The dance in *The Rainbow* echoes this passage directly. The insistent references to fusion are picked up in the *Rainbow* passage quoted above, and the room that seems to be "under sea" in the revised "White Stocking" becomes "a vision of the depths of the underworld, under the great flood" (R 316) in *The Rainbow*.

In the revised text, Whiston seems like a "guardian angel" to Elsie. She is "also conscious, much more intimately and impersonally, of the body of the other man moving somewhere in the room" (PO 241). Elsie and Whiston quarrel briefly: he wants to take her home, but she is enjoying herself too much. When the time comes for Adams to dance with her again, the language becomes sexual even before the music begins: "Oh, the delicious closing of contact with him, of his limbs touching her limbs, his arm supporting her. She seemed to resolve" (PO 243).

In the magazine text, Adams, still humiliated by his behavior over the spilled coffee, is "very stiff and martial, his excessive joviality gone" (SS 104), when he comes to dance with Elsie once more. The dance never takes place because of the incident with the white stocking: "Sam Adams, laughing outright, picked up the fallen stocking, and held it at arm's length. There was a shout of laughter down the room. Elsie stood crimson with shame . . ." (SS 105). The final paragraph tells us abruptly that "they had married shortly afterward when Whiston had got another job. There had been one child, which had died" (SS 105).

The sexual overtones of the white stocking incident are carefully developed in the revised text:

Then in an instant, Adams picked it up, with a little, surprised laugh of triumph.

"That'll do for me," he whispered—seeming to take possession of her. And he stuffed the stocking in his trousers pocket, and quickly offered her his handkerchief. (PO 243)

Elsie feels "weak and faint" during her last dance with Adams, "but it was peace" (PO 243–44). She dances with him again even after he has taken symbolic possession of her before everyone.

In place of the abrupt ending of this section in the magazine text, Lawrence has added two pages of dialogue between Elsie and Whiston. Whiston is enraged, but Elsie weeps, repeating only that she doesn't want to go home. It is implicit in both versions that Elsie accepts Whiston because she feels guilty about her behavior at the party and is fearful that it will happen again, but in the revised text this motivation is more successfully dramatized.

"Ted!" she whispered, frantic: "Ted!"

"What, my love?" he answered, becoming also afraid.

"Be good to me," she cried. "Don't be cruel to me."

"No, my pet," he said, amazed and grieved. "Why?"

"Oh, be good to me," she sobbed.

And he held her very safe, and his heart was white-hot with love for her. His mind was amazed. He could only hold her against his chest that was white-hot with love and belief in her. So she was restored at last. (PO 246)

Elsie and Whiston embark on marriage on a very shaky basis. It is not surpising to find that a new conflict has erupted between them. The ambiguous reconciliation at the end of Section II of the revised story prepares the reader for exactly the same ambiguity at the end of the story. There is passion beneath the surface of a marriage that the social code cannot keep in check. Lawrence treats this passion more clearly and centrally in his revised text and, in doing so, greatly improves the story.

Section III brings us back to the present. In the revised text Lawrence tells us at the beginning of this section that Elsie and Whiston were married a few weeks after the Christmas party before he inserts some revealing sentences: "She loved him with passion and worship, a fierce little abandon of love that moved him to the depths of his being, and gave him a permanent surety and sense of realness in himself. He did not trouble about himself any more: he felt he was fulfilled and now he had only the many things in the world to busy himself about. Whatever troubled him, at the bottom was surety. He had found himself in this love" (PO 246). This passage could be a description of the first two years of the marriage between Lawrence and Frieda. In fact, it is a more apt description of their relationship than of the first years of marriage of Elsie and Whiston. The passage describes a period of great strength and harmony that Elsie and Whiston are not likely to have experienced. The alliance with Frieda allowed Lawrence to shake off his past and to achieve an equilibrium both emotionally and artistically. *The Rainbow* and the final revisions of the *Prussian Officer* stories are written out of the new "surety" he had found. Lawrence, whether or not he knows it, is speaking of himself.

The stage is set for the climactic scene between husband and wife. Whiston is "depressed" and "in a state of suppressed irritation" (SS 105–6, PO 248). After brooding all day, he has come home to fight it out. When he challenges Elsie about the white stockings, she runs upstairs to put them on and do battle with him. In the magazine text she stands "in front of him, holding up her skirt" (SS 106). In the revision she "picked up her skirts to her knees and twisted round, looking at her pretty legs in the neat stockings" (PO

249). Elsie's dance continues the dance motif of the second section. The dance is brief in the magazine version: she merely "danced a jig round the room, flinging up her white-stockinged ankles" until Whiston tells her to "sit down, and don't be a fool" (SS 106). The expanded revision greatly heightens both the sexuality and the tension:

> And she looked over her shoulders at her pretty calves, and the dancing frills of her knickers.
>
> "Put your skirts down and don't make a fool of yourself," he said.
>
> "Why a fool of myself?" she asked.
>
> And she began to dance slowly round the room, kicking up her feet half reckless, half jeering, in ballet-dancer's fashion. Almost fearfully, yet in defiance, she kicked up her legs at him, singing as she did so. She resented him.
>
> "You little fool, ha' done with it," he said. (PO 249)

In the revision Elsie's dance amounts to open warfare—and it is a war that strikes deeply at Whiston's manhood. Even after he orders her to stop, she dances "round the room doing a high kick to the tune of her words" (PO 250). Elsie's dance is an extended sexual taunt, and Whiston is goaded into calling his wife a "nasty trolley" and a "stray-running little bitch" (PO 250–51). In the magazine version he breaks off, "afraid lest he should get hold of her and hurt her," and goes outside (SS 107). In the revised version much stronger passion has been unleashed: "Her jeering scorn made him go white-hot, molten. He knew he was incoherent, scarcely responsible for what he might do. Slowly, unseeing, he rose and went out of doors, stifled, moved to kill her" (PO 251). He goes "white-hot" with rage—just as he had gone "white-hot" with love at the end of Section II of the revision. At this point the two texts part ways. Both end in what seems reconciliation, but they take different paths in reaching this conclusion.

In the magazine text, Elsie dreads "the mischief that she might have done" and goes outside looking for Whiston. She calls his name but cannot see him. He refuses to answer but begins to feel "sorry for her" (SS 107). He goes in after her and they stand confronting each other:

Taking courage, she went to him. He held her fast against his breast, so fast, she could not move, and was afraid. He did not say anything, but stood quite rigid, with a curious fine tremor in his body, holding her fast. She could not quite understand, and was afraid and unsure. She did not trust these high pitches of emotion.

Again, making an effort, she put her arms round his neck and drew down his head, kissing him.

"My love, my love," she murmured. (SS 107-8).

"A little wonder" wakes in her heart, and she marvels over the way he "clings to" her. The reference to the "powerful vibration of her husband's body" (SS 108) is the only hint at the end of the magazine story of the irrational forces beneath the surface of love and marriage. The ending of the magazine version of "The White Stocking" is pat and a little sentimental:

But she loved him. Oh, down in the very kernel of her, she loved him. It had never gone so deep before. She was glad. It made her feel so much bigger.

Next day she sent back both stockings and earrings. She never told her husband about the latter. (SS 108)

This is unsatisfactory: Lawrence gained full control over the materials of the story only when he revised it in 1914.

At the conclusion of the *Prussian Officer* text, Elsie does not go out in search of Whiston. He leans against the garden fence,[7] "unconscious with a black storm of rage," before going in to renew the battle. He threatens to break her neck, and she announces "with a queer chirrup of mocking laughter" (PO 252) that Adams had sent her both an amethyst brooch and the pair of earrings. This information brings on the final crisis:

---

7. Cf. Alfred Durant just before his mother's death in "Daughters of the Vicar" and Paul Morel at the end of *Sons and Lovers* for other uses of this motif.

He seemed to thrust his face and his eyes forward at her, as he rose slowly and came to her. She watched transfixed in terror. Her throat made a small sound, as she tried to scream.

Then, quick as lightning, the back of his hand struck her with a crash across the mouth, and she was flung back blinded against the wall. The shock shook a queer sound out of her. And then she saw him still coming on, his eyes holding her, his fist drawn back, advancing slowly. At any instant the blow might crash into her.

Mad with terror, she raised her hands with a queer clawing movement to cover her eyes and her temples, opening her mouth in a dumb shriek. There was no sound. But the sight of her slowly arrested him. He hung before her, looking at her fixedly, as she stood crouched against the wall with open, bleeding mouth, and wide-staring eyes, and two hands clawing over her temples. And his lust to see her bleed, to break her and destroy her, rose from an old source against her. It carried him. He wanted satisfaction. (PO 253)

Whiston's "lust to see her bleed, to break her and destroy her" and his desire for "satisfaction" are obviously and violently sexual. The battle of the sexes has passed beyond metaphor. Too much has been written about the dishes Lawrence and Frieda sometimes threw at each other, but we do know that Lawrence believed that a strong passional impulse should not be resisted. When George Orwell read the story he "deduced the moral that women behave better if they get a sock on the jaw occasionally,"[8] an interpretation that might not have upset Lawrence. At any rate, the addition of the blow makes the story more psychologically persuasive and greatly increases its effectiveness. The blow provides a needed catharsis.

The relationship between Elsie and Whiston in the story's final text is analogous in many ways to that of Schöner and the Captain in "The Prussian Officer." Tension

8. George Orwell, review of a paperback reprint of *The Prussian Officer* in the *Tribune* (London), 16 November 1945, reprinted in *The Collected Essays, Journalism, and Letters of George Orwell,* ed. Sonia Orwell and Ian Angus (New York, 1968), IV, 31.

between two people builds until only violence can release it. The violence in "The Prussian Officer" produces murder. In "The White Stocking" violence is a transgression of the mores of modern domestic life, and Elsie and Whiston are shocked back to social reality.

Elsie "mechanically" (PO 253) wipes her bleeding mouth and begins to weep quietly. She is "yielded up to him," her will gone. At the same time a "weariness" comes over Whiston, he is "dreary and sick" and does not "care any more" (PO 254). The rhythm of the final scene is that of sexual arousal and detumescence: after Whiston hits her, Elsie recognizes that "the passion had gone down in him" (PO 255). Both of them seem to be in a trance. The reconciliation takes place suddenly. Lawrence's art here is more convincing than the couple's reconciliation:

"I'm sleeping down here," he said. "Go you to bed."

In a few moments she lifted her tear-stained, swollen face and looked at him with eyes all forlorn and pathetic. A great flash of anguish went over his body. He went over, slowly, and very gently took her in his hands. She let herself be taken. Then as she lay against his shoulder, she sobbed aloud:

"I never meant—"

"My love—my love—" he cried, in anguish of spirit, holding her in his arms. (PO 256)

The long day is over, but the future is uncertain. Lawrence had set his magazine story "forty years ago" (SS 97), but the final version belongs emphatically to the world of modern love and marriage.

The marriage of Ted and Elsie Whiston is not a facsimile of the marriage of D. H. and Frieda Lawrence, and yet it is the experience of the first two years of this marriage that gave Lawrence the insights that allowed him to transform "The White Stocking" into a first-rate story. He had learned firsthand that there are powerful tensions that any marriage must resolve—and that it is difficult to build a marriage that provides strong support for both partners while maintaining essential freedom. In the late spring of 1914 Lawrence was convinced that he and Frieda had come through to something fine. From this vantage point he was able to give "The White Stocking" a new shape that promised well for his future as a writer.

The powerful energies generated in the story are exactly the energies that dominate the Lawrentian universe. The achievement of "The White Stocking" is in its author's ability to integrate this vision of the impersonal forces that govern all of existence with a loving, sympathetic portrayal of ordinary people living an ordinary life. This is the same blending—the cosmic and the everyday—that is so important to the achievement of *The Rainbow*. Lawrence could only find the story when he had found himself—or, to put it another way, when he had found the style, the language, and the vision of his mature identity as an artist.

Chapter VII

"The Prussian Officer"
and "The Thorn in the Flesh"

"I am here in Bavarian Tyrol, near the mountains. They stand up,
streaked with snow, so blue, across the valley"

Lawrence and Frieda eloped to the Continent on 13 May
1912. He wrote six stories that reflect the first months in
Europe. Three of them—"A Chapel Among the Mountains,"
"A Hay Hut Among the Mountains," and "Once"—were
never published in his lifetime, appearing for the first time
in the posthumous *Love Among the Haystacks and Other Pieces.*
"A Chapel Among the Mountains" and "A Hay Hut Among
the Mountains" are slight autobiographical transcriptions
of related incidents from the walking tour Lawrence and
Frieda took through Germany to Italy. "Once" is based on
an experience of Frieda's young womanhood in Germany,
before her marriage to Weekley. "The Mortal Coil," written
slightly later, is a melodramatic tale about an aristocratic
second lieutenant and his mistress. The other two stories
that use German material are two of the finest in *The Prussian
Officer*, "The Thorn in the Flesh" (originally "Vin Ordinaire")
and "The Prussian Officer" itself (originally "Honour and
Arms").

On about 10 June 1913, Lawrence wrote Garnett from
Germany that he had "written the best story I have ever
done—about a German officer in the army and his orderly.
Then there is another good autobiographical story. I think
it is good: then there is another story in course of completion. . . . " (CL 209). The story about the officer and the orderly
is the first form of "The Prussian Officer." The original
"Thorn in the Flesh" could be either the "good autobiographical story" or the "story in course of completion."

The "good soldier story" (CL 221) Lawrence had sold to

Austin Harrison at the *English Review* two months later is almost certainly "Honour and Arms." This story and "Vin Ordinaire" had both been purchased by Harrison by 6 October, for by that day Lawrence had asked Ezra Pound to send "Once" along to the *Review*, where it "would go excellently well with the two soldier stories" (CL 229). Late in the same month Lawrence reported that Harrison "has got three soldier stories, which he is going to publish in a sort of series—perhaps four—so he says—which will make a book afterwards" (CL 234–35). The fourth story, in Lawrence's "mind for a long time" (CL 229), was probably written out later as "The Mortal Coil." Harrison's idea for a little book of four Prussian stories must have been related to the growing tension with Kaiser Wilhelm's Germany, but the project never materialized. The *English Review* did publish both "Honour and Arms" and "Vin Ordinaire," but "Once" never appeared. As Lawrence feared, the subject matter was doubtless too bold for the times.

"The Prussian Officer" marks a significant breakthrough in Lawrence's art. Some critics, noticing the differences between the magazine and book versions of the tale, have talked about Lawrence's skill in revision as a way of accounting for the breakthrough. However, if they had examined a revised holograph of the story owned by Humanities Research Center of the University of Texas at Austin, they would have reached a strikingly different conclusion. Although sixty years have passed since Lawrence wrote this story, some of the most basic groundwork for critical appraisal still needs to be laid. In contrast, a study of the development of "The Thorn in the Flesh" offers a particularly radiant example of Lawrence's remarkable—and by this time familiar—growth at this crucial point of transition.

Lawrence's artistic breakthrough with "The Prussian Officer" is important to my argument, but, for reasons that will shortly become apparent, I will be relegating my specific discussion of the textual evolution of the story to Appendix A. Most of this chapter will be devoted to a consideration of the following versions of "The Thorn in the Flesh":

1. "Vin Ordinaire." Originally written in mid-June 1913. Magazine text of the story, published in the *English Review*, June 1914.
2. "The Thorn in the Flesh." July 1914 revision; Hopkin proof version.
3. "The Thorn in the Flesh." Hopkin proof text revised in October 1914 for inclusion in *The Prussian Officer*. Final text.

"The Prussian Officer," which is almost certainly the inspiration for Hemingway's little short story "A Simple Enquiry," has proven curiously elusive to critics. It has been discussed in terms of psychological theory, homosexuality and *Blutbrüderschaft*, and German militarism.[1] A letter Lawrence wrote Garnett in the autumn of 1912 bears directly on the homosexual element of the story:

I wanted to get into a corner and howl over the *Jeanne d'Arc* [a play written by Garnett]. Cruelty is a form of perverted sex. . . . And soldiers, being herded together, men without women, never being *satisfied* by a woman, as a man never is from a street affair, get their surplus sex and their frustration and dissatisfaction into the blood, and *love* cruelty. It is sex lust fermented makes atrocity. (CL 156)

In "The Prussian Officer," clearly enough, "sex lust fermented

1. Ann Englander has written an article entitled " 'The Prussian Officer': The Self Divided" (*Sewanee Review*, 71 [1963], 605–19) in which she sets up a model of Lawrence's psychological theory and then attacks the story for not conforming to it. Frank Amon ("D. H. Lawrence and the Short Story," in *The Achievement of D. H. Lawrence*, ed. Frederick J. Hoffman and Harry T. Moore [Norman, Okla., 1953], pp. 227–28) is among the critics who have pointed out the homosexual overtones of the story, while Mark Spilka (*The Love Ethic of D. H. Lawrence* [Bloomington, Ind., 1955], p. 172) says "there is nothing homosexual about this relationship." Harry T. Moore (*D. H. Lawrence: His Life and Works* [New York, 1964], pp. 95–96) discusses the story in terms of "Lawrence's attitude to militarism, particularly of the German brand," and Anthony West (*D. H. Lawrence* [London, 1950], p. 98), rather remarkably praises it for arriving at "something generally true about Germans."

makes atrocity." The homosexual implications of the tale seem
to be purposive, and a case can be made for interpreting
the story in the light of psychological speculation and even
of antimilitarism. However, I feel that Lawrence's sensibility
is engaged at a deeper level.

"The Prussian Officer" is a fully achieved embodiment
of Lawrentian metaphysic—of the dualistic vision so centrally
significant to his best art. The Captain and his orderly are a
complementary pair. The Captain, dominant and masculine,
is fair, tall, and slender, with challenging blue eyes. Schöner,
submissive and feminine, is short and swarthy, with heavy
limbs and receptive dark eyes. These pairs of opposites function within the larger framework of antitheses that give the
story structure: the valley and the mountains, heat and cold,
life and death. The orderly has "dark, expressionless eyes, that
seemed never to have thought, only to have received life
direct through his senses, and acted straight from instinct"
(PO 4). In the story, his awakening into consciousness is a
violent experience that produces murder and his own death.

Lawrence's dualistic habit of mind has often been remarked,
and critics are coming to realize its critical importance in his
art and thought. The *Study of Thomas Hardy*, written in 1914
after the final revision of the *Prussian Officer* stories, is primarily
an occasion for Lawrence to explore aspects of his dualistic
universe. The final *Prussian Officer* revision is of course part
of the same creative moment. The interesting point here is
that the sexual and metaphysical polarities of "The Prussian
Officer" itself predate both the first draft of *The Rainbow* and
the *Study of Thomas Hardy*. In writing the story, he seems to
"find" the metaphysic complete and fully articulated. The
dualistic vision at the heart of the story is a version of the
dynamic polarity between the Brangwen men and the
Brangwen women. It also prefigures the dualistic speculations
of such works of the twenties as *Fantasia of the Unconscious*.[2]

2. Also consider the following passage from Lawrence's review of Trigant
Burrow's *The Social Basis of Consciousness*, published in 1927: "The real
trouble lies in the inward sense of 'separateness' which dominates every

Schöner, the young soldier of "The Prussian Officer," can also be found playing the role of a Bavarian peasant in "The Crucifix Across the Mountains," the first essay of *Twilight in Italy.* The earlier version of the piece, "Christs in the Tirol," was written in August or September of 1912 and was first published in the *Saturday Westminster Gazette* in March 1913, but the peasant emerged only when Lawrence transformed the piece into "The Crucifix Across the Mountains" for inclusion in the travel book. This revision probably dates from the autumn of 1915, over two years after the composition of the story. The language and symbolic structure of the story are taken over intact into the travel essay, and Lawrence's evocation of the Brangwen men also comes to mind. The peasant's body is a "hot welter of physical sensation," his mind is flushed "with a blood heat, a blood sleep." This "flow of sensuous experience" at last "drives him almost mad." In contrast, "overhead there is always the strange radiance of the mountains": "the ice and the upper radiance of snow are brilliant with timeless immunity from the flux and the warmth of life." "The Prussian Officer" is the story of the journey Schöner makes from the warm valley of life to the icy eternity of death when he is awakened from his "sleep, this heat of physical experience" by his captain. Schöner's progression to violence and death parallels the peasant's "crucifixion."[3] As in so much of Lawrence's best work, the crucifixion is the tragic split between our mental and sensual being.

A reader does not need to know about Lawrence's dualistic

---

man. At a certain point in his evolution, man becomes cognitively conscious: he bit the apple: he began to know. Up till that time his consciousness flowed unaware, as in the animals. Suddenly, his consciousness split" (*Phoenix,* p. 378).

3. *Twilight in Italy,* quoted from *D. H. Lawrence and Italy: Twilight in Italy, Sea and Sardinia, Etruscan Places,* p. 5. Copyright 1972 by The Viking Press, Inc. Copyright 1921 by Thomas Seltzer, Inc., renewed 1949 by Frieda Lawrence. All rights reserved. Reprinted by permission of Laurence Pollinger Ltd., the Estate of the late Mrs. Frieda Lawrence, and The Viking Press, Inc.

vision or quasiphilosophical speculation in order to respond
to "The Prussian Officer." Lawrence successfully translates
his ideas into a compelling, almost expressionist, narrative
charting the course of an intense relationship between two
men. Theory is not obtrusive, but it does form the foundation
of the story. "The Prussian Officer" is a splendid early example
of the interplay of Lawrentian art and metaphysic. The
metaphysic involved anticipates *The Rainbow* and Lawrence's
greatest work as a novelist.

In January 1958 an article by Roger Dataller entitled
"Mr. Lawrence and Mrs. Woolf" appeared in *Essays in
Criticism*. Dataller contends that Woolf's low opinion of Lawrence's style was a blind spot and argues for Lawrence's
conscious craftsmanship by means of a lengthy comparison
of the magazine versions of two short stories with the versions
of the same tales as they appeared in *The Prussian Officer and
Other Stories*. The stories that form the basis of his argument are
"The Prussian Officer" and "The Thorn in the Flesh."

"Mr. Lawrence and Mrs. Woolf" contains a fundamental
error that stands as a warning to the Lawrence scholar to
beware the textual pitfalls of the early short fiction. Dataller
reports that "since there are two printed versions of each
story, one for magazine publication and the other for the book,
we are able by following Lawrence's revision to note the interplay of his mind and technique. The themes were not fundamentally changed, but there were significant readjustments.
'The Prussian Officer' he extended by no less than 1,500
words. . . . "[4] However, if Dataller had had access to the
Humanities Research Center, he would have learned that
a comparison of magazine and book versions of "The Prussian
Officer" cannot possibly give us any insight into the "interplay of [Lawrence's] mind and technique." The 1,500 words
"added" to the book version can be found in a holograph

---

4. Roger Dataller, "Mr. Lawrence and Mrs. Woolf," *Essays in Criticism*,
8 (1958), 50. Dataller is generally accurate about "The Thorn in the
Flesh," but the essay suffers from a yearning to make Lawrence more like
Woolf and Joyce.

that antedates both magazine and book texts. Lawrence cut
these words before magazine publication and subsequently
restored them when the story was to be included in his book.
In comparing magazine and book texts we are not really
"following Lawrence's revision." Instead we are merely
discovering which passages of the story were left out of the
English Review and were then put back for *The Prussian Officer
and Other Stories.*

The evidence that this is what took place is definitive.
The story of the curious textual history of "The Prussian
Officer" will be found in Appendix A, along with a consideration of the extant texts. Certainly these texts—revised holograph, magazine version, Hopkin proof text, final text—all
differ one from the other, but they do not differ in a way that is
revealing, that brings us any significant news about Lawrence's
art or his growth to maturity. "The Prussian Officer" is the
most famous story in Lawrence's first collection of tales;
perhaps it's the best. However, the important fact concerning
the story for this study is that, unlike the other major stories
in the collection, it required no fundamental reseeing, no
systematic revision. Lawrence did not need to return to trans-
port the story into that terrain beyond the old stable ego of
the character, for the story needed no transporting. It was
structured by his metaphysic even in its original holograph
form dating from the late spring of 1913. Lawrence's excited
comment on first completing the story—"I have written the
best story I have ever done" (CL 209)—indicates an awareness that he has achieved something radically different from
the earlier tales. "The Prussian Officer" reverses the significant
pattern that is the primary occasion of this book. But in doing
so, it also prefigures what would happen one year later when
Lawrence decided to transform the other strong stories in the
Prussian Officer collection.

In contrast the transformation of "Vin Ordinaire" into "The
Thorn in the Flesh" is one of the most fascinating studies
in the making of the *Prussian Officer* stories and a *locus classicus*

for the emergence of the mature Lawrence. A consideration
of the three extant versions of the tale offers definitive evidence
that rewriting was to Lawrence nearly as creative as original
composition.

"Vin Ordinaire" appeared in the *English Review* in June
1914. The story, perhaps obliquely influenced by Thomas
Hardy's "The Melancholy Hussar of the German Legion,"[5]
concerns a young soldier's act of rebellion against the military
and his flight to his sweetheart. Bachmann's fear of heights
leads to his humiliation during a scaling exercise and causes
him, inadvertently but instinctively, to knock his sergeant from
the top of the earthworks into a moat far below. He flees to
his sweetheart and spends the night with her before he is
recaptured the next morning. The simple outline of the action
is a constant in all versions, but even though he had written
the story a year earlier, he revised and recast it extensively
and changed its title to "The Thorn in the Flesh" before
sending it off to Garnett for inclusion in *The Prussian Officer*.
We know from the letter to Garnett on 4 July 1914 that it
was in fact the last story to be revised. Lawrence found "it
wants writing over again, to pull it together" (AH 201). The
revision of the story successfully tightened it—and in the
process it became a remarkably different work of art.

For reasons of clarity, I will build my argument on the
dramatic contrast between the magazine and *Prussian Officer*
versions. The text of the story found in the Hopkin proofs is
the direct result of Lawrence's attempt to "pull it together"
in July. Lawrence truly seems to have "found" his story in this
revision, but there is nevertheless much verbal variation
between the proof and final versions, a good deal of which
serves to focus the central themes more sharply. Although I
will be concentrating on magazine and *Prussian Officer* texts,
I will also be referring to the proof versions for illustrative
purposes. The story achieved its full narrative intensity only
in the revision of the proofs in October.

5. "The Young Soldier with Bloody Spurs," a poem sent to Edward
Garnett in August 1912 and left unpublished in Lawrence's lifetime,
also deals with similar materials. See AH 51–55.

One interesting incidental feature of the Hopkin proof version is its two overt references to the "thorn" of the story's revised title, an image directly associated with Bachmann's shame. At the end of the first scene between Bachmann, Emilie, and Ida, the soldier "dared not touch it, probe it, draw out the thorn, and bear the hurt to its depth" (H 263). After the night spent with his sweetheart he thinks about the freedom he has won: "he had drawn the thorn from his body, the stigma from his shame" (H 273). The *Prussian Officer* text contains no direct allusion to the title. When Lawrence revised the tale for the last time in October 1914, he decided to let the title stand on its own, thereby expanding its symbolic resonances. We have already observed that he was so taken with the new title—and the new story—that he suggested it as the title for the entire collection.[6]

The method of recasting the story is a more drastic version of that used in the final revision of "The White Stocking." "Vin Ordinaire" has five sections, "The Thorn in the Flesh," six. The revision of Sections I and II is a free rewriting that at the same time carefully follows the earlier text. The second paragraphs of the two texts display the characteristic pattern of revision:

"Vin Ordinaire"	"The Thorn in the Flesh"
The barracks were a collection of about a dozen huts of corrugated iron, that sweltered like Dutch ovens on the hot summer plain, but were gay with nasturtiums climbing ambitiously up. The soldiers were always outside, either working in the patch of vegetable garden, or sitting in the shade, when not at drill in the yard enclosed by the wire fence. (VO 298)[7]	Among the fields by the lime trees stood the barracks, upon bare, dry ground, a collection of round-roofed huts of corrugated iron, where the soldiers' nasturtiums climbed brilliantly. There was a tract of vegetable garden at the side, with the soldiers' yellowish lettuces in rows, and at the back the big, hard drilling yard surrounded by a wire fence. (PO 34)

6. Lawrence to Edward Garnett, 17[?] July 1914, unpublished letter in the Henry W. and Albert A. Berg Collection of the New York Public Library.

7. The abbreviation VO refers to "Vin Ordinaire," published in the *English Review* in June 1914 (vol. 17, pp. 298–315).

Barracks, climbing nasturtiums, vegetable garden, and drill yard enclosed by wire fence are common to both passages. The content of these two paragraphs is so similar that Lawrence must have had the first one before him when writing the second. Yet something much less mechanical than spot retouching took place. The material is the same, but Lawrence has completely rewritten the paragraph.

Paragraphs in the first two sections of "The Thorn in the Flesh" are based on paragraphs in "Vin Ordinaire." The sequence of events of these sections is nearly identical, the content is close, and the language has much in common—and yet the sections are very different. "Vin Ordinaire" serves as a jumping-off point. It is altered but never completely abandoned. The changes in these sections of the story are more than a revision but less than a complete rewriting. All of Sections I and II of the texts can be laid out in parallel, as can Section V of the magazine text with Section VI of the book text.[8]

The middle sections of the story reveal a different pattern of revision, and it is here that the tale fully attains its new shape. Sections III and IV of "Vin Ordinaire" are deleted and are replaced by new material in Sections III, IV, and V of "The Thorn in the Flesh," with only a few verbal echoes remaining from the earlier version. The new material carries an entirely different burden of meaning, and the story is completely transformed. The first five paragraphs of Section VI of "The Thorn in the Flesh" also have no precedent. The sixth paragraph of Section VI of the final text links up with Section V of "Vin Ordinaire," and for the rest of the story "The Thorn in the Flesh" follows the text of its predecessor in the same way the first two sections of the stories are related.

In tightening up "Vin Ordinaire," Lawrence more sharply focused character, motivation, and action. The blurred meaning of "Vin Ordinaire" gives way to the clear, almost programmatic meaning of "The Thorn in the Flesh." In the

8. This does not take into account paragraphs that are deleted and new paragraphs that are added.

summer of 1914 he transformed his story into a kind of parable of a man's relation to his woman and to the demands of his society.

In "Vin Ordinaire" the handsome Bachmann has "something young and conceited about him, something swagger and generous" (VO 299). He easily fills his weekly postcard to his mother. In "The Thorn in the Flesh" his "youthful swagger" is "in suppression now." Instead there is a "self-conscious strain in his blue eyes, and a pallor about his mouth." He "mechanically" scribbles a few lines to his mother but, nervous about the wall-scaling ahead of him, breaks off, able to "write no more. Out of the knot of his consciousness no word would come" (PO 35). The Bachmann of "The Thorn in the Flesh" has been made more awkward and self-conscious than his predecessor and much less able to function smoothly in the military machine. In "Vin Ordinaire" it is made clear that in spite of his panic, he is about to make it over the wall on his own when he is pulled up from above. There is no hint in "The Thorn in the Flesh" that Bachmann would have succeeded by himself. Lawrence sacrifices a touch of irony and drama for clearer characterization.

In "The Thorn in the Flesh" the shame the young soldier feels because of his failure is a key structural principle. Driven by shame because of his disgrace, he finds fulfillment with Emilie and realizes how irrelevant his shame had been. Shame hardly figures as a motivation in the earlier version. In "Vin Ordinaire," after being pulled up, he is at first "still too stunned to know anything but shame," but this soon gives way to "a fierce, self-destroying rage" and to "hate and self-justification" (VO 303). In the revision the only emotion left in this passage is "tension of shame" (PO 40). The revised version of the key passage in which the climbing Bachmann realizes that he has involuntarily urinated also heightens the emphasis on shame: shame is mentioned only once in the magazine passage, four times in the revision. In "The Thorn in the Flesh," when the soldier runs away after knocking the sergeant into the moat, he feels "the steady burning of shame in the flesh," the "raw, steady-burning shame" (PO 42). At the same point in "Vin Ordinaire" Bachmann feels hatred for the army and worries about the shame his failure will cause his mother. Lawrence so greatly heightened the emphasis on Bachmann's shame with the resolution of his revised story well in mind. He wanted to equip his soldier with a sharper sense of failure in order to make the ultimate wholeness and harmony all the more wonderful.

In "The Thorn in the Flesh" the soldiers become automatons: the first soldier to scale the wall has a "blank, mechanical look," the sergeant sees Bachmann "as a mechanical thing" (PO 38). However, there is nothing mechanical about Bachmann's experience as his climbs the ladder. Lawrence devotes twice as many words to this description in the revised text. The "blind gush of white-hot fear" that almost melts "his belly and all his joints" has no precedent in "Vin Ordinaire," nor does the moment when "all of him, body and soul, . . . [grows] hot to fusion point" (PO 39). This is the language of the back-washing scene in "Daughters of the Vicar" and of the scenes of passion in *The Rainbow*.

In the second section of the story, Bachmann goes to seek shelter at the Baron's house, where Emilie is the servant. His "static" (PO 43) look as he rides the tram toward his sweetheart was added only when Lawrence revised the Hopkin proofs in October—a change that introduces the theoretical vocabulary of this period. Emilie has been greatly altered in revision. Lawrence devotes most of the third section of "The Thorn in the Flesh" to describing the background of Emilie and of Bachmann, but even in the second section she has acquired a larger quantity of Lawrentian vitality. In "Vin Ordinaire" she is "very dark, with closely-banded black hair, proud, almost cold grey eyes, and the faint shadow of hair darkening her upper lip" (VO 306). In "The Thorn in the Flesh" her eyes are "the proud, timid eyes of some wild animal, some proud animal," and she has "strong maiden breasts" (PO 44). In "Vin Ordinaire," when Bachmann says he would like to hide for a night before trying to escape to France,

Emilie lowers her eyes; at the same point in "The Thorn in the Flesh" she gazes at him "with steady, watchful grey eyes" (PO 45). In "Vin Ordinaire" the soldier watches Emilie's "proud, straight back, her strong loins" (VO 307) as she leaves the room. In the revised text he looks at her "flat, straight back and her strong loins" (PO 45) as she bends over the stove, a suggestively sexual position. Bachmann becomes "bashful and strained" (PO 44) when he explains his situation in "The Thorn in the Flesh" and feels within himself "the dross of shame and incapacity" (PO 46), for the awkward young soldier is still psychologically short of manhood. In four short paragraphs added to the revised text, Bachmann's awkwardness and sense of failure are posed directly against Emilie's pride of bearing:

> "You could sleep with me," Fräulein Hesse said to her.
> Emilie lifted her eyes and looked at the young man, direct, clear, reserving herself.
> "Do you want that?" she asked, her strong virginity proof against him.
> "Yes—yes—" he said uncertainly, destroyed by shame. (PO 46)

Emilie is proud, reserved, and somewhat remote. In the Hopkin proof text of July, Lawrence had even emphasized her foreignness by having her speak a little pidgin English—"I come soon" (H 262)—a decision he wisely reconsidered.

One of the most striking alterations of "Vin Ordinaire" is the passage describing Emilie's little room and Bachmann's response to it. A lifelike crucifix is the most noticeable detail in the room. This is made much of in "Vin Ordinaire":

> His senses quickened, he perceived for the first time in his life that the carved figure on the Cross was that of a young man, thin and wasted and cramped. It was a crucifix carved by a peasant-worker in Bavaria. The Christ was lean and rather bony, with high cheekbones and a dead face, the mouth hanging slightly open. He was a common man. Bachmann had seen many a peasant who might have been his brother. And it startled him. He was shocked to think of the cramped torture the man must have gone through. He wondered what Emilie . . . thought when she looked at the naked,

dead man carved there. "It might be me," thought the soldier.[9] (VO 309)

In "Vin Ordinaire" Bachmann, an uncomfortable stranger in the room, is upset about Emilie's religion and becomes "violently Protestant" (VO 309). In "The Thorn in the Flesh" the same bedroom is "foreign but restoring to him" (PO 47). The violent Protestantism is excised, and the description of the crucifix is greatly abbreviated (with the heavy-handed linking of Bachmann to Christ eliminated): "He looked at the crucifix. It was a long, lean, peasant Christ carved by a peasant in the Black Forest. For the first time in his life, Bachmann saw the figure as a human thing. It represented a man hanging there in helpless torture. He stared at it, closely, as if for new knowledge" (PO 47–48). In the revision Bachmann feels "safe, in sanctuary" (PO 47) in Emilie's room, the place where he is to attain manhood and human fulfillment: as late as the Hopkin proofs he had felt "safe, and yet out of place" (H 262). When he goes to the window, he sees a "shimmering, afternoon country" (PO 47) outside. The "shimmeriness" suggests Lawrence's vital, kinetic universe.[10] Bachmann's vision as he looks out the window is a hint that he is about to have an experience that will put him in closer contact with the forces of the Lawrentian cosmos.

Section II of "Vin Ordinaire" ends with Bachmann partially undressing and lying down to rest, hoping fervently that Emilie

9. Like "The Prussian Officer," "The Thorn in the Flesh" makes use of Lawrence's memories of his walk through Southern Germany with Frieda, and Emilie's crucifix is a leaner version of a crucifix described in "Christs in the Tirol."

10. Cf. Paul Morel's painterly vision of the universe: "Only the shimmeriness is the real living. The shape is a dead crust" (SL 152). When Lawrence's sister Ada was going through a religious crisis in 1911, he wrote her a consoling letter in which he defined God as "a vast, shimmering impulse which waves onwards towards some end" (CL 76). As late as *Mornings in Mexico.*, "everything, everything is the wonderful shimmer of creation." From *Mornings in Mexico* (London: Secker, 1927; New York: Alfred A. Knopf, Inc., 1927), p. 113 (N.Y. ed.). Copyright 1927 by Alfred A. Knopf, Inc. Quoted by permission of Laurence Pollinger Ltd. and the Estate of the late Mrs. Frieda Lawrence.

will come. At the same point in "The Thorn in the Flesh," Bachmann's flesh burns with "restless shame," making him feel "unutterably heavy." He "mechanically" takes off boots, belt, and tunic, lies down and falls into "a kind of drugged sleep" (PO 48). The sleep signals the significant change in being that is about to come to pass. Lawrence ends this section brilliantly. Emilie appears briefly to look in on him "sunk in sleep": "She saw his pure white flesh, very clean and beauti-ful. . . . His legs, in the blue uniform trousers, his feet in the coarse stockings, lay foreign on her bed. She went away" (PO 48). It is the social man who is entrammeled in uniform trousers and coarse stockings. The "pure white flesh, very clean and beautiful," belongs to the man himself. The tableau of the sleeping soldier is an image of the two poles of the story, and it is Emilie who will be instrumental in the liberation of the real man.

Lawrence was displeased with the third and fourth sections of "Vin Ordinaire," and when he revised the story for inclusion in *The Prussian Officer*, he completely dispensed with them. Section III describes a scene of passion between Bachmann and Emilie, Section IV contains their thoughts as they lie awake after they have separated. It is hard to find fault with Lawrence's decision to eliminate these sections.

Much of Lawrence's passion-prose does not read very well half a century later, but he is not entirely to blame. In the England of 1915 *The Rainbow* was suppressed as an obscene book. Physical love is essential throughout the Lawrence canon, but until *Lady Chatterley's Lover* he did not dare to describe it without a good deal of indirection. The main complaint to be leveled against the passion-prose, its fuzziness and imprecision, is at least partly attributable to its obscurantist function. The passion-prose in Section III of "Vin Ordinaire" is par-ticularly awkward:

He was kissing her throat. She did not know what she was panting for, waiting for. But his mouth, with the soft moustache, was moving across her throat to her cheek, and at last their mouths met. She met him in the long, blind, final kiss that hurt them both. And then in positive pain, blind, unconscious, she clutched him to her. She did not know what it was that hurt her with sheer pain. He, shuddering slightly, was growing afraid, so unconscious and awful she seemed. With trembling fingers he unbuttoned her bodice to feel the breasts that had been in his consciousness so long, buttoned firm under her cotton dress. He found them, and she started with agony.

Then her mouth met his mouth again. And now she was sheer instinct. It was so powerful that she would have died if she had to be taken from him at this moment. It went through her limbs till she felt she was sinking loose. (VO 311)

It is impossible to know exactly what is happening in the above paragraph. However, Section IV makes it clear that the love is not consummated. Emilie returns home bearing Bachmann "some deep, unfathomed grudge" (VO 311). She lies awake all night suffering "the slow, mean misery of half-satisfaction" and "burning almost with hate of him." "The whole woman in her" is "like a thing bound down" because Bachmann did not "finish what he had begun." Meanwhile Bachmann sleeps "uneasily" through the night. His earlier failure has been compounded by his failure with Emilie. He lies in bed "feeling without honour and without worth" (VO 312).

The middle sections of "The Thorn in the Flesh" transform the earlier story into an entirely new work of fiction. Section III, as noted above, is devoted to sketching in the background of Emilie and Bachmann. Emilie is a "foundling, probably of some gipsy race, . . . a naive, paganly religious being" (PO 48–49). She is "naturally secluded in herself, of a reserved, native race" and is "primitive" and "fiercely virgin" (PO 49). She is repelled by the casual sex she sees all around her between soldiers and "the common girls" (PO 50). She is "virgin," "shy," "primitive," and needs "to be in subjection" (PO 51): "Her whole nature was at peace in the service of real masters or mistresses. For her, a gentleman had some mystic quality that left her free and proud in service. . . . Her desire was to serve" (PO 50). Swarthy men replete with life-giving qualities that are lacking in unawakened English heroines abound in Lawrence's fiction of the 1920s. In "The Thorn in the Flesh" it is Bachmann who is unawakened. Emilie is a heroine of the same species as Joe Boswell of "The Virgin and the Gipsy," Phoenix and Lewis of "St. Mawr," and the peasant of "Sun," to name only a few. However, the question of whether Lawrence may have supplied his heroine with a few too many impressive Lawrentian antecedents and credentials legitimately arises. In reshaping the character of Emilie according to his new version of the story, he went a little too far and made her background too schematic. Interestingly, most of the language of servitude quoted above was added only in the October revision of the proofs—and this language seems rather questionable.

Nor was he content to leave Bachmann an ordinary soldier:

... He came of a rich farming stock, rich for many generations. His father was dead, his mother controlled the moneys for the time being. But if Bachmann wanted a hundred pounds at any moment, he could have them. ... The family had the farming, smithy, and waggon-building of their village. They worked because that was the form of life they knew. If they had chosen, they could have lived independent upon their means.

In this way, he was a gentleman in sensibility. ... He had, moreover, his native, fine breeding. (PO 50–51)

As a natural aristocrat, Bachmann is qualified to play master to Emilie with her need "to be in subjection." This unattractive conception of the relationship between man and woman seems forced onto the story, nor is it unique in the canon. With Lawrence's own working-class background in mind, Bachmann's innate gentility and "native, fine breeding" take on unpleasant overtones. The information about Bachmann's background does not improve the story and tends to schematize its art. It is odd that he should have added this element to the final version of "The Thorn in the Flesh" at the same time he was deemphasizing class in "Daughters of the Vicar."

In Section IV of "The Thorn in the Flesh," when soldiers come round to inquire after Bachmann, the governess and

Emilie say they have not seen him. In the Hopkin proofs Emilie is troubled that "the lover, Bachmann, who should be to her a new and a closest giver of authority, was only dependent on her" (H 267). This is changed strikingly in the *Prussian Officer* text: "the lover, Bachmann, who was he, what was he? He alone of all men contained for her the unknown quantity which terrified her beyond her service" (PO 52). This last-minute alteration raises ultimate questions about human identity. One thinks of Mrs. Bates as she washes the body of her dead husband, Louisa Lindley as she washes Alfred Durant's back, John Adderley Syson as he lies on the "dry brown turf" (PO 172) and wonders about his transformed sweetheart.

Lawrence sends the Baron and Baronness out for the evening so that Emilie may go up to Bachmann undisturbed. The passion-prose takes an extreme form even before Bachmann touches her: "The moment she entered the room where the man sat alone, waiting intensely, the thrill passed through her, she died in terror, and after the death, a great flame gushed up, obliterating her" (PO 53). As late as the Hopkin proofs of July we read only that "the thrill passed through the passionate, secluded girl" (H 268). In the final text Lawrence also finds a printable way to record the first contact persuasively and even movingly in language reminiscent of *The Rainbow*: "As she came quite close, almost invisibly he lifted his arms and put them round her waist, drawing her with his will and desire. He buried his face into her apron, into the terrible softness of her belly. And he was a flame of passion intense about her" (PO 53–54). There is no ambiguity about what happens between Bachmann and Emilie in "The Thorn in the Flesh." The love is consummated, and consummated beautifully: "And he was restored and completed, close to her. That little . . . clasp of acknowledgment that she gave him in her satisfaction, roused his pride unconquerable. They loved each other, and all was whole. She loved him, he had taken her, she was given to him. It was right. He was given to her, and they were one, complete" (PO 54). Emilie, the perfect servant, feels "reverence and gratitude." For Bachmann, "shame and memory" vanish in the "furious flame of passion," and his "pride unconquerable" is "roused." He sits on the side of the bed, "escaped, liberated, wondering, and happy" (PO 54). Only in the October revision of the Hopkin proofs do the lovers rise for the first time "transfigured with happiness" (PO 54). Literal escape from the army is no longer important, for now Bachmann is inwardly free. The art of "The Thorn in the Flesh" contains something like a Lawrentian program for the social man and the private man.

In Section v of "The Thorn in the Flesh" plans are laid for escape but they no longer matter, for now Bachmann has "the inner satisfaction and liberty" (PO 55). As in "Daughters of the Vicar," the lovers plan to flee to North America. The soldier goes out to mail the postcard to his mother—an important detail not present in "Vin Ordinaire"—and then sits down to ponder the events of the day. He has come through to self-acceptance and true manhood:

Still, a flush of shame came alight in him at the memory. But he said to himself: "What does it matter?—I can't help it, well then I can't. If I go up a height, I get absolutely weak, and can't help myself." Again memory came over him, and a gush of shame, like fire. But he sat and endured it. It had to be endured, admitted, and accepted. "I'm not a coward, for all that," he continued. "I'm not afraid of danger. If I'm made that way, that heights melt me and make me let go my water"—it was torture for him to pluck at this truth—"if I'm made like that I shall have to abide by it, that's all. It isn't all of me." He thought of Emilie, and was satisfied. "What I am, I am; and let it be enough," he thought. (PO 56)

The fire of shame has yielded to the fire of passion: fittingly, Bachmann and Emilie make love again at the end of the section. In the embrace of passion they find "victory" and "deep satisfaction" (PO 57). In the proofs she lies "close" to him "in peace" (H 272); in the final text she "lies close in her static reality" (PO 57)—another detail, probably not an improvement, that shows the late insertion of Lawrentian metaphysic.

At the end of the fourth section of "Vin Ordinaire," Bachmann stands "looking out of the window" (VO 313) and
hears the bugle sounding from the barracks. At the beginning
of the sixth section of "The Thorn in the Flesh," Bachmann
and Emilie look out the window *together*. She loves his body,
"proud and blond and able to take command," and he loves
hers, "soft and eternal." Emilie is now "in a new world of her
own" and is "curiously happy and absorbed" (PO 57) as she
does her work, which seems like "a delicious outflow,
like sunshine." Bachmann muses again about the unimportance
of "absolute, imperious freedom" now that he has "won to
his own being, in himself and Emilie" and "drawn the
stigma from his shame" (PO 58). One crucial change in this
passage came only in October. In the proofs Bachmann is "free
of" himself (H 273); in the final text he is "beginning
to be himself" (PO 58). Freedom is achieved by discovery of
self, not by escape from self. Bachmann's reverie is dramatically
interrupted: "Suddenly he heard voices, and a tramping of feet.
His heart gave a great leap, then went still. He was taken.
He had known all along" (PO 58). In "Vin Ordinaire"
Bachmann's capture is presented undramatically. At the point
of capture, the entirely new material in "The Thorn in the
Flesh" ends. The first paragraph of Section v of "Vin
Ordinaire" links up loosely with the sixth paragraph of Section
vi of "The Thorn in the Flesh" and the two versions follow each
other until the end of the texts.

At the beginning of 1871 Frieda's father received a wound in
his right hand that prevented him from ever again being
a soldier.[11] The Baron of the story, whose "right hand had
been shattered in the Franco-Prussian War" (VO 313), seems to
be a fictional version of Baron Friedrich von Richthofen.
This character becomes more sympathetic in the revised text.
Where he rails at Emilie in "Vin Ordinaire" for hiding a soldier
in her room, he prepares himself "for what he could do"
(PO 61) in "The Thorn in the Flesh." The Baron of the revised

11. Harry T. Moore, *The Priest of Love: A Life of D. H. Lawrence* (New
York, 1974), p. 142.

version even seems on the side of the lovers. He is changed primarily because Bachmann and Emilie have changed. Lawrence does not want the fulfillment they have experienced to be undercut by too much bullying at the end of the story.

Lawrence uses the last section of "The Thorn in the Flesh" to bring his thematic lines into final focus. In "Vin Ordinaire," when asked about Bachmann, Emilie stands "like a slave, by herself" (VO 314). In the revision she stands with "her whole naked soul before him" (PO 59). When the Baron confronts Bachmann in "The Thorn in the Flesh," Lawrence adds that he sees "the same naked soul exposed, as if he looked really into the *man*" (PO 60). In "Vin Ordinaire" he has been totally recaptured by the military machine and goes "obediently," his "expressionless face . . . raised in obedience" (VO 314). The revised text makes it clear that the Prussian army cannot touch the real man: "He stood at attention. But only the shell of his body was at attention. A curious silence, a blankness, like something eternal, possessed him. He remained true to himself" (PO 60). The "curious silence, a blankness, like something eternal" was added only in October.

As Bachmann is led by Emilie in "Vin Ordinaire," she holds her face "a little averted." He does not "want to look at her" even though her presence is "very real to him" (VO 315). The dominant note in the early version of the story is humiliation: humiliation at the fortification, humiliation in bed, humiliation at recapture. In "The Thorn in the Flesh" he does not look at her but only because he does not need to. They have achieved a peace and harmony beyond anything conceivable in the earlier version: "There Emilie stood with her face uplifted, motionless and expressionless. Bachmann did not look at her. They knew each other. They were themselves" (PO 61). In "Vin Ordinaire," when the Baron turns to Emilie after her lover has been taken out, she stands "more withdrawn than usual, as if waiting to defend herself" (VO 315). At the same point in "The Thorn in the Flesh," she looks up at him from "cutting bread," an emblem of life's fullness. Her eyes are "scarcely seeing": "She was too much herself.

The Baron saw the dark, naked soul of her body in her unseeing eyes" (PO 61).

Bachmann and Emilie have fought through to a truer world than the world of everyday life, to a world in which Bachmann's capture does not matter. Because they have found this world, Bachmann is "true to himself" and Emilie is "too much herself." It is of course significant that the soul the Baron discerns in Emilie's unseeing eyes is the "naked soul of her body." It is through our bodies that we make vital contact with the universe. The "blankness, like something eternal" that possesses Bachmann and the emptiness of Emilie's eyes express the impersonality of the love and passion they have experienced. "Transfigured" (PO 54) by their love-making, they relate to each other more deeply than at the level of human personality.

Lawrence's newfound interest in "the non-human in humanity" (CL 281–82) is apparent in the transformed "Thorn in the Flesh." The characters of Bachmann and Emilie are blurred and unfocused in "Vin Ordinaire," but Lawrence systematically clarifies them in his revision. The social roles of Bachmann and Emilie have no meaning. In the intensity and, paradoxically, in the impersonality of their relationship to each other, they discover their real selves. The many references to naked souls and being true to self demonstrate the author's attempt to make the theme of his story "carbon": that which is essential in male and female and in their conjunction. At the same time, perhaps curiously, the Bachmann and Emilie of the revised text seem more fully human.

"Vin Ordinaire" did need to be tightened up technically, and, with the clear exception of the intrusive third section, "The Thorn in the Flesh" is a far superior story. The story is made more dramatic, diction is improved, and excess verbiage is eliminated. Nevertheless, the real improvement is in its thematic and structural transformation. As I have argued, the insights that shaped the rewriting of "Vin Ordinaire," part of the creative moment that produced *The Rainbow*, are also related to the fulfillment Lawrence found with Frieda.

The letter Lawrence wrote A. W. McLeod shortly before revising "Vin Ordinaire," in which he states that "the only re-sourcing of art, revivifying it, is to make it more the joint work of man and woman," could be an explication of what he was attempting in revising the story of Bachmann and Emilie. "The source of all life and knowledge is in man and woman, and the source of all living is in the interchange and the meeting and mingling of these two: man-life and woman-life, man-knowledge and woman-knowledge, man-being and woman-being" (CL 280). There is no mistaking Frieda's importance in this turning point of Lawrence's career. The transformation of "Vin Ordinaire" into "The Thorn in the Flesh" is a dramatization in miniature of this moment of transition.

In *Pansies* Lawrence wrote a little poem urging each man to turn his breast "straight to the sun of suns" and another proclaiming that women should declare themselves "sun-women" (CP 525–26). These poems from the late 1920s are simply more glorified expressions of the "man-life" and "woman-life" mentioned in the letter to McLeod and dramatized in "The Thorn in the Flesh." Except for the period of *Aaron's Rod, Kangaroo,* and *The Plumed Serpent*—those years when Lawrence seems to have lost his way—he was to celebrate essential "man-life" and essential "woman-life" for the rest of his career.

Chapter VIII

Conclusion: End of Apprenticeship

"It's the end of my youthful period"

A distinction drawn by James Thorpe in "The Aesthetics of Textual Criticism" provides a useful vocabulary for considering the nature of the *Prussian Officer* revisions:

The basic proposition which I submit about works created by authorial revision is that each version is, either potentially or actually, another work of art. It remains a "potential" work of art—it is in process, it is becoming—so long as the author is still giving it shape, in his mind or in successive drafts or interlineations or in whatever manner he suspends those works which he is not yet ready to release to his usual public. On the other hand, the "actual" work of art is a version in which the author feels that his intentions have been sufficiently fulfilled to communicate it to the public, as his response to whatever kinds of pressure bear on him, from within or without, to release his work into a public domain.[1]

In nearly every instance the occasion for revising the *Prussian Officer* stories was external in origin: Austin Harrison's demand for the alteration of "Odour of Chrysanthemums," the October 1911 revision of "Daughters of the Vicar" so that Edward Garnett could try to place it, the concerted effort in 1913 to get old, unpublished short fiction into print, the Duckworth contract for *The Prussian Officer and Other Stories*. Nevertheless, with the possible exception of the required revision of "Odour of Chrysanthemums," the real pressure to revise came from within. Every new effort to publish an unsold story provoked new revision. Lawrence felt that personally and artistically he had moved on in the interim; consequently he needed to rewrite in order to register the advances.

Lawrence defended *The Rainbow* in a letter to Garnett early in 1914 by declaring that he was "changing, one way or the

1. James Thorpe, "The Aesthetics of Textual Criticism," *PMLA*, 80 (1965), 477–78.

other" (CL 263). Art was a process in exactly the same way that life was a process, and the two couldn't be separated. Personal change was immediately translatable into artistic change. There is no evidence that Duckworth required that he revise the twelve stories to be collected in *The Prussian Officer*: the important pressure was internal. Lawrence believed with entire justice that his work had entered a phase of important new original achievement. At such a moment he did not want his first collection of tales to be an assortment of relics from the past.

In 1914 Lawrence was ready to release his stories to the public, but only after they had received a final, transforming revision. Only then could potential move solidly into actual. The artistic integrity of these stories owes a good deal to Lawrence's progress toward self-knowledge. This period in which he felt so strongly that he had come into his own is characterized by rare poise and confidence—personally, aesthetically, and intellectually. That is the major reason that the best of the *Prussian Officer* stories, works that had remained in process for so many years, at last came to be truly and definitively completed.

In his article on the significance of the *Prussian Officer* volume, J. C. F. Littlewood imagines an ideal reader of Lawrence taking home the short story collection in December 1914 and starting in on it: "He has followed the earlier work and vividly remembers *Sons and Lovers*. He is astonished by this development, which seems to have been so assured as well as so rapid. The young author appears to have resolved a nagging problem of personal integration and gained a new freedom."[2] Littlewood accurately characterizes the great advance Lawrence made over his earlier fiction, as well as over the earlier versions of the stories. We have dwelt so long in the tangled thicket of particular textual revisions that it is well to keep such an overview in mind. The ease and assurance are unmistakable, doubly so if the final stories

2. J. C. F. Littlewood, "D. H. Lawrence's Early Tales," *Cambridge Quarterly*, 1 (spring 1966), p. 112.

are contrasted with the earlier versions. The *Prussian Officer*
tales, as we have seen, are a study in the emergence of Lawrence vision. One reviewer's complaint concerning the "want
of variety . . . about the motifs"[3] is really a negative perception
of the strong unity of the collection, a unity that emerged only
with the revisions of 1914. The vision of passionate communion across the gulf of human isolation, the new theoretical
framework that supports such a vision, and the new language
and heightened narrative intensity that express it: it is in these
qualities that the unity of *The Prussian Officer* can be located.

The late revisions of the stories and of *The Rainbow* seem to
me to parallel what happened in the process of the composition
of *Moby-Dick*. As Leon Howard has described it, "Melville . . .
began to revise his romantic narrative of the whale fishery
at a time when his reading of Hawthorne's stories and his
meeting with their author had just served as catalytic agent
for the precipitation in words of a new attitude toward human
nature which his mind had held in increasingly strong solution
for some years."[4] Lawrence experienced a similar leap forward.
In his case the catalysts seem to have been the sharply articulated quarrel about his new fictional theory with Edward
Garnett plus his awareness of the intense personal satisfaction
he was enjoying with Frieda. In *The Prussian Officer, The
Rainbow*, and *Moby-Dick* one can feel the writer reaching
higher, daring more, and achieving more than he ever had
before. The excitement of the new artistic launching-out
as well as of the emergence of the "new attitude toward
human nature" communicates itself almost tangibly. The
three books are also supreme examples of the artist's faith in his
medium: there is no sense of the writer imposing himself on his
work but rather a powerful feeling of the creation itself fighting
through to its own appropriate form.

The dynamic equilibrium of the *Prussian Officer* tales,
The Rainbow, and *Moby-Dick* was difficult to maintain. The

3. Review of *The Prussian Officer* in the *Bookman* (London), 47 (March 1915),
183.
4. Leon Howard, *Herman Melville: A Biography* (Berkeley, 1951), p. 169.

destructiveness of *Women in Love* and *Pierre* seems in fact to be partly directed against the aesthetic and visionary wholeness of the works immediately preceding them—or rather against the notion that such wholeness is possible. *Women in Love* and *Pierre* are both filled with a repressed violence that seems related to the authors' inability to reduplicate the powerfully harmonious artistic experience of *The Rainbow*, the best of the *Prussian Officer* tales, and *Moby-Dick*.[5]

Lawrence was to publish two other collections of short stories in his lifetime, as well as a volume containing three novellas. These later collections—especially *England, My England* and the *Ladybird* volume—have a definite unity, but there is no parallel to what we have witnessed in the long and complicated process of the making of the *Prussian Officer* volume. So much more was at stake during the *Prussian Officer* years. The creation of *The Rainbow* and of the final versions of the best of the stories was indeed the central act of self-discovery in Lawrence's artistic career. With these works he rightly believed he was attaining full artistic independence. He had defined and articulated his special gifts and powers and had found his true voice, and the letters of this period demonstrate that he knew it.

Emile Delavenay's description of the improvement found in the final revisions of the *Prussian Officer* tales misses the essential point of Lawrence's development:

Everywhere Lawrence has sought to achieve a more objective perspective, to efface those personal traits he subsequently found too obvious or too naive; he has worked over his dialogue to make it more natural, less verbose . . . ; he has developed the characters and made the incidents more probable, elaborating the detail and placing it more firmly in context. . . .[6]

Although the fact of such general technical improvement is

5. *Thieves of Fire* (New York, 1974), Denis Donoghue's study of the "Promethean imagination" in literature, explores some of the other similarities between Lawrence and Melville.

6. Emile Delavenay, *D. H. Lawrence, the Man and His Work: The Formative Years, 1885–1919* (Carbondale, Ill., 1972), p. 205.

undeniable, Delavenay has made the process too mechanical. The final revisions of these stories tell a tale of aesthetic and personal discovery, not of diligent repairs produced in a spirit of detached and dispassionate craftsmanship. Technical improvements were a *by-product* of the process of revision—of reseeing and reengagement—not the purpose toward which Lawrence directed his energies. As he wrote while Garnett was laboring at the scaling down of *Sons and Lovers*, "Trim and garnish my stuff I cannot—it must go" (CL 176).

Revision did involve much local retouching, but it was not conceived of in terms of such retouching. The point was to bring a fresh creative flow to his work in progress. If he found the right imaginative engagement, the story was apt to be enriched and transformed—and, along the way, tightened and improved technically.[7] I do not believe that he embarked on the last revision of "The White Stocking" with the purpose of heightening the sexuality or that he revised "Daughters of the Vicar" intent upon establishing a new theoretical framework. Only in the heat of fresh discovery did he see his stories anew. The technical refinements were a by-product of the new confrontation with the text.

The developmental, "exploratory" nature of Lawrence's imagination is crucial to an understanding of his art, never more so than during this transitional period. For example, the insights garnered from the final revision of the *Prussian Officer* stories contributed directly to the abstract exposition of the *Study of Thomas Hardy*, and in turn the *Study*—as well as the fresh immersion in Hardy's fiction—helped shape *The Rainbow*. With *The Rainbow* Lawrence achieved as much artistic resolution as he was ever to enjoy, but, as we have observed, he kept moving onward. The 1915 revisions of the earlier Italian essays include the first complex expression of Lawrence's mature racial and historical theories (though these theories were hinted at in a few of the *Prussian Officer* tales). The revisions of *Twilight in Italy* introduce and develop some

---

7. This did not always happen: witness the strident, ill-conceived ending of the 1911 *English Review* version of "Odour of Chrysanthemums."

of the ideas that achieve more systematic statement in *The Crown*. In *Twilight in Italy* the ideas are still related to a narrative sequence, but *The Crown* is like the *Study* in being abstract and expository. Both *Twilight* and *The Crown* in turn have a direct impact on *Women in Love*. My point in this blow-by-blow account is to illustrate the highly organic nature of Lawrence's development, as well as the perpetual intertwining of art and idea. It is finally not possible to separate Lawrence the artist from Lawrence the "thinker."

Of course Lawrence's "pseudo-philosophy" is anything but a practical guide to living. If the Lawrentian metaphysic is to be taken seriously as an ethos, many a confirmed Lawrentian would probably begin to entertain second thoughts. The ideas he was working with during this period comprise an honest attempt to open people up to the larger possibilities of life, to lead them to more intense perception and to fuller experience. At the same time, there is no mistaking the fact that the ideas embody a deep suspicion of ordinary human relationship.

Impersonality is a key concept in the Lawrentian metaphysic because Lawrence felt badly scarred by the personal relationships in his life. He had concluded that a love relationship conducted on a personal basis can only result in possessiveness and exploitation: that had been his own experience with his mother and with Jessie Chambers. Will and Anna relate to one another in the sheaf-stacking scene in *The Rainbow*, not as man and woman, but as elemental beings out of the great unknown. Such a relationship may make sense when encountered safely within the confines of a novel, but it's difficult to imagine living a life in such terms.

The finely realized cherry-tree scene in the "Test on Miriam" chapter in *Sons and Lovers* helps illuminate this problem. Though the passage lacks the foundation in metaphysic that would come later in Lawrence's work, it nevertheless anticipates the artistic world of *The Rainbow*. The scene vividly dramatizes some of the central issues in the "pseudo-philosophy" that would soon be emerging.

At the beginning of the cherry-tree scene, Paul, characteris-
tically tormented, wishes to leave "himself to the great hunger
and impersonality of passion," but Miriam calls "him back
to the littleness, the personal relationship" (SL 284). He
climbs

> high in the tree, above the scarlet roofs of the buildings. The wind,
> moaning steadily, made the whole tree rock with a subtle, thrilling
> motion that stirred the blood. The young man, perched insecurely
> in the slender branches, rocked till he felt slightly drunk, reached
> down the boughs, tore off handful after handful of the sleek, cool-
> fleshed fruit. Cherries touched his ears and his neck as he stretched
> forward, their chill finger-tips sending a flash down his blood.
> All shades of red, from a golden vermilion to a rich crimson, glowed
> and met his eyes under a darkness of leaves. (SL 285)

Miriam comes out exclaiming that the sunset is "wonderful"
and "beautiful," and Paul, chuckling demonically, pelts
her with cherries.

   The scene isn't hard to "read." Paul, oppressed by Miriam's
possessiveness and spirituality, is attempting to escape to
the otherness of nature. The scene is impressive for its intense
physicality. One experiences the dark energies of nature
only through physical contact. The cherries have "finger-tips"
in order to complete the circuit with Paul. The moaning
wind and rocking tree seem embodiments of the impersonal
otherness of the universe. The rhythmic motion is intoxicating.
Paul is able to lose himself, to abandon himself to the flow, to
feel part of the basic, elemental process of life.

   Lawrence endorses his hero's behavior clearly enough.
Miriam's breathless delight is there to reveal her limitations.
Even more obviously, the author carefully places "four dead
birds" next to Miriam and calls attention to "some cherry
stones hanging quite bleached like skeletons" (SL 285). Paul
is open to "life"; poor clumsy Miriam isn't.

   But if Lawrence seems unequivocally on his hero's side,
most readers will feel some shade of discomfort. The four dead
birds and the cherry stones seem forced and intrusive. Lawrence's thumb is in the balance in his effort to make us assent

to Paul. And the point is that Paul's escape to the impersonal involves an escape *from* the personal, an escape from his own feeble efforts at self-integration and his attempts to do justice to his sweetheart. It is perhaps all too easy to climb a tree and commune with the cosmos. It is rather more difficult to confront and come to terms with problems of human relationship in a way that is fair to the other person involved. From this perspective, the visionary mode seems almost escapist. The search for cosmic order is revealed as a search for self-protection.

The ideas that feed into *The Rainbow* and the best of the *Prussian Officer* stories are rather abstract and remote from human experience. If these are the building blocks for Lawrence's best fiction, isn't that fiction itself somewhat suspect? The answer would be yes if these works were as totally experimental as is suggested by Lawrence's theorizing about the old stable ego of the character. However, no one could possibly interpret this famous letter to Garnett as the whole truth about Lawrence's art during this period. Although the letter does help make sense of important aspects of the novel and the tales, *The Rainbow* and the *Prussian Officer* stories are also populated by recognizable human characters who relate to one another in traditional fictional ways. As a statement of what's going on in the novel, the letter is extreme and somewhat distorted. It must be understood for what it is: a first articulation of an exciting intellectual breakthrough, heavy ammunition in an ongoing quarrel.

If Lawrence were interested in human beings exclusively as elemental fragments of matter and energy thrown off by the great inhuman will at the center of life, it is hard to imagine he would be a very readable novelist, much less a great one. Surely Eugene Goodheart overstates when he describes Lawrence's "whole imaginative career" as a "repudiation of art which is content to imitate already enacted life."[8] Lawrence never ceased to be interested in the real world and in

8. Eugene Goodheart, *The Utopian Vision of D. H. Lawrence* (Chicago, 1963), pp. 14–15.

real men and women and their problems of relationship. Though the metaphysic took him in a direction away from everyday human experience, he remained firmly rooted in the traditional domain of the novelist. The metaphysical substructure of *The Rainbow* and the best *Prussian Officer* stories adds considerable strength and substantiality, but the metaphysic is simply an extra dimension in fictions that are otherwise understandable in terms of late nineteenth-century conventions. Novel and tales are mixtures of tradition and experiment, or, to put it in another framework, of ordinary human experience and the impersonal reality subsuming it. The artistic breakthrough of 1914 expresses itself primarily as an attempt to understand the larger ordering beyond the flux of time, the larger meaning beyond the everyday.

I would venture that the effort to reconcile the everyday with the transcendent is one of the central issues in *Women in Love*. Birkin argues for ultimate marriage, for a mystic conjunction, for star-polarity—for a relationship beyond love and somehow beyond the flux of time. Ursula gives battle against Birkin's abstractness and preachiness. She holds out for a relationship that includes love, tenderness, and personal feeling. In the course of the novel she learns the sentimentality and insufficiency of her idea of love. But if she is educated by Birkin, he, in turn, is educated by her: Ursula helps heal Birkin by bringing him back down to earth. Love must be personal as well as impersonal, human as well as inhuman, here and now as well as transcendent.

The failure of the leadership novels of the twenties can be measured in terms of Lawrence's strange reluctance to build his fictions on the real world he was so skilled at evoking. The felt life of Mexico in the first four chapters of *The Plumed Serpent* is a remarkable achievement, but Kate's mythic voyage across Lake Chapala is a journey to Never-Land. The rest of the novel seems to take place in a vacuum and reads like shrill fantasy. Without commonsensical Kate Leslie, the pull of reality would go completely slack. *The Plumed Serpent*, Lawrence's major sustained effort in the novel form during the last decade of his life, can only testify to how badly he had lost his way.

Goodheart calls attention to another problem with Lawrence's metaphysic when he notes that "the movement into space in which men and women have passionate encounters is often not *realized* in the language." Whenever Lawrence moves beyond the old stable ego of the character, he does so with the awareness that he is attempting, paradoxically, to express in language what cannot be expressed in language. The prose he invented to express the inexpressible tries to be "as suggestive and as evocative as possible, and its intention is to communicate a restless sense that there is a much greater world beyond it that it has only partially illuminated."[9]

Sometimes there is too much generalized connotation and not enough denotation in Lawrence's rendering of the ineffable. Sometimes he seems to launch out too drastically into a realm of verbal abstraction and imprecision. The incremental repetition and the unrelenting intensity of Lawrentian passion-prose regularly risk the danger of reader exhaustion. Both *The Rainbow* and *Women in Love* offer abundant examples of the faults I am describing. Yet both novels are so firmly grounded in the bedrock of reality that artistic catastrophe is avoided. Lawrence returns speedily to the real world from even his most grandiose flights.

The *Prussian Officer* stories occupy a somewhat anomalous position in Lawrence's artistic career because of their accretive nature. They include writing from the earliest years mixed in with writing that is an essential component of the creation of *The Rainbow*. Stories that began in an idiom of symbolic realism took on, in the end, visionary qualities as well as the additional freight of the abstract and idiosyncratic specula-tion embodied in the metaphysic.

Indeed the addition of metaphysic to the stories raises the specter of an enduring Lawrence controversy. He may have believed that "the highest form of art should be true

9. Goodheart, pp. 33, 32.

unweighted conflict, an exploration not an assertion,"[10] but in practice there was a tendency for assertion to creep—or to enter forcibly—into his art. How, finally, do the *Prussian Officer* stories appear when seen in this light?

Not surprisingly, the latest of the stories to be written, the two Prussian tales, seem most obviously composed against a doctrinal framework. "The Prussian Officer" itself is the most obvious and important case in point. Here the characteristic Lawrentian dualism constitutes both the meaning and the structure. This fully achieved dualistic vision enters Lawrence's fiction with remarkable wholeness. It is this dualism that he developed and expanded in all the writing—both fictional and expository—culminating in *Women in Love*. The story is also notable for its perfect blending of art and metaphysic. For once the two comprise a seamless whole, and art and idea are indistinguishable: there isn't an intrusive detail anywhere. The original version was so finely realized that Lawrence felt no need to revise it significantly for his book of short stories.

The same cannot be said for some implications of both "The Thorn in the Flesh" and "Daughters of the Vicar." Final revision in 1914 brought greater clarity and artistic success to both stories, but nevertheless they also contain areas in which metaphysic threatens to impinge on art. Bachmann and Emilie are characters when we see them in action, but their sketched-in background, written in schematic accordance with Lawrence's emerging racial theory, almost succeeds in denying them life. Mr. Massy, the clergyman of "Daughters of the Vicar," exists only as a crudely embodied abstract idea, and we have observed other details from the story in which metaphysic is incompletely integrated. These flaws in otherwise first-rate fictions can be profitably understood in terms of an imbalance between art and ideas. The background of Bachmann and Emilie and the abstractly conceived

10. Mark Kinkead-Weekes, "The Marble and the Statue: The Exploratory Imagination of D. H. Lawrence," in *Imagined Worlds: Essays on English Novels and Novelists in Honour of John Butt*, ed. Ian Gregor and Maynard Mack (London 1968), p. 385.

character of Massy are as intrusive as, say, Count Psanek's long, pedagogical monologue in *The Ladybird* or Clifford's paralysis in *Lady Chatterley's Lover*. Stridency and thinness are often the result when Lawrence abandons his scrutiny of the real world and becomes a full-time prophet. He doesn't always follow his own good advice about trusting the tale; sometimes he imposes his will on it instead.

Most writers—Wordsworth is a classic example—discover at one time or another the double-edged seductiveness of ideas. Ideas are in an instant both liberating and imprisoning: capable of providing a necessary order, susceptible to rigidifying into "message." The temptation to use his art as a platform was a violation of Lawrence's finer instincts, but this was a temptation to which he sometimes succumbed. If, however, the details I have pointed out in the *Prussian Officer* volume tend in exactly that direction, on balance those stories—in fact most of the stories he wrote—are free of didacticism.

At the very least, I hope that this study has demonstrated the necessity of mastering the intricate chronology of Lawrence's writings before passing judgment on his developing art and ideas. The particular accretive and exploratory nature of his art makes this a requirement, but many critics seem not to have taken the time and trouble. R. E. Pritchard's attempt to provide a comprehensive interpretation of Lawrence's career depends on beginning with an accurate chronology, but he stumbles over the *Prussian Officer* stories. We are told that *The Prussian Officer* "goes further" than *Twilight in Italy*, even though the travel book was written after the revision of the tales, and even though the travel book is both more systematic and more unresolved than the stories. Similarly, Keith Alldritt seems to have the relationship between the revised *Twilight* and *The Rainbow* reversed. Stephen Miko devotes an entire book to Lawrence's development from *The White Peacock* through *Women in Love* without so much as glancing at the role of the *Prussian Officer* and *Twilight in Italy* revisions. The Biographical Note in Frank

Kermode's little study of Lawrence informs us that Lawrence "wrote stories for *The Prussian Officer*" in 1913. Under the circumstances, this remark can only confuse the serious student of Lawrence. He "wrote" only two of the stories that year; he revised a number of them, but the important revisions took place the following year.[11] Lawrence's exploratory imagination makes it imperative that the critic be accurate in his chronology.

I also hope that this study has done away with an entrenched misconception about the *Prussian Officer* volume. F. R. Leavis is the best spokesman for this error when he remarks that the stories "were written during [Lawrence's] first creative years."[12] We have observed in considerable detail how deceptive a half-truth this statement is. Lawrence may have originally composed most of the stories at the beginning of his career, but the final, major revisions of "The White Stocking" and "Daughters of the Vicar" (two of the tales Leavis is ecstatic about), as well as of "Odour of Chrysanthemums," "The Shades of Spring," and "The Thorn in the Flesh," were carried out in the early summer of 1914, a time when Lawrence had already completed three versions of *The Rainbow*. The final versions of all the substantial tales in the collection were forged at the same smithy as *The Rainbow*.

Leavis's approach to the *Prussian Officer* stories is colored by his lack of knowledge of their compositonal history. He believes "the title story and 'The Thorn in the Flesh' are in an early Lawrence vein that he soon outgrew; sultrily overcharged, sensuously and emotionally, they seem to associate with *The Trespasser*." Actually the stories were the last to be written and the last to be revised. Their published versions followed the final revision of *The Trespasser* by almost two-and-a-half years, and the style of "The Thorn in

11. R. E. Pritchard, *D. H. Lawrence: Body of Darkness* (London, 1971), p. 60; Keith Alldritt, *The Visual Imagination of D. H. Lawrence* (Evanston, Ill., 1971), p. 145; Stephen Miko, *Toward* Women in Love: *The Emergence of a Lawrentian Aesthetic* (New Haven, 1971); Frank Kermode, *D. H. Lawrence* (New York, 1973), p. xiv.

12. F. R. Leavis, *D. H. Lawrence: Novelist* (New York, 1956), p. 78.

the Flesh" in particular has little to do with that of the novel. Leavis praises the back-washing scene in "Daughters of the Vicar" and marvels that it was written "nearly twenty years before the passage about the 'body' in *Apropos of Chatterley's Lover.*"[13] His date is off by five years: this passage in the story did not emerge until the 1914 revisions. Leavis's tendency to dismiss most of the early volume of stories almost certainly affects his reading of "Odour of Chrysanthemums" too, for, not expecting much in it, he does not find much:

"A Sick Collier," "The Christening," and "Odour of Chrysanthemums" show Lawrence as the portrayer of the life he knew earliest, that of the miner's home. The presentment has the quality that I discussed in examining "The Daughters of the Vicar": this is working-class life—to render it in its distinctiveness (as he so incomparably does) is certainly Lawrence's preoccupation. . . . [14]

Leavis links "Odour of Chrysanthemums" with a brief sketch and a satiric *jeu d'esprit*, praises it for its faithful rendering of working-class life and for its absence of snobbery—and completely overlooks the central meaning of the story, which has nothing at all to do with class. I believe that his preconceived attitude about the collection as a whole is responsible for this oddly shallow reading of one of Lawrence's greatest stories.

Harry T. Moore, the most ardent and influential Lawrence advocate in the United States, is equally in error in his assessment of the *Prussian Officer* volume. Moore suggests, for example, that only the Prussian stories in the collection exhibit "the growing mastery of rhythm and of color usage that is also noticeable in the prose of *Sons and Lovers.* The other stories resemble *The White Peacock* stylistically: the writing is simple and competent, but it lacks the distinction of Lawrence's later idiom." Even the most casual reader should be able to notice the immense difference between the style of *The White Peacock* and of the *Prussian Officer* versions of

13. Leavis, pp. 308, 102.
14. Leavis, p. 308.

such stories as "Daughters of the Vicar" and "The Shades
of Spring." Harry Moore of all people should have known
better, but it was easier to categorize the stories as representative
of "Lawrence's earlier phase rather than his post-*Sons
and Lovers* period." The assertion that "virtually all the stories in
The Prussian Officer are at this same level of excellent
workmanship"[15] is supported neither by the texts nor by the
facts of their composition.

Graham Hough makes the same erroneous assumption about
the volume in *The Dark Sun*, though he is slightly more
circumspect:

> As far as date is concerned, the relation can be briefly
> outlined. There is an early group of stories (they mostly appear in
> the *Prussian Officer* volume, some in the posthumous collection
> called *A Modern Lover*) very closely connected with *The White Peacock*
> and *Sons and Lovers*, both in themes and treatment. There is a second
> group, collected under the title *England My England*, all written during
> the war, showing a similar but less intimate connection with *The
> Rainbow* and *Women in Love*.[16]

The lines are not nearly so neat, and of course the most
significant association between short story collection and novel
is that between *The Prussian Officer* and *The Rainbow*. Some
of Hough's assessments of individual stories seem related to
the idea that they are early works. He states, for example, that
"The White Stocking" and "Odour of Chrysanthemums" display "little trace of the characteristic Lawrentian promise"[17]—
a curious viewpoint indeed.

I have cited these examples from Leavis, Moore, and Hough
because they are three of the most influential critics of Lawrence of the last twenty years. The periodical literature is also
replete with articles on the *Prussian Officer* tales that operate
on similar assumptions. Most often the critic will set out with
the belief that the stories are early works and therefore not

15. Harry T. Moore, *D. H. Lawrence: His Life and Works* (New York, 1964),
p. 97.
16. Graham Hough, *The Dark Sun: A Study of D. H. Lawrence* (New
York, 1957), pp. 168–69.
17. Hough, pp. 169–70.

up to the level Lawrence was later to achieve. Occasionally the opposite mistake is made, and a critic will read more systematic Lawrentian attitudes of the 1920s into works in which they are not present. Actually, the process of revision of the stories was so gradual, drawn-out, and complicated that it is difficult to make one general statement that will cover all the tales. But a critic must certainly understand that a volume of stories, most of which were thoroughly revised in 1914 in accordance with the emerging artistic aims of *The Rainbow*, cannot be dismissed as early works.

In the 1914 revisions the themes of human isolation, of salvation through human contact, and of the celebration of the powerful dark forces in the universe emerged with full Lawrentian intensity. The final revisions of the best stories are exciting because they seem to be an integral part of the moment in which he became the Lawrence we know. The time of apprenticeship was past. The best stories in the collection must be measured against the finest short fiction he ever wrote.

Appendixes
Index

Appendix A

The "Prussian Officer" Texts

"I have written the best story I have ever done"

The ultimate source of "The Prussian Officer" is probably found in the life of Friedrich von Richthofen, Frieda's father. As a young officer, the baron served in the Franco-Prussian War. The diary he kept of his war experiences includes two entries that suggest "The Prussian Officer." On 10 November 1870, he wrote, "A mad scene this evening at the 'Horse.' I whipped an artillery officer with my sabre." An entry on the next day reads: "Heinrich [his servant] got drunk and I beat him."[1] From such minute suggestions emerged one of Lawrence's most ambitious and fully achieved short stories.

Lawrence had suggested that "Goose Fair" be the title of his collection, but Garnett, hoping to improve sales, changed "Honour and Arms" to "The Prussian Officer" and gave the same title to the book. Lawrence's own title is borrowed from an aria from Händel's oratorio "Samson." The aria is sung by Harapha, the giant of Gath, who taunts the blind Samson. Lawrence meant the text of the aria to resonate against his own story:

> Honour and arms scorn such a foe,
> Though I could end thee at a blow,
> Poor victory, to conquer thee,
> Or glory in thy overthrow!
> Vanquish a slave that is half slain!
> So mean a triumph I disdain.[2]

1. Harry T. Moore, *The Priest of Love: A Life of D. H. Lawrence* (New York, 1974). It may also be relevant that Frieda's paternal grandmother was a Polish countess; the Captain's "mother had been a Polish Countess" (PO 3).

2. G. F. Händel, *Samson: An Oratorio in Vocal Score*, Novello's Original Octavo Edition (London and New York, n.d.), pp. 87–91. Muriel begins to play "Honour and Arms" in "A Modern Lover" until she is interrupted by Mersham's request for "something quiet" (CSS, p. 16).

The revised holograph of the story in the collection of the University of Texas Library dates from the early summer of 1913. Lawrence published the magazine text of "Honour and Arms" in the *English Review* of August 1914 and in the *Metropolitan* three months later. The story of course also appears in the Hopkin proofs. The final text is that found in the *Prussian Officer* volume.

The holograph of "Honour and Arms" in the collection of the University of Texas is written in different inks on four different kinds of paper. Extensive interlinear revision found throughout shows that the manuscript is an amalgam of work Lawrence did on the story at several discrete points in time. Lawrence wrote the first half of the holograph in a large, clear hand, but in the last pages his writing is extraordinarily small and cramped, as if he was running out of paper. Douglas Clayton's name and address are written in Lawrence's hand on the back of the last leaf. Clayton and his mother typed a number of Lawrence's manuscripts for him, so it is likely that the Texas holograph was sent to the Claytons to have a typescript made for the *English Review*. This dates the holograph in the summer of 1913.

An earlier stage of "Honour and Arms" is concealed beneath the slashes the author made as he revised the story to send to his typist. These cancellations are extensive, but the words and phrases that are replaced offer few revelations. In most instances the canceled passages could be restored without seriously affecting the story. Lawrence was in full imaginative command of the dualistic vision he wished to develop before he began; the revisions in manuscript in no way transform this vision.

A typical revision in manuscript is the description of the Captain. Diction is improved, but the story is not altered:

Texas holograph, canceled passage	Texas holograph, revised passage
His moustache was also cut short and bristly over a full, almost brutal mouth. His face was rather rugged, the cheeks thin. His fair eyebrows	His moustache also was cut short and bristly over a full, brutal mouth. His face was rather rugged, the cheeks thin. Perhaps the man was

stood bushy over his light, bluey-grey eyes, which were always ready to catch fire, haughtily, overbearingly, or to stare coldly. The man was handsome, and perhaps more so for the irritable tension of his brow, and the deep lines in his face, that looked almost careworn.

the more handsome for the deep lines in his face, the irritable tension of his brow, which gave him the look of a man who fights with life. His fair eyebrows stood bushy over light-blue eyes that were always flashing with cold fire. (Hol 2)[3]

A canceled passage at the beginning of the second section of the story reads "The scent of green rye soaked in sunshine made him feel sick." In the manuscript the last four words are amended to "came like a dizziness" (Hol 10). The magazine text was changed further to "came like a sickness" (HA 32),[4] which put Lawrence nearly back where he started. Such alterations are characteristic of the holograph revisions. They do not affect the larger design of the story.

The revised Texas holograph of "Honour and Arms" is very close in detail to the version of the story published in the *English Review* in August 1914. There are a good number of changes in words and phrases, but they in no way alter the basic thrust of the story.[5] Some of these slight variations are interesting, however. The radiance of the mountains seems "quite natural" (Hol 10) at the beginning of the second section of the manuscript. In the magazine text it seems "almost supernatural" (HA 33). Several of the changes display errors in transcription, unless Lawrence himself retouched some details on the basis of aural association. The mountains "drew gradually nearer" (Hol 1) in the manuscript; is the magazine text they "grew gradually nearer" (HA 24). The Captain's "dithering" smile (Hol 7) becomes a "withering" smile (HA

3. The abbreviation Hol refers to the holograph of "Honour and Arms" at the Humanities Research Center, The University of Texas at Austin.

The change in eye color from "bluey-grey" to "light-blue" is probably worth noting. Blue eyes in Lawrence are regularly associated with abstraction, intellectuality, and willfulness.

4. The abbreviation HA refers to the magazine text of "Honour and Arms," published in the *English Review* in August 1914 (vol. 18, pp. 24–43).

5. These changes were probably made on the typescript Lawrence received from the Claytons.

30). In the manuscript, when the orderly thinks about his officer's harassment in regard to his girl, he is "much too dumb even to want to cry" (Hol 4); in the *English Review* text he is "much too done" (HA 31). In the holograph "all the life of this morning" (Hol 12) is concentrated in the figure of the captain; in the magazine text "all the light" (HA 34) of the morning is concentrated in him. These are variations that the future editor of Lawrence should know about.

Nevertheless, even though revised holograph and magazine text are close in detail, the two versions of the story are radically different. This is because of the 1,500 words that appear in that manuscript but are simply not to be found in the story published in the *English Review*. These missing words comprise approximately fifteen paragraphs located throughout the holograph. Two of the paragraphs omitted from the magazine text are particularly noticeable to the reader familiar with the story, for one is the flashback in which the orderly knocks over the wine bottle—an important episode, replete with sexual symbolism, in the developing tension between the men—and another is the lovely description of the squirrels near the end of the tale.

These missing paragraphs do appear both in the Hopkin proofs of July 1914 and in the final version of the story published in *The Prussian Officer and Other Stories* in December 1914, although Lawrence has slightly retouched the wording of several of the paragraphs in the latter version. No pattern or common property characterizes the omitted paragraphs. There is no artistic reason that they have been left out. One such paragraph, for example, is a brief description of Schöner's hallucinations as he marches with the company after his kicking: "The soldiers were tramping silently up the glaring hillside. Gradually his head began to revolve, slowly, rhythmically. Sometimes it was dark before his eyes, as if he saw this world through a smoked glass, frail shadows and unreal. It gave him a pain in his head to walk" (Hol 11, PO 18).

There can be no doubt about what happened. Every writer

of short fiction has to contend with the problem of space requirements of magazine editors. Lawrence could not place "Daughters of the Vicar" because it was too long, and "Love Among the Haystacks" suffered the same fate. In August 1913 Lawrence wrote Garnett that the Northern Syndicate had sent back "two stories as not being of the right length" (CL 219). Mitchell Kennerley, editor of the *Forum*, made the situation crystal clear in a letter answering Garnett's complaints about his rate of payment. The *Forum* paid ten dollars per thousand words, and the maximum payment was fifty dollars, no matter how long the story was. Kennerley would always "prefer a story of five thousand words rather than one of ten."[6] Small wonder that Lawrence once remarked "about magazines—I can't help feeling a hatred of their ways and means and all that" (CL 660).

For reasons of space or simply because it was felt that "The Prussian Officer" would profit from being more concise, the *English Review* cut the story—and without so much as asking the author's permission. Lawrence seems to have discovered what had happened only when he obtained a copy of the magazine. A letter to J. B. Pinker, his agent at the time, on 15 September 1914 makes this clear: "I have asked my sister to send a duplicate typed copy of Honour and Arms. The English Review made me furious by cutting it down."[7]

Apart from this letter and the evidence of the manuscript, we even know the identity of the man who did the cutting. The person responsible for the magazine form of "The Prussian Officer" was—of all people!—Norman Douglas, at the time Harrison's assistant at the *English Review*, ultimately an outright enemy of Lawrence. Contemporary criticism generally sees incremental repetition and prose artistry in the tale. In his informal autobiography, *Looking Back*, Douglas

6. Mitchell Kennerley to Edward Garnett, 30 June 1913, unpublished letter in the Henry W. and Albert A. Berg Collection of the New York Public Library.

7. Lawrence to J. B. Pinker, 15 September 1914, quoted in the *D. H. Lawrence Review*, 5 (1972), 331.

remembered only redundancy: "He sometimes turned up at the *English Review* office with stories like the *Prussian Officer* written in that impeccable handwriting of his. They had to be cut down for magazine purposes; they were too redundant; and I was charged with the odious task of performing the operation. Would Lawrence never learn to be more succinct, and to hold himself in hand a little?"[8] Lawrence was justifiably angry, but at least he could be secure in the knowledge that the full text would be published in his first collection of tales at the end of the year.

Anyone lacking access to the Texas holograph, the Pinker letter, or Norman Douglas's autobiography must necessarily arrive at a totally wrong conclusion about the difference in length between magazine and book versions of the story. A critic who has not studied this manuscript can only surmise that the fifteen paragraphs not present in the *English Review* text are expansions of the story in the final version. The three "extensions" Roger Dataller quotes in "Mr. Lawrence and Mrs. Woolf"[9] are all of course to be found in the Texas manuscript. He proceeds to show how each of these passages, in adding to the intensity of the atmosphere and sharpening the thematic focus, reveals Lawrence's growth as an artist. But each of the passages is present in the earliest extant manuscript of the story.

The transformation of "Honour and Arms" into "The Prussian Officer" reveals a final process of revision involving the omitted manuscript paragraphs as well as the *English Review* text. The Hopkin proof version of July 1914 is almost word-for-word identical with the revised holograph and needn't be considered here. There was spot retouching throughout the final revision in October, but nothing major occurred. The basic design—and the story's "metaphysical" implications—had been firmly in mind from the beginning.

8. Norman Douglas, *Looking Back: An Autobiographical Excursion* (London, 1933), p. 345.
9. The Dataller essay appears in *Essays in Criticism*, 8 (1958), 48–59. George Ford makes the same mistake on page 65 of *Double Measure* (New York, 1965).

Early in 1913 Lawrence told Garnett that his writing must "come more and more to shape each year" since "trim and garnish my stuff I cannot—it must go" (CL 176). Very few of the revisions of "The Prussian Officer" seem to be based on any systematic reseeing of the story. Rather they show Lawrence in the process of letting his tale "go": the final revisions seem nearly as spontaneous as the original composition. Perhaps the most significant knowledge that emerges from a careful scrutiny of the different versions of "The Prussian Officer" is the fact that the "best short story" Lawrence had ever done was cut for magazine publication without his knowledge or permission. The story was first written in June 1913 and was revised for the final time sixteen months later; the surviving holograph, the unpublished proof version, and the two published texts show no thematic differences. There was no need for major recasting or for systematic revision. It's as if Lawrence saw "The Prussian Officer" whole the first time he sat down to write it. The special nature of that "wholeness" points the way to the revisions of the best of the other stories collected in the *Prussian Officer* volume.

The Origins of "The Christening"

"Thank God . . . I've been saved from that"

"The Christening," an extended jeer at conventional moral-ity, is one of the stories Lawrence had in mind when he wrote Garnett from Germany on 29 June 1912: "I wonder if any-body would have a short story now. While here, I've written three. But, under the influence of Frieda, I am afraid their moral tone would not agree with my countrymen" (CL 133). "The Christening" presents a black-comedy version of family life. The sardonic tone sustained throughout the tale culminates in the wonderfully acid description of the baptism of the illegitimate child. The 1912 date of the story's compo-sition is made conclusive by the amusing story of a good friend of Lawrence's with a remarkable proclivity for bastardy. This friend was fruitful and mutiplied outside the marriage bond in both 1906 and 1912, and each time he seems to have had an impact on the fiction of the young writer. Lawrence's very different responses to his friend's two bastards give an inkling of how much Lawrence grew up between the ages of twenty and twenty-six.

The friend in question is George Henry Neville, a Law-rence schoolmate in Eastwood and Nottingham High School. He was also a member of the Pagans, the social and cultural circle that formed in Eastwood around the young Lawrence. Neville's nickname was "Teufel," and more than one turn-of-the-century Midlands maiden must have believed he deserved it. He fathered his first illegiti-mate child in the spring of 1906. At the time, Lawrence—by his own confession something of a prig—was deeply troubled. Jessie Chambers recorded his response in detail:

On an evening of that same spring (when Lawrence was in his twenty-first year) his sister cycled up to the farm. She had come to tell me something that shocked us all very much. A friend of theirs was in deep disgrace—in A's conventional phrase he had "got a girl into trouble." On the following evening Lawrence came himself, looking white and upset. As soon as we were alone he asked me if I had heard about his friend—they had been High School boys together. He seemed relieved that I knew. He said his mother had told him about it that morning. He was very distressed. His mother had said how terrible might be the consequences of only five minutes' self-forgetfulness. And it seemed to add to the tragedy that the young people had only seen one another on Sunday evenings after chapel—so Lawrence said. He told me these things in a voice that sounded sick with misery, and I felt very concerned, wondering why he should take it so to heart. Then he startled me by bursting out vehemently:

"Thank God . . . I've been saved from that . . . so far."

I was puzzled, feeling in the dark about the whole business, and very sorry for Lawrence's distress. He seemed relieved after he had told me about it.[1]

No doubt Jessie included this story as part of her strategy of redressing the balance after her portrayal in *Sons and Lovers,* but it certainly has the ring of authenticity. Seventy years after the fact, however, it is hard to read this passage without smiling. Mrs. Lawrence's "five minutes' self-forgetfulness" formula belongs to a lost world of moral earnestness that is especially amusing if one bears Neville's character (or at least his recurrent tendency toward "self-forgetfulness") in mind. The "tragedy" of illicit love "on Sunday evenings after chapel" sounds like something Samuel Butler inadvertently omitted from *The Way of All Flesh.* Nevertheless, one must note Lawrence's pale countenance and voice "sick with misery." In the spring of 1906, he had not begun his rebellion against the accepted morality—or against its embodiment in his life, his mother.

Neville produced his second bastard six years later, early in 1912. Lawrence wrote Garnett about him on 8 March 1912, just a month before he met Frieda:

1. ET, pp. 125–26.

And —— my very old friend, the Don Juanish fellow I told you of—went and got married three months back, without telling a soul—and now boasts a son: "Jimmy, a very fine lad." He writes me eight pages, closely packed, this morning. The girl is living at home, with "Jimmy" in Stourbridge. The manager asked —— to resign his post, because of the blot on the scutcheon. He said he'd "see them frizzled first." In the end, he was removed to a little headship on the Stafford-Derby border—has been there six weeks—alone—doing fearfully hard work. Don Juan in hell, what ho! He implores me to go and stay a week with him. I suppose I'll have to. This has upset me—one never knows what'll happen. You know —— has already got one illegitimate child. It's a lovely story, the end of it: the beginning was damnable. She was only nineteen, and he only twenty. Her father, great Christian, turned her out. —— wouldn't acknowledge the kid, but had to pay, whether or not. That's five years back. Last October, I am told, the girl got married. Before the wedding—two days or so—she went to ——'s home with the child, and showed it to Georgie's father and mother.

"I've come, Mr. ——, for you to own this child. Who's the father of that?" pushing forward the small girl.

"Eh bless her, it's just like him," cried old Mrs. ——, and she kissed the kid with tears.

"Well, Lizzie," said —— to the girl, "if our George-Henry says that isn't his'n he's a liar. It's the spit and image of him."

Whereupon Lizzie went away satisfied, got married to a collier, and lives in Cordy Lane. She, with one or two others, will rejoice over George's final nabbing. Isn't it awful?

All this, by the way, is quite verbal truth. (CL 103)

Lawrence's melodramatic "Thank God . . . I've been saved from that . . . so far" in 1906 has become simply "That has upset me—one never knows what'll happen." At that, it is hard to believe he was really upset, for the letter to Garnett treats the story of George and his illegitimate children in a vein of satire and comedy; indeed the letter all but launches into a short story. The jocular tone of the letter shows how far Lawrence had come since 1906. "The Christening" was written in much the same flippant tone just a few months later and contains a similar slash at Christianity.

The news of his friend's latest bastardy brought illegitimacy to mind in 1912 and helped provide the germ of the fiction. The madness of art indeed.[2]

Although no manuscripts exist for "The Christening," Harry T. Moore has pointed out that a "somewhat different version of this story comprise[s] one of the episodes in an early draft of *The White Peacock*"[3] now owned by The Bancraft Library of the University of California, Berkeley. Moore's description is somewhat inaccurate, for episode and short story are too unlike to be classified as versions of the same story. Nevertheless, the episode in the fragment at Berkeley, Lawrence's first conception of a comic baptism scene, is clearly a prefiguration of "The Christening" and Lawrence's first attempt to deal with its materials.

Lawrence began *The White Peacock* as *Laetitia* at Easter of 1906 and was finished with this version by June 1907. He had completely rewritten it by the end of April 1908. Lettie is the central character in the fifty-eight page fragment at Berkeley; the language of this holograph is even more mawkish than that of the final version. The fragment sounds like a piece of the novel Lawrence described to Blanche Jennings in a letter dated 4 May 1908: "Well, when my boyhood . . . began to drop from me, . . . then I began to write. Consequently I wrote with crude sentimentality, being sick, having lost the health of my laddishness, all the humour that was the body of my mind's health dead. . . . Much of *Laetitia* is poor stuff, I fear, and I shall have it all to do over again" (CL 9).

George Neville's bastard son struck a resonant chord in Lawrence's imagination in the spring of 1912 and contributed to a story about the christening of an illegitimate

---

2. Lawrence made further use of George Henry Neville's experiences in *The Married Man*, the clumsy four-act comedy that also dates from 1912. George Grainger, the Don Juanish protagonist, loses his job because of a scandal over a bastard child—a son named Jimmy—and meanwhile he has gotten another girl pregnant.

3. Harry T. Moore, *D. H. Lawrence: His Life and Works* (New York, 1964), p. 99.

grandson. I think it probable that the same friend's bastard daughter, so upsetting to Lawrence in the spring of 1906, found her way into the first draft of *The White Peacock* as Lettie's illegitimate daughter. The fragment of this draft at Berkeley was begun at Easter 1906. The christening scene itself is treated broadly in the fragment, but otherwise the illegitimate child is immersed in a hearts-and-flowers atmosphere fully in keeping with Lawrence's deep but maudlin concern over his friend's trouble in the spring of 1906.

The holograph of the *Laetitia* fragment is a fascinating, if not very skillful, piece of writing. The earliest extant example of Lawrence's prose, the story it tells is vastly different from the published version of *The White Peacock*.[4] The christening scene occupies eight pages in the middle of the fragment. Although in general the presentation of Lettie's misfortune is engulfed by great sorrow and solemnity, Lawrence was unable to resist the opportunity to satirize the clergyman who comes to christen the baby. The caricature of the minister is broad indeed:

We heard a timid rap at the door, and Mrs. Worthington hurried to admit a man exceedingly tall, enveloped in an old black macintosh. He wished us Good-day, and hoped we were well in a Yorkshire voice of much variety. He hung on some words as

4. In the published novel, Lettie marries Leslie, becomes a good but dissatisfied wife, and seeks her fulfillment in motherhood. The rejected George marries beneath himself and becomes a drunkard by early middle age. In the *Laetitia* fragment, Lettie has had an illegitimate child by Leslie, but she does not love him and they do not marry. Instead she marries George, who understandably feels second best. In one scene snatched from *Uncle Tom's Cabin*, the distraught Lettie runs across a frozen pond with her baby, falls into the water when the ice cracks, and is fished out by George. Later Leslie and a lady in a dark dress with white furs arrive for a melodramatic encounter with Lettie and her baby near a wishing well; this is the first time Leslie has seen his child. At the end of the fragment (clearly the end of this version of the novel), Leslie settles £500 on the baby, and George and Lettie emigrate to Canada. Thus, the *Laetitia* fragment, Lawrence's first known prose work, is also the first to end with a characteristic departure.

if he loved the sound thereof, as if the sound were a benediction to the hearers; he slid up and down his sentences as if he chanted a psalm with ever-varying tune. Having removed his macintosh and wide-awake, he stood smiling on us, the queerest man in the world, hairless, gaunt, having immense bones and no flesh, and a holy, pastoral air. He seemed to crack into several huge parts as he sat down, still smiling on us from his small, hairless face, and twisting his immense fingers nervously, not knowing what to say. From his mountainous feet great rivers trickled and formed seas. This caused him evident discomfort; he shifted about, and made many seas instead of one ocean.[5]

The minister does not realize that the child is a bastard, so his homilies on the holiness of love and sacredness of marriage are amusingly ironic. Much of the comedy in the scene is at the expense of the minister's Yorkshire accent. In "The Christening" the baby's strong-willed patriarchal grandfather completely overshadows the minister, but in the *Laetitia* fragment the minister is the whole scene. The problem is that the broad caricature is so out of keeping with the "crude sentimentality" of everything else in the draft. Basic changes in the novel's plot dictated the scene's excision, but Lawrence almost certainly would have cut it anyway. Nevertheless, the baptism scene in the early draft of the novel stands as the prototype of the story.

The most casual reading of the completed "Christening" is sufficient to reveal that the tyrannical old collier is the center of interest. He is a character of great vitality, but his overpowering will has crippled three of his children. His vitality is destructive rather than life-giving. The oldest daughter, a schoolteacher with a heart condition, is mainly concerned with salvaging the family's respectability in the face of her sister's humiliation. The sullen, resentful youngest daughter is ashamed of her disgrace and despises her child's father. She is redeemed only by her natural love for her baby. The son seems primarily motivated by malice.

5. *The White Peacock (Laetitia)*, holograph in the collection of The Bancroft Library, University of California, Berkeley, p. 44.

("Pat-a-cake, pat-a-cake, baker's man," he sings, knowing full well that the "baker's man at Berryman's" [PO 278–79] is the father.) Only the middle sister has emerged unscathed. The old man's prayer over his grandchild reveals his guilt about the fates of his children. Yet when the minister asks for the child's name, the retired collier lifts his head "fiercely" and says, "Joseph William, after me" (PO 276). The new child will bring no regeneration to the family. "The Christening" describes a baptism without rebirth.

The culmination of the story is the father's long, guilty, inchoate prayer—a masterpiece of woozy religiosity—over his bastard grandchild. I will quote only the first few sentences of this extensive religious ramble: "'We ask Thee, Lord,' the old man cried, 'to look after this childt. Fatherless he is. But what does the earthly father matter before Thee? The childt is Thine, he is thy childt. Lord, what father has a man but Thee?'" (PO 277). This prayer seems to look forward to another Lawrentian patriarchal monologue, Tom Brangwen's speech about marriage at the wedding party of his nephew Will and Anna Lensky. Tom is a little in his cups, but his speech is central to the theme of the novel. "Marriage is what we're made for—" he begins, and he concludes by declaring that it seems to him that "a married couple makes one Angel." An "Angel is the soul of a man and woman in one: they rise united at the Judgment Day, as one Angel—" (R 133–35). Other Brangwens mock him throughout this harangue, but he persists until he has finished his simple, moving affirmation of life on earth. I am convinced that the old collier's wordy prayer in "The Christening"—another simple man's naive formal discourse on the workings of the universe—served as a curious trial run for Tom's speech.

"The Christening" is a nicely realized and underrated little story, remarkable partly because Lawrence has adopted his jeering tone without lapsing into pseudofacetiousness or intrusiveness. Its "doctrinal" content is insignificant, and yet if Lawrence is seen as a "passionately religious man" intent on clearing away the rubble of the old values, his corrosive portrayal of family life and religion in the tale is worth examining. The story's background constitutes an interesting perspective on Lawrence's growth toward emotional and artistic maturity. What seemed Midlands tragedy in 1906 had become the stuff of comedy by 1912. The intersections of art and life are myriad, but not every young writer has a friend so ready to provide him with opportunities to reflect on the moral significance of illegitimacy.

A *Prussian Officer* Calendar

This calendar provides a chronological history of all the *Prussian Officer* stories, along with the major dates pertaining to the novels Lawrence wrote in the same years and some key dates from his biography. One asterisk denotes the original composition of a story or stories; two asterisks designate the date of the magazine publication.

I have also tried to account here for all the extant manuscripts of all twelve stories. Warning: these manuscripts include a few that did not figure in my discussion of particular stories.

	1885
September 11	Lawrence born in Eastwood, Nottinghamsire.
	1898
September 14	Enters Nottingham High School.
	1901
summer	Meets Jessie Chambers ("Miriam").
July	Leaves Nottingham High School.
	1902
autumn	Becomes pupil-teacher at British School in Eastwood.
	1904
Easter[?]	Beginning of engagement to Jessie Chambers.

	1906
Easter	Begins *The White Peacock* as *Laetitia.*
September	Enters Nottingham University College.
	1907
*October	Writes "Legend" (the first version of "A Fragment of Stained Glass"), "The White Stocking," and "A Prelude" for the *Nottinghamshire Guardian* short story contest. The holograph of "The White Stocking" now in the collection of W. H. Clarke is probably the text Lawrence submitted to this contest.
December 7	"A Prelude" published in the *Nottinghamshire Guardian,* Lawrence's first appearance in print.
	1908
April	Completes second version of *The White Peacock.*
June	Awarded teacher's certificate by Nottingham University College.
*summer[?]	Original composition of "The Shadow in the Rose Garden" as "The Vicar's Garden." The fair copy now at the University of Texas probably dates from the same time.
summer[?]	Fair copy of "Legend" (now at the University of Texas).

October 9	Asks Blanche Jennings where he should send short stories.
October 12	Begins teaching at Davidson Road School in Croydon.
*[?]	"Second Best" probably dates originally from some time in 1908 or 1909.

1909

before June	Writes "A Modern Lover," which was never published until the posthumous *Modern Lover* collection (1934).
June	Jessie Chambers submits Lawrence poems to the *English Review*.
*early summer	Writes "Goose Fair"—probably a collaboration with Louie Burrows.
late October	Sends third version of *The White Peacock* to Ford Madox Ford.
November	Suite of poems (submitted by Jessie in June) published in the *English Review*: Lawrence's first nationwide publication.
*before December 9	MS fragment of "Odour of Chrysanthemums" in Lawrence's hand on the back of a holograph fair copy of the story (now at the University of Texas). This is probably a piece of the original draft.
December 9	Sends the original version of "Odour of Chrysanthemums" along with the holograph of "Goose Fair" (now at the

University of Nottingham) to the *English Review*.

1910

by January 23	Rewrites the original "White Stocking."
**February	"Goose Fair" published in the *English Review*.
March	Begins *The Trespasser* as *The Sorrows of Siegmund* and finishes it within three months.
March 10	The original "Odour of Chrysanthemums" set in proof by the *English Review*.
spring	Final revision of *The White Peacock*.
October	Begins *Sons and Lovers* as *Paul Morel*.
November	Breaks off the six-year engagement with Jessie Chambers.
before December	First version of *The Widowing of Mrs. Holroyd*.
December 3	Becomes engaged to Louie Burrows.
December 9	Death of Lawrence's mother.

1911

January	*The White Peacock* issued by Duffield in New York and by Heinemann in London.
March 30–April 2	Revises the original magazine proofs of "Odour of Chrysanthemums." This set of revised proofs is now at the Universtiy of Nottingham.
April 1	Completes the transcript of the magazine version of "A

	Fragment of Stained Glass" (now at the University of Nottingham).
early April	Louie Burrows writes out a fair copy of the revised "Odour of Chrysanthemums" proofs to be sent to the *English Review*. This fair copy is now at the University of Texas.
April 12	Finishes rewriting the magazine version of "The White Stocking."
after April 12	Sends the revised holograph of "Second Best" (now at the University of Nottingham) to the *English Review* along with "Odour of Chrysanthemums," "A Fragment of Stained Glass," and "The White Stocking."
**June	"Odour of Chrysanthemums" published in the *English Review*.
June 2	Secker writes offering to publish a volume of short stories.
*July 15–16	Writes "Daughters of the Vicar" as "Two Marriages." The holograph fragment (manuscript *A*) in the collection of George Lazarus is probably this draft.
July 21	Finishes correcting the magazine proofs of "A Fragment of Stained Glass" and sends the Nottingham transcript of the story to Louie.
August	Edward Garnett writes asking

	for stories for the *Century Magazine.*
**September	"A Fragment of Stained Glass" published in the *English Review.*
September 25	Sends rough draft of "Two Marriages" to Garnett.
early October	Revises "Two Marriages" to have a typescript made.
mid-October	Meets Garnett.
November	Completion of "Two Marriages" typescript. The extant pages of this typescript are now part of the *B* manuscript in the collection of George Lazarus.
*ca. December 25	Writes "The Shades of Spring" as "The Soiled Rose."
by December 30	The *Century Magazine* rejects "Two Marriages."

1912

January	Convalescing in Bournemouth; decides to abandon career as schoolmaster.
January-February	Revises *The Trespasser.*
**February	"Second Best" published in the *English Review.*
*February or March	Composition of "A Sick Collier."
March 6	Talks of going to Germany with ultimate goal of secondary school teaching.
by March 8	The revised typescript of "The Soiled Rose" (now in the collection of the New York

	Public Library) completed and accepted by the *Forum*.
early April	Meets Frieda von Richthofen Weekley.
April	Finishes first version of *Paul Morel*.
May	*The Trespasser* published by Duckworth.
May 3	Elopes with Frieda to Germany.
*May or June	Writes "The Christening" as "The Baker's Man."
August 5	Lawrence and Frieda leave Icking for hiking tour through the Tyrolese Alps to Italy.
August	Begins *Paul Morel* again.
September 18	Established at Gargnano, Lago di Garda.
November	Finishes *Paul Morel* as *Sons and Lovers* and sends it to Duckworth on November 13.
November 19	Writes Louie Burrows from Italy that he has been with Frieda for six months.
late December	Begins *The Lost Girl* as *The Insurrection of Miss Houghton*. Set aside in March 1913 and not completed until 1920.

1913

February	*Love Poems and Others* published by Duckworth.
**March	"The Soiled Rose" published in the *Forum* (and in the *Blue Review* in May).

March	Begins the first version of *The Rainbow* as *The Sisters*.
May	*Sons and Lovers* published by Duckworth.
early June	Finishes first version of *The Sisters*.
*before June 11	Writes "The Prussian Officer" as "Honour and Arms." The Texas holograph of this story is probably the revised draft sent to Douglas Clayton to be typed some time during the summer.
*after June 11	Writes "The Thorn in the Flesh" as "Vin Ordinaire."
mid-June to early August	In England before returning to continent. During this period of intensive short story revision, "The Vicar's Garden" becomes "The Shadow in the Rose Garden," "The Baker's Man" becomes "The Christening," and "Two Marriages" becomes "Daughters of the Vicar." (The revised typescript and holograph fair copy material now in George Lazarus's *B* manuscript comprise the latter revision.) "A Sick Collier" is among the other stories revised at this time.
August	Revises *The Widowing of Mrs. Holroyd*.
by August 25	One of the Prussian stories (probably "Honour and Arms") sold to the *English Review*.

September	Begins second version of *The Sisters.*
**September 13	"A Sick Collier" published in the *New Statesman.*
by October 6	Both "Honour and Arms" and "Vin Ordinaire" sold to the *English Review.*
autumn	Ezra Pound sells "The Christening" and "The Shadow in the Rose Garden" to the *Smart Set.*

1914

by January	Finishes second version of *The Sisters.* Third version of *The Rainbow* begun in February as *The Wedding Ring.*
**February	"The Christening" published in the *Smart Set.*
**March	"The Shadow in the Rose Garden" published in the *Smart Set.*
April	*The Widowing of Mrs. Holroyd* published by Mitchell Kennerley in New York and Duckworth in London.
by mid-May	Completes *The Wedding Ring,* now called *The Rainbow.*
**June	"Vin Ordinaire" published in the *English Review.*
June 5	Writes the letter to Garnett propounding his new theory of characterization.
late June	Returns to England and is unable to leave again until after World War I.

late June	Sale of *The Rainbow* to Methuen. Contract with Duckworth for *The Prussian Officer and Other Stories.*
first half of July	Extensive revision of "The White Stocking," Odour of Chrysanthemums," "Daughters of the Vicar," "The Soiled Rose," "Honour and Arms," and "The Shadow in the Rose Garden" for publication in *The Prussian Officer.* "Vin Ordinaire" is revised a few days later. Retouches some of the other five stories in the collection. This revision produced the Hopkin proof text now in the collection of the Nottinghamshire County Library.
July 13	Marriage to Frieda.
July 14	Letter to Garnett about the stories he wants to collect for *The Prussian Officer.* Proposes *Goose Fair* as title.
July 17[?]	Extensive revision of "Vin Ordinaire," transforming it into "The Thorn in the Flesh." Proposes *The Thorn in the Flesh* as title for the collection.
**August	"Honour and Arms" published in the *English Review* (and in the *Metropolitan* in November).
early August	Methuen rejects version of *The Rainbow* it had received.
by September 5	*Study of Thomas Hardy* begun.

	Completed in November, though Lawrence planned to rewrite it.
** October	"The White Stocking" published in the *Smart Set*.
mid-October	Revises the Hopkin proofs of *The Prussian Officer* to produce the final versions of the stories. Proposes *The Fighting Line* as title.
by December 4	Begins fourth and final revision of *The Rainbow*.
December	*The Prussian Officer and Other Stories* published by Duckworth. (The first edition actually dated November 26.) Garnett had retitled "Honour and Arms" and had also given the new title to the collection.

1915

| by March 2 | Completes the fourth version of *The Rainbow*. |
| September 30 | *The Rainbow* published by Methuen. |

Indexes

Q3

30/8/

T. Thomas
in